HEALTHY COOKING FOR TWO
(or just you)

HEALTHY COOKING FOR TWO
(or just you)

Low-Fat Recipes with Half
the Fuss and Double the Taste

By Frances Price, R.D.

Rodale Press, Inc.
Emmaus, Pennsylvania

Printed in the United States of America on acid-free ∞ , recycled paper ♻

Cover and Book Designer: Elizabeth Otwell
Cover Photographer: Ellen Silverman
Cover Food Stylist: Anne Disrude
Cover Prop Stylist: Betty Alfenito
Illustrator: Julie Paschkis
Cover Recipe: Bronzed Cornish Hen (page 166) with Thai Peach Salsa (page 167)

Library of Congress Cataloging-in-Publication Data

Price, Frances.
    Healthy cooking for two (or just you) : low-fat recipes with
half the fuss and double the taste / by Frances Price.
        p.   cm.
    Includes index.
    ISBN 0–87596–274–2   hardcover
    1. Low-fat diet—Recipes.   I. Title.
RM237.7.P746   1995
641.5′638—dc20   95–17216

Distributed in the book trade by St. Martin's Press

2 4 6 8 10 9 7 5 3 1   hardcover

OUR MISSION

We publish books that empower people's lives.

RODALE  BOOKS

Contents

A Few Notes from the Editor

The first thing that you'll probably notice about the recipes in this book is that they're arranged in column format. The first measurement column of each recipe is meant for those cooking for one; the second reflects cooking for two. There's a reason for this format. You've got enough to do when measuring ingredients, chopping food and tending pots and pans without having to do arithmetic in your head to scale down standard recipes.

The second thing you'll notice is that sometimes this format translates to more than one serving per person. That was certainly done on purpose. Frances is a great believer in making good use of her time and ingredients. She knows that it's worthwhile to prepare larger amounts of dishes that require extra time on the stove or that store well. Soups, muffins, quick breads, salad dressings and long-cooking meat dishes are good examples.

Unless otherwise indicated in the directions, the pan, bowl and other equipment sizes given work for both the smaller and larger quantities. Sometimes you do need to make an adjustment when preparing the larger quantity. If so, that information will be noted in parentheses in the directions. To make salad for one person, for example, you might use a small mixing bowl; if you are making it for two people, you might need a medium mixing bowl. Here's how the directions would read: Toss the salad in a small (or medium) mixing bowl.

Don't be concerned when you see

ounce amounts specified for ingredients such as canned beans, tomato products, tuna and such or frozen vegetables. You needn't get out a kitchen scale. The amounts refer to common can and frozen package sizes. Wherever possible, Frances created recipes that use an entire container of a packaged food to cut down on wasteful leftovers.

   The nutrient analyses included with the recipes are intended to help you plan healthy menus. Here are some things to keep in mind when looking at them.

- 🌶 If alternatives are given in the ingredient list, the first ingredient listed is the one upon which the analysis is based. For example, if a recipe calls for butter or margarine, either ingredient will work in the recipe, but the nutrient analysis will reflect the nutrient value of butter, the first ingredient listed.
- 🌶 Ingredients not specifically listed in the recipe are not reflected in the nutrient analysis. For example, if you add salt to the water when you cook pasta or frozen vegetables that you will be using in a recipe, the sodium content of your finished dish may be higher than the one listed for the recipe.
- 🌶 If an ingredient is listed as "optional" or "to taste," that ingredient will not be figured into the nutrient analysis. Salt very often fits that description.
- 🌶 The nutrient analysis gives the values of a single serving, regardless of how many servings the recipe makes.
- 🌶 The figures given are for meat, poultry and fish that have been pre-pared, cooked and served according to the instructions in the recipe.

Learning to

Cook for Two

*O*ne of the hardest lessons I ever had to learn, in a lifetime that's included some pretty tough lessons, was how to cook for "just me." Not that I couldn't cook the pans off just about everyone I knew by the time my nest emptied. For almost two decades, I'd cooked volumes for my four girls, two sequential husbands and a hungry host of grateful friends and relatives.

On the job, I'd made a successful career of telling other people how to cook and what to eat, as a food writer and executive dietitian. Even so, I found downsizing my cooking so disorienting that I opened a restaurant rather than relearn to cook for just me.

It was a drastic solution I wouldn't recommend to my worst enemy—or first husband. But I *did* learn to cook for one, an order at a time, in sauté pans and individual casseroles, using a palette of prepped ingredients that ranged from chopped raw onions to velvety velouté sauce. Cooked-to-order specialties included grill-broiled salmon and asparagus trumped with orange hollandaise as well as pasta primavera with 13 fresh vegetables, 3 kinds of cheese and a cup of golden Guernsey cream. You'll find these specialties in this book, lightened for fat but not for flavor. You'll also find slow-simmered favorites like Amish Baked Steak and microwave quickies like Carolina Casserole of chicken and rice.

After the roof quite literally fell in on the restaurant, I had to find other employment, at a time in my life when age and disposition had rendered me unemployable. Surely, I reasoned, there must be some way I could wring a living from all that cooking—possibly by providing recipes and answers to cooking-related questions I was getting increasingly?

Most of the questions came from live-alones who seemed to think I must have the answers since I was both single and a professional cook. I called my friend Louis Mahoney, food editor at the Richmond newspapers, and asked if she was interested in a weekly column on cooking for one. She was. So was Ann Hoffman at the *Virginian Pilot* in Norfolk and Ginger Johnston of the *Oregonian*'s "FoodDay" section. And so it was that from the beginning, in 1986, my column, "One and Only Cook," has appeared in newspapers coast to coast, though coverage in the nation's midsection remains thin to this day.

In the early days of the column, before fat reared its ugly head, I reprised recipes that were heavy with butter and cream and red meat. My readers were as unconcerned about healthy cooking as I was. They wanted small-size recipes for prime rib and "death by chocolate." Then, early in 1988, national concern over healthier eating styles began showing up in their letters to me. Fully a year before commercial processors brought out turkey sausages, a Florida reader wrote to ask for recipes for making his own turkey sausage. I responded with a recipe for turkey country sausage.

A reluctantly trim M.D. who makes his living vaporizing fat from others wanted recipes for low-fat baked goodies—for himself. For him, I developed Biscotti Allegro. Readers prodded me into making a right turn toward a healthier way of cooking.

Years earlier, I'd been a card-carrying member of the American Dietetic Association but had dropped out in the 1970s when no one, absolutely no one, gave a hoot about nutrition. Over a year and a half in the early 1990s, I success-fully completed four courses in advanced nutrition and the stiff test required by the ADA. I'm very glad I did, because now I'm that rare combination of chef and registered dietitian. As such, I'm in a perfect position to balance good taste with good health.

As a chef, I place good taste above all other con-siderations. It's my firm belief that nutrition is only as good as it tastes. Nutritious food that's left on a plate because it has no taste doesn't do anyone any good. So you'll find butter listed before margarine in my recipes and fresh whole eggs instead of egg substitutes.

As a dietitian, I've made it my business to keep up with what's really healthy and what's hype in nutrition. My recipes reflect sound scientific evidence, not the latest fads. I use an abundance of healthy ingredients like fresh fruits and vegeta-bles and grains that, coincidentally, are loaded with good taste.

As a single cook, I refuse to invest huge chunks of time cooking for "just me"—or dirtying up pots and pans for guess-who to wash up. That's why most of the recipes in this book are fast. They're for people who don't necessarily love to cook but love to eat. You can choose recipes that match your inclination. And I've

Learning to Cook for Two

streamlined cooking methods to get you from point A to point B as quickly as possible. I've kept instructions brief but with enough detail to guarantee you'll get good results.

These recipes are *basic* and *simple*, for a generation that grew up without learning to cook. They're *fresh*, made with mostly seasonal ingredients you can find in any reasonably well-stocked supermarket.

One other thing. Entirely too many so-called healthy recipes arrive at their low-fat ratings with impossibly small portions. So you'll find portion sizes in my recipes that are *realistic*, even *generous*, by many standards. You won't get up from the table feeling hungry.

Whether you've cooked for others for a lifetime and are now relearning to cook for yourself, or you're a kitchen novice trying to impress the one you love at the table, don't be afraid to get in that kitchen and rattle those pots and pans. I'll be right there with you in spirit, and in the recipes and menus that follow. Good luck in the kitchen. Good cooking. And most especially, good eating, for life!

Kitchen

Basics

Why bother to cook for yourself—or for two? The top six reasons for scratch-cooking are:

- Home cooking wakes up your taste buds with new, improved flavors.
- It puts you in charge of what goes into your body.
- It cuts down the expense of prepared foods.
- It accentuates positives, such as vitamin C and beta-carotene.
- It eliminates negatives, such as excessive sodium and fat.
- It takes less time than reading the labels on processed foods. (Well, just about!)

You pay more for convenience food than you probably realize, and it often takes less time to make similar foods from scratch than television ads have led us to believe. In two minutes you can make your own vinaigrette dressing from extra-virgin olive oil and red wine vinegar. And even if you buy the finest-quality ingredients, your homemade dressing will still cost you less than half of what you would pay for a bottled dressing that lists water as a major ingredient.

You can pinch pennies by adding pinches of your own herbs and spices to casseroles instead of relying on packaged helpers for hamburger and tuna—which are generally nothing more than a blend of herbs, spices, artificial flavors, sugar and salt.

If you've never cooked before, go straight to the chapter on soup. Soups are very forgiving. If you fumble the seasonings or amounts, you can correct your mistakes as you go, adding a pinch of your favorite herb to a bland soup or a potato to an overseasoned soup. You'll do just fine in the kitchen if you never, ever oversalt your food and if you stay away from complicated stuff like puff pastry (which you have no business messing around with anyhow, since it's astronomically high in fat).

Shopping Rites

Coping with family-size packaging can be a real problem when there's only one or two of you. The following tips should make shopping less onerous, help you save grocery money and cut down on leftovers.

Meat and Poultry

Ring that bell over the meat counter at your supermarket and when a human being appears, order the amount you need—and only the amount you need, whether it's two chops or one chicken breast or eight ounces of lean ground beef. Don't settle for family-size packs that mean instant leftovers. Shopping will take a little longer, but if enough of us ring enough bells, supermarket managers will get the message that over half of all American households consist of one or two people. Eventually, we'll find more meat and poultry packaged in small amounts.

If such supermarket activism isn't your style, get your meat and poultry at a supermarket custom counter or at a local butcher shop. You'll pay a little more, but you won't pay for what you don't need.

Fruits and Vegetables

Shop where fresh fruits and vegetables are sold in bulk, rather than prepackaged, so that you can buy only the amounts you'll actually use. Look for produce on special. Low produce prices often accompany peak season, when flavor and freshness are at their height.

For the freshest produce at the lowest prices, buy fruits and vegetables at the source: at pick-your-own farms, farmers' markets and roadside stands. When shopping at the source isn't possible, look for the supermarket in your area that consistently stocks the best produce. An increasing number of chains are upgrading produce sections in response to rising consumer demand for quality and variety.

A well-stocked, well-run salad bar can be an excellent source of ready-to-cook ingredients that can get dinner off to a flying start. Many supermarkets are offering salad bars, and although you do pay more for prepped ingredients, you'll save time and eliminate waste when you shop the salad bar on busy nights. Many of the recipes in this book give suggestions for fresh, prepped ingredients that can be purchased at the salad bar on your way home from work.

Fish and Seafood

Buy fish and seafood the day you are going to cook it (or, at most, one day before) from an independent fish market or enlightened supermarket that cares

Storing Fruits & Vegetables

- Store fruits that need further ripening, such as avocados, peaches and pears, at room temperature. Place them in paper bags (to hasten ripening and discourage fruit flies) until they have ripened to your taste; then store them in the refrigerator.

- Store bananas, which blacken in the refrigerator, at room temperature.

- Store vegetables (except onions and potatoes) and fully ripe fruits in the refrigerator. Place them in the vegetable crisper or in perforated plastic bags. (Perforated plastic lets raw fruits and vegetables, which are living organisms, "breathe," hence stay fresh longer.)

- Store onions (including garlic and shallots, but not green onions) in a cool, dry, well-ventilated place.

- Store potatoes in a cool, dark, well-ventilated place that's slightly humid. Do not refrigerate them or they'll turn sweet. It's best not to store potatoes next to onions, as natural gases given off by the onions may cause the potatoes to go bad.

- Once vegetables and fruits have been cooked, store them in tightly covered containers in the refrigerator for no more than three to five days.

enough to train employees in handling this highly perishable food.

Display cases should be antiseptically clean, uncluttered with an overabundance that usually signals slow-moving, hence less-than-fresh, fish and seafood. Ideally, finfish should be stored on crushed ice and lightly covered with more ice to retain moisture and flavor and to wash away bacteria that grows faster on un-iced fish.

When it comes to judging fish, your nose knows, so don't be afraid to use it! Ask to smell your intended purchase before you buy from a showcase. Fresh fish and seafood should smell clean and pleasant — reject any fish that doesn't.

Storing Staples

- Store canned goods and other staples on shelves at room temperature. Follow the safety rule of "first in, first out" by arranging your most recent purchases behind earlier purchases.
- Bulging cans indicate the presence of gases formed by harmful bacteria and should be discarded. So should dented cans, which may be contaminated.
- Bulky dry goods, such as flour, cornmeal and sugar, should be transferred from their original packaging to dry canisters or jars with tightly fitting lids for storage.

Staples

Shop with a grocery list in hand to avoid costly impulse purchases. But stay flexible. You can save money by stocking up on sale items that you use regularly. Canned tomatoes and dry pasta are excellent items to stock abundantly because so many recipes call for them. On the other hand, blueberry pie filling isn't a bargain unless you are really going to make those blueberry-cheese blintzes and a couple of pies.

Be adventurous and browse ethnic markets for bargains in oils, cheeses and condiments. I buy Parmigiano-Reggiano, the king of cheeses, at half the price I'd pay in my supermarket from a Greek grocery, where I also stock up on large cans of extra-virgin olive oil. At home I funnel the oil into clean wine bottles and refrigerate all but the bottle in use. Olive oil, like all other oils, will cloud up in the refrigerator, but it clears as it warms to room temperature.

Ethnic markets also offer bargains on staples like soy sauce, dried mushrooms, basmati and Arborio rices, bulgur, couscous, canned chilies, pimentos, artichoke hearts, dried and canned beans and many other specialty items.

Bottom-Line Basics

The foods that you keep in your kitchen are as unique as your thumbprint; no two people cook, or eat, exactly the same way. The following list is my personal pantry list (in alphabetical order). These are the basics I keep on hand that you'll encounter over and over again in the recipes ahead. A little planning makes a big difference when you're looking for fast, healthy meals. If you keep some of these basics on hand, you'll reduce trips to the store, though you'll still need to shop once a week for fresh, perishable foods.

Pantry Foods

Baking powder and baking soda. For leavening baked goods.

Barbecue sauce. For chicken, meat loaf, salad dressings and vegetables.

Beans and peas (dried and canned). Red or white kidney, black, pinto, Great Northern, navy, chick-peas, split peas; for dips, salads, soups and casseroles. Buy canned beans in 15- or 16-ounce cans. Cook big batches of dried beans and freeze them in small containers.

Bulgur wheat. Fine or medium; for casseroles, salads and as an alternative to potatoes.

Chicken broth. For soups, stews, sauces and casseroles.

Cocoa. Unsweetened; for baking and for hot cocoa made with 1% low-fat milk when you have to have something chocolate.

Cornmeal. Yellow or white; for cornbread and cornmeal dumplings and for thickening chili.

Flour. All-purpose; for baking and thickening soups, gravies and sauces.

Honey. For smoothies, granola and baked goods.

Oats. Old-fashioned rolled; for granola and for microwaving a breakfast in three minutes.

Oils. Olive and neutral-flavored canola; for salad dressings, sautés, sauces and general cooking.

Onions, shallots and garlic. For savory dishes, snacks and soups. Unlike most produce, which should be refrigerated, these necessities should be kept in a cool, dark place like a closet or pantry because they will sprout in the refrigerator.

Pasta. Thin spaghetti or linguine as well as short, chunky elbow macaroni or rotini; for main courses, casseroles, salads and side dishes.

Potatoes. Baking and waxy boiling; store in a cool, dark closet or cabinet; for casseroles, soups and side dishes.

Reduced-fat biscuit mix. For biscuits, dumplings and shortcakes.

Rice. Long- or medium-grain white and brown rice; for side dishes, entrées, risottos and casseroles.

Sugar. Granulated and light or dark brown; for baked goods.

Tomatoes. Whole or in pieces (15- or 16-ounce cans); for soups, sauces, chili, casseroles and vegetarian entrées.

Is It Still Good?

Nothing is forever, especially foods held in the freezer section of an apartment-size refrigerator. Label everything that goes into your freezer with its name and the date of storage, using a black marker. Use or discard frozen foods within three months unless you have a freezer that you're sure maintains a *constant* temperature of 0°. In that case, label everything and use it within a year.

Tomato paste. 6-ounce cans; for adding color and flavor to sauces, stews and soups.
Tuna. Water-packed solid or chunk-style (3¼- or 6½-ounce cans); for salads, casseroles and pasta dishes.
Vinegars. Choose one or more from among red or white wine, rice, cider, balsamic, tarragon and raspberry; for low-fat dressings and sauces.

The Refrigerator

Butter or stick margarine. For cooking and baking. Soft margarine isn't appropriate for the recipes in this book; it has too low a melting temperature and too much liquid.
Carrots. In 1-pound polybags; for snacks, soups, sauces, casseroles and salads.
Celery. By the bunch; for snacks, soups, casseroles, sauces and salads.
Citrus fruit. Including lemons and limes for salad dressings, drinks and desserts plus oranges or orange juice concentrate for juice, snacks, sauces and dressings.
Dairy products. Including 1% low-fat milk for beverages, cereals, cooking and baking plus nonfat or low-fat yogurt for cereals, smoothies, salad dressings and baking.
Dijon mustard or coarse-grain mustard. For dressings and sauces.
Eggs. Large, by the dozen or half dozen; for use within one week from expiration date stamped on carton; store in the carton, in the refrigerator.
Fruit. Fresh and in season; for salads, snacks, desserts and eating out-of-hand.
Ginger root. Fresh; for stir-fries, oriental dishes, salad dressings and baked goods.
Ketchup and chili sauce. For low-fat condiments.

Mayonnaise. Light or regular; for salads, dressings and low-fat condiments.

Parmesan or Romano cheese. In a wedge, tightly wrapped in film; for grating over pasta, pizza, salads and soups. Buy other cheeses sparingly, when needed, to avoid high-fat snacking.

Parsley. Washed, well-drained and stored in a tightly covered container; for sauces, stocks, soups and salads.

Tahini (sesame paste). For salad dressings, dips and spreads.

Frozen Assets

Breads. Several varieties including flour tortillas and pita; for sandwiches and personal pizzas; store tightly bagged in plastic.

Homemade chicken broth. Store in tightly sealed 1- and 2-cup containers.

Peas and other vegetables. Loosely frozen and polybagged: for stews, soups, salads and side dishes.

The Spice Rack

Herbs or spices? What's the difference? Herbs are from green and leafy plants generally grown in temperate climates, while spices include the seeds, roots, bark and flower buds of trees and plants grown in the tropics. A pinch or two of the appropriate herb or spice can turn the ordinary into the extraordinary. But use caution in adding "the praise of cooks" to your culinary creations; although a little is good, too much can mean disaster.

Fresh herbs are increasingly available by the bunch at supermarkets and by the pot at farmers' markets. And though fresh herbs have a brighter flavor than dried herbs, most recipes, including mine, call for dried herbs because that's what most people have on hand. You can substitute finely chopped fresh herbs for dried in any recipe by doubling or tripling the amount called for.

As for storing dried herbs and spices, be aware that heat (from your kitchen stove) and direct light (from a sunny window) destroy flavor. Verily, you cannot save thyme in a bottle for much over a year, so do be brave and throw away ancient seasonings that have lost their savor. How do you know when that moment arrives? When dried herbs smell flat and dusty rather than pungent, it's time to say good-bye.

Basic Herbs and Spices to Keep on Hand

Basil. Use this most Italian of herbs in any nonsweet recipe of Italian origin: pastas, pizza, tomato and other sauces, eggplant and zucchini casseroles, frittatas and salad dressings. Sprinkle it

BASIL

over fish for broiling or poaching and over raw vegetables and salads, especially tomatoes.

Bay leaves. These are indispensable for seasoning chicken broth. A leaf or two turns plain beef or lamb stew into fancy ragout. Use bay in combination with thyme or basil in tomato sauces, vegetable soups, marinades, pot roasts and seafood chowders.

Cinnamon. Use this for any apple-based dessert, rice pudding, bread pudding, granola and oatmeal cookies. A tiny pinch turns a cup of coffee into a dieter's dessert.

Cumin. This has become a shelf staple with the growing popularity of Mexican, vegetarian and Indian cooking. Use ground cumin in chili and curries. Make your own blend of chili powder by adding oregano, paprika and ground hot pepper. Use toasted cumin seeds, whole or partially crushed, in curries, steamed vegetables, rice and couscous.

Pepper. Keep two kinds handy. Have black pepper, preferably in the form of whole peppercorns, for grinding fresh. Choose one or more types of hot red pepper: ground red pepper, Creole pepper, crushed red-pepper flakes or whole dried pepper pods. Go easy until you know how hot your peppers really are.

Thyme. This is the herb that I'd choose if I could have only one on the shelf. Thyme goes well with everything from shrimp Creole to roast chicken. Use it in soups, stocks, stews, oven roasts and pot roasts and with pork, lamb, veal, beef, fish, cheese and egg dishes. Add thyme to seafood chowders and broiled fish. Thyme brings out the flavor of potatoes, green beans, carrots, cauliflower and tomatoes; it also substitutes nicely for sage in recipes for poultry, pork and stuffings.

Special Seasonings—For Serious Cooks

Cloves. Add two or three whole cloves to chicken stock, hot tea or stewed dried fruits; a pinch of ground cloves perks up pork, ham and tomato dishes.

Coriander. The seed of feathery cilantro, ground or whole coriander is to Indian cooking what thyme is to French cooking and what basil is to Italian cooking. Use it in pea soups, dried bean casseroles, curries, Mexican and Indian dishes and in fruit salads and pickles.

Dill. I prefer dill weed, which is the dried leaves, to dill seeds. Dill is wonderful with cucumbers or fish, particularly salmon, and in beet borscht. It jazzes up tomato soup, tuna and potato salads.

Fennel. This is a major flavor component of Italian sausage. Try fennel seeds in combination with basil or oregano in tomato and marinara sauces. Add it to fish, particularly tuna and sea bass, and to pork with sauerkraut.

Ginger. Keep ground ginger on hand for gingerbread, cookies, soups and curries. Be aware that the flavor of ground ginger differs from that of fresh ginger root, so the two aren't really interchangeable.

Nutmeg. Add a pinch of nutmeg to any variety of cream of vegetable soup as well as creamed spinach or onions. Use it with or instead of cinnamon in apple desserts; sprinkle it over hot milk with honey for a nightcap.

Oregano. Similar to thyme but more pungent, oregano is made for Greek dishes, including salads, broiled fish and lamb. Also important in Italian and Mexican cooking, oregano can be used in combination with or instead of basil. Add it to bean soups, stews, chili and casseroles. It's particularly good with green peppers and onions—with or without Italian sausage.

Paprika. Made of ground mild red peppers, paprika colors broiled fish, deviled eggs or any pale dish. Bittersweet and scarlet, it's a major component of Hungarian goulash and chicken paprikash.

Rosemary. Tasting faintly of pine, rosemary boosts the flavor of dried beans, chicken, lamb and veal dishes. Also try it in clam and fish chowders and tomato-based bouillabaisse.

Sage. Lay in a goodly supply only if you make your own sausages and cheese bread. Otherwise, substitute thyme for sage in recipes for roasts and stuffings. Fresh sage is superior to dried, which can have a musty flavor.

SAGE

Tarragon. This is a fine French touch for fish, chicken, veal, eggs and salads. Add tarragon to broccoli or cauliflower before cooking. Heat it briefly with white vinegar to make your own tarragon vinegar.

Cooking Gear

Most kitchen gadgets are a waste of money and counter space for smaller kitchens. With an electric can opener, for example, the blade is eternally dirty, and if your kitchen is as tiny as most one- or two-person kitchens, the opener can take up half your counter space. Better to spend half the money to buy a heavy-duty hand-powered can opener, the two-handled sort that clamps over the lip of a can for opening, washes up with the dishes and stays conveniently put in a drawer until needed. Another example is a food processor, which takes longer to assemble and clean than it would take you to hand-chop ingredients for small recipes.

Having the right equipment, however, can make cooking easier and faster. Many small utensils, such as can openers and potato peelers, can be purchased inexpensively at supermarkets and discount variety stores. Good-quality pots, pans and knives, however, are relatively expensive but worth every penny you'll save in time and replacements; they will reward you with consistently good results.

Choose heavy pots and pans made of cast iron, aluminum, enameled iron, anodized aluminum or stainless steel. Thin, flimsy pots and pans have hot spots that cause food to stick and scorch. My personal choice for stockpots and saucepans is stainless steel, with copper laminated over the bottoms. I got custody of a set given to me and the first mister as a wedding gift many years ago; it has outlasted two marriages and gives every indication of continuing life as a family heirloom when I pass on.

But I must tell you my preference for this moderately priced cookware is considered déclassé by most members of the food establishment. They prefer higher-priced, less durable enameled iron and anodized cast aluminum.

For the eight-inch and ten-inch heavy nonstick skillets on which I am fixated, choose slope-sided sauté pans with metal handles that can go directly into the oven.

Good knives, with blades made from a carbon steel or vanadium, can be sharpened repeatedly to a fine edge with a steel, though all knives need to be professionally sharpened occasionally. Many people go crazy when it comes to knives—it seems that every fruit and vegetable requires a special knife. In most circumstances, I've learned to get along with just three: a chef's knife, a serrated bread and tomato knife and a paring knife.

Department stores are a good source for high-quality cookware. Look for bargain prices during housewares sales. A restaurant supply house is another good source—and an excellent classroom for learning about cookware when clerks aren't busy and are in a good mood. They can answer all sorts of questions and be of tremendous help in guiding your selections. Not all restaurant supply houses sell retail, so call before you go and stick to your list of bare necessities when you get there. It's all too easy to get carried away and come home loaded with pineapple corers, barding needles and other arcanery that you'll never, ever use. Believe me, I know.

I must also confess that when it comes to kitchen gear, I'm just a junk store junkie. I can't resist a bargain like the two-foot paella pan, hand-hammered from rusty tin in Spain, that was mine for only $2.48 in an East Baltimore thrift shop. Nobody in East Baltimore wanted it, but it will sure come in handy whenever I get around to inviting a dozen people over to dine on authentic paella.

Lucky for me, most of the stuff that I haul home for pennies on the dollar is infinitely more practical, which is why I make a bimonthly sweep of several secondhand stores run by worthy nonprofit organizations. If you're outfitting a kitchen on a budget, you might want to do the same.

Bare Essentials: Pots and Pans
- 10″ heavy nonstick skillet or sauté pan
- 7″ or 8″ heavy nonstick skillet or sauté pan
- 8″ heavy iron skillet, for cornbread and browning meats and fish
- 1-quart saucepan with lid
- 2-quart saucepan with 1-quart double-boiler insert and lid (insert doubles as a mixing bowl)
- 4-quart stockpot or saucepan with lid
- 2-quart enameled, cast-iron casserole with lid, for small pot roasts, stews and chili
- 2-cup ovenproof round casseroles, 2″ deep, for individual entrées, vegetable casseroles and desserts
- 2-cup shallow, oval, ovenproof casseroles or gratin pans, for individual entrées, casseroles and desserts
- 4- or 6-ounce individual microwave-safe, ovenproof soufflé dishes or custard cups
- 8″ × 8″ baking pan, for baking and roasting chicken
- 9″ × 13½″ baking pan, for granola, biscuits and roasting vegetables and meats
- 2-cup mixing bowl or oversized soup bowl
- 2-quart mixing bowl
- Colander, for draining pasta, salad greens, produce

Necessary Knives and Gadgets
- Chef's knife, 8″ to 12″ blade, for slicing, dicing, mincing, chopping and crushing
- Paring knife, 4″ blade, for peeling vegetables and slicing and dicing small foods like shallots
- Serrated-edge knife, 12″ to 14″ blade, for slicing bread, tomatoes and cooked meats
- Chopping board, at least 12″ × 12″, although 12″ × 18″ is better
- Sharpening steel, for sharpening knives
- 2 wooden spoons (1 slotted), for use with nonstick skillets

- Rubber spatula, for scraping down bowls and blenders
- Broad metal and plastic spatulas or pancake flippers, for turning eggs, meats, fish and pancakes
- Metal slotted spoon, for stirring, removing poached eggs from liquid
- Wire whisk
- Spoon tongs, for turning meat, poultry and fish during cooking and for lifting cooked pasta from water
- Cooking fork, for turning meat and poultry and lifting foods
- 4-sided upright grater, for grating and shredding vegetables, citrus rind and cheese
- Heavy-duty manual can opener
- Set of graduated measuring spoons (¼, ½ and 1 teaspoon and 1 tablespoon)
- Set of graduated measuring cups (¼, ⅓, ½ and 1 cup), for measuring dry ingredients
- Microwave-safe, heatproof glass measuring cups, 1-, 2- and 4-cup sizes for measuring liquids and for microwave cookery
- Wire-mesh strainer, for sifting flour and draining small amounts of fruits, vegetables and pasta
- Corkscrew, for wine and vinegar
- Bottle opener, punch-type, for opening cans of juice
- Garlic press
- Swivel-bladed vegetable peeler, for peeling potatoes, apples and such
- 2 heavy pot holders

Small Equipment
- Blender, for salad dressings, sorbets, smoothies, pureed vegetables, pestos and soups; also for grating cheese, crumbling bread and chopping nuts
If I had to choose one small appliance, it would be my blender.
- Hand-held mixer: for mixing batters and mashing potatoes

Bread

and Breakfast

*T*here are two simple things that you can do to get on the road to a healthier lifestyle — this morning: *Do* eat your breakfast and *don't* butter your bread.

You may think that skipping breakfast will save you calories in the long run. And that might be a logical assumption, except that people who skip breakfast tend to consume the same amount of calories over a 24-hour period as those who eat it. But going without eating for extended periods of time lowers your metabolic rate, which means that people who skip breakfast don't burn calories as fast or efficiently as people who eat the morning meal.

Rev up your engine in the mornings. If you're chronically short on time, bake a batch of Apricot and Almond Granola or Apple-Walnut Bran Muffins on a weekend or evening when you do have time. Then eat it with yogurt and fruit on mornings when you're rushed. Or spend the three minutes it takes to make and inhale Breakfast in a Glass or a Strawberry-Banana Smoothie before you dash out the door.

The staff of life is making a comeback, now that we've been given the green light to eat complex carbohydrates (read "starchy foods"). The problem, it turns out, was never the bread but the butter (or margarine) that we spread on it. Invest in good-quality, whole-grain breads and do as the French do: Skip the butter. They don't need it, because they use freshly baked French bread to mop up sauces and vitamin-infused juices that we Americans usually leave on our plates.

So get to know the taste of real bread from a good bakery — and from your own kitchen. Always insist on honest bread with flavor enough to stand on its own. It doesn't have to take hours to bake; you can get Southern Skillet Cornbread into the oven in about five minutes and read the paper or watch TV while it bakes.

Strawberry-Banana Smoothie

You can enjoy this smoothie year round. Just substitute an equal measure of unsweetened, whole frozen strawberries when good fresh ones aren't available.

Ingredients	For 1 serving	For 2 servings
Nonfat plain yogurt	¾ cup	1½ cups
Strawberries, capped	½ cup	1 cup
Banana, peeled and sliced	1 small	1 large
Honey	1 teaspoon	2 teaspoons
Grated nutmeg (optional)	dash	⅛ teaspoon

Place the yogurt, strawberries and bananas in a blender. Drizzle the honey over the fruit. Process the mixture on high speed about 15 seconds, or until the fruit is blended. If honey clings to the sides of the blender, scrape down the sides and process for another 5 to 10 seconds. Serve in tall glasses, sprinkled with the nutmeg (if using).

Per serving: 213 calories, 0.7 g. total fat, 0.2 g. saturated fat, 4 mg. cholesterol, 122 mg. sodium, 11.1 g. protein, 44.4 g. carbohydrates, 3.3 g. dietary fiber.

Breakfast in a Glass

No time for making (or eating) breakfast? Zip this up in less than 5 minutes and take it with you. You'll fuel up on wheat germ, yogurt and orange juice. Best of all, this tastes mighty like an old-fashioned Orange Julius.

Ingredients	For 1 serving	For 2 servings
Nonfat plain yogurt	1 cup	2 cups
Wheat germ	2 tablespoons	¼ cup
Frozen orange juice concentrate	2 tablespoons	¼ cup
Honey	2 teaspoons	4 teaspoons

Place the yogurt, wheat germ, orange juice concentrate and honey in a blender. Process the mixture on high until thoroughly blended, about 30 seconds. Serve in tall glasses.

Per serving: 300 calories, 1.6 g. total fat, 0.3 g. saturated fat, 6 mg. cholesterol, 182 mg. sodium, 19.7 g. protein, 54.8 g. carbohydrates, 2.2 g. dietary fiber.

Four-Seasons Smoothies

In summer my favorite breakfast is a tall, cool smoothie, bursting with fresh strawberries or blueberries or peaches. But don't wait for hot weather to enjoy smoothies. And don't save them for breakfast. A smoothie can be a grand healthy stand-in for late-night ice cream. In winter, cooked dried fruit and compotes make delicious fiber-rich smoothies.

Tangy yogurt, abundant with calcium, blends beautifully with most seasonal fruits. Compose your own smoothies for every season following the basic directions given for my Strawberry-Banana Smoothie. When your favorite fruit comes into season, substitute it for the strawberries and banana called for in the recipe. (Frozen fruit also works well.)

Experiment with quantities and fruit combinations to come up with your own signature smoothie. Here are some ideas and measurements for one serving to get you started.

- 1 cup cantaloupe or honeydew cubes
- 1 medium peach, pitted and sliced
- ½ cup applesauce
- 2 large plums, halved and pitted
- ⅓ cup prunes, cooked and pitted
- ⅓ cup stewed apricots (with juice)
- ½ cup blueberries, stemmed

Apricot & Almond Granola

Why should you bake your own granola instead of buying ready-made? Because homemade granola tastes twice as good and costs half as much. And you can cut the fat down considerably when you make it yourself. Homemade or store-bought, most granolas are high in fat; in this recipe, a small amount of canola oil and crunchy almonds add flavor but keep calories from fat at 30 percent. For a robust breakfast, top this granola with low-fat milk or yogurt and fresh fruit. Or for a snack, enjoy it plain.

Ingredients	For 4 cups	For 8 cups
Dried apricots	½ cup	1 cup
Rolled oats	3½ cups	18 ounces
Sliced almonds	6 tablespoons	¾ cup
Wheat germ	¼ cup	½ cup
Ground cinnamon or grated nutmeg	¼ teaspoon	½ teaspoon
Canola oil	1 tablespoon	2 tablespoons
Honey	2½ tablespoons	⅓ cup

Preheat the oven to 325°.

With oiled scissors, snip the apricots into pea-size pieces; set them aside.

In a large mixing bowl, combine the oats, almonds, wheat germ and cinnamon or nutmeg. Mix well.

Pour the oil into a measuring cup and stir in the honey. Drizzle evenly over the oat mixture, turning with a spoon to coat the oats evenly. Don't worry if clumps form; they will be broken up during baking.

Spread the granola evenly in a 9″ × 9″ (or 9″ × 13″) baking pan and bake for 25 to 30 minutes, or until it is golden brown. (Every 10 minutes or so during baking, turn the granola with a metal spatula so that it toasts evenly and the clumps are broken apart.)

Transfer the pan to a wire rack and cool the granola to room temperature. Stir in the apricots. Store the granola in a tightly covered container for up to 1 month.

Per ½ cup: 204 calories, 6.9 g. total fat, 0.8 g. saturated fat, 0 mg. cholesterol, 3 mg. sodium, 7.5 g. protein, 29.7 g. carbohydrates, 3.1 g. dietary fiber.

Irish Fruit & Fiber

Have you checked the prices of breakfast cereals lately? Now, I believe in getting plenty of dietary fiber, but I'm not ready to take a vow of poverty to get that fiber in ready-to-eat cereals. Instead, I treat myself to bountiful bowls of luscious fruit and fiber that I make on the cheap, with steel-cut Irish or Scotch oatmeal.

Purchase your Irish oatmeal in bulk at a health food store or co-op. Avoid the high-priced fancy tins sold in specialty shops and the gourmet section of grocery stores. The oats are the same; they just cost more.

Be wary when you buy Irish oatmeal. If the label says "quick-cooking," the oats aren't Irish. Irish oats take a long time to cook because unlike rolled oats, which have been partially cooked and flattened with rollers to speed cooking, Irish oats are uncooked and whole.

Since it takes about half an hour to cook up a batch of Irish oatmeal, I make a big batch once a week in the dead of winter and store it in my refrigerator, then reheat a bowlful at a time in the microwave for a quick, low-fat breakfast. For fiber, try prunes, raisins or dried cherries, cranberries, peaches or apples. For extra goodness, stir in a small spoonful of honey, brown sugar or maple syrup and a heaping spoonful of nonfat yogurt.

> ⅔ cup Irish (steel-cut) oats
> ⅔ cup chopped dried apricots
> 2¾ cups water

In a heavy 2-quart saucepan, combine the oats, apricots and water. Bring the mixture to a boil over medium-high heat. Reduce the heat to low and cover the pan. Cook, stirring occasionally to prevent sticking, for 30 minutes, or until the oats are tender. Serve the cereal right away or keep it for up to 1 week in a covered container in the refrigerator.

Makes 4 servings

Per serving: 126 calories, 1 g. total fat, 0.2 g. saturated fat, 0 mg. cholesterol, 7 mg. sodium, 3 g. protein, 28.7 g. carbohydrates, 0.6 g. dietary fiber.

Apple-Walnut Bran Muffins

Any good baking apple works well in this recipe; I like Granny Smith, Rome Beauty and Winesap. Leave the skin on the apple; it adds fiber, color and texture to the muffins. For easy breakfasts at home or healthier coffee breaks at work, bake and freeze a batch of these tender muffins. They are extra good spread with yogurt cheese, light cream cheese or apple butter.

Ingredients	For 6 muffins	For 12 muffins
Apple	½	1
Whole-wheat flour, unsifted	¾ cup	1½ cups
Baking soda	½ teaspoon	1 teaspoon
Grated nutmeg	⅛ teaspoon	¼ teaspoon
Water	½ cup	1 cup
Wheat bran, fine	½ cup	1 cup
Eggs	1 large	2 large
Nonfat buttermilk	½ cup	1 cup
Honey	2½ tablespoons	⅓ cup
Walnut or canola oil	½ tablespoon	1 tablespoon
Chopped walnuts	2 tablespoons	¼ cup

Preheat the oven to 350°.

Line 6 (or 12) 2½″ muffin cups with fluted paper liners.

Core the apple and chop it into pea-size pieces; set aside.

Sift the flour, baking soda and nutmeg onto a piece of wax paper and set aside.

Bring the water to a rolling boil in a small saucepan; stir in the bran and set the mixture aside.

In a medium mixing bowl, beat the eggs until foamy, then beat in the buttermilk, honey and oil. Beat in the cooled bran mixture, then the apples and walnuts.

Gently stir the flour mixture into the batter just to moisten. Do not overmix the batter or the muffins will be tough and lumpy.

With a ⅓-cup measure, transfer the batter to the muffin cups and bake for 25 to 30 minutes, or until a wooden toothpick inserted in the center of a muffin comes out clean. Cool the muffins on a wire rack.

Per muffin: 115 calories, 4.1 g. total fat, 0.6 g. saturated fat, 36 mg. cholesterol, 91 mg. sodium, 5 g. protein, 17.5 g. carbohydrates, 2.9 g. dietary fiber.

Muffin Tips

Don't follow your natural inclination to beat muffin batter until it's smooth. Too much mixing activates the gluten in flour, which in turn produces tough, flat muffins filled with "tunnels." For tender muffins with pebbly, rounded tops and a coarse-grained yet tender texture, combine the liquids, then stir them into the mixed dry ingredients only enough to moisten the flour mixture — a few lumps are fine.

To freeze muffins, let them cool to room temperature on a wire rack. Freeze them in a single layer on a baking sheet, then transfer the frozen muffins to a heavy-duty, resealable plastic bag and store in the freezer. They will keep up to three months.

Reheat frozen muffins in a microwave or a preheated 350° oven until warmed through.

Pecan Brancakes with Cider Syrup

Even if you're home alone next Sunday, make the larger batch of pecan brancakes so you'll have extra to freeze and reheat in a toaster oven or microwave. (Freeze the brancakes in a single layer on a baking sheet, then bag them in resealable plastic bags. Store them for up to 2 months.) These low-fat, high-fiber pancakes make a quick, substantial breakfast or light supper. To make blueberry brancakes, omit the pecans and stir fresh or frozen blueberries into the batter, allowing ½ cup for every 6 brancakes.

Ingredients	For 6 brancakes	For 12 brancakes
Cider syrup		
Cider or apple juice	1 cup	2 cups
Pecan brancakes		
All-purpose flour, unsifted	⅓ cup	⅔ cup
Baking soda	½ teaspoon	1 teaspoon
Ground cinnamon	¼ teaspoon	½ teaspoon
Wheat bran, fine or coarse	½ cup	1 cup
Eggs	1 large	2 large
Low-fat plain yogurt	¾ cup	1½ cups
Molasses or honey	1 tablespoon	2 tablespoons
Chopped pecans	2 tablespoons	¼ cup
Canola oil	1 teaspoon	2 teaspoons

To make the cider syrup: Pour the cider or juice into a 1-quart (or 2-quart) saucepan and boil it down rapidly over high heat until the liquid is reduced by half. Remove it from the heat.

To make the pecan brancakes: Sift the flour, baking soda and cinnamon into a medium mixing bowl. Stir in the bran.

In another medium mixing bowl, beat the eggs until foamy, then beat in the yogurt and molasses or honey. Pour into the flour mixture and stir just enough to moisten. Add the pecans; do not overmix.

Place a heavy, 10″ nonstick skillet over medium heat for 3 to 5 minutes, then brush the skillet lightly with ½ teaspoon of the oil. With a ⅓-cup measure, scoop the batter into the skillet to form thick brancakes about 3″ across. Cook the brancakes for 3 to 4 minutes, or until they are browned on the bottom. Flip them and cook them for 2 to 3 minutes, or until both sides are brown. Remove the first batch of brancakes from the skillet.

Easy Low-Fat Spreads & Toppings

Instead of butter, try these quick, low-fat toppings on your breads.
- Low-fat cottage cheese mixed with preserves, jam or applesauce
- Honey blended with tahini (sesame seed paste) or almond butter
- Sweetened sliced fruit (such as strawberries) mixed into nonfat yogurt or yogurt cheese

Repeat until you've used all the oil and batter.

Warm the cider syrup and drizzle it over the hot brancakes just before serving.

Per 3 brancakes with ¼ cup cider syrup: 344 calories, 11.5 g. total fat, 2.3 g. saturated fat, 112 mg. cholesterol, 302 mg. sodium, 12.6 g. protein, 53.2 g. carbohydrates, 2.9 g. dietary fiber.

Southern Skillet Cornbread

Well-made Southern cornbread has crumbly, moist innards with an exterior so crisp it crackles, produced by pouring the batter into a sizzling-hot cast-iron skillet. I prefer cornbread made with the fine Southern white cornmeal. If you are making this recipe with coarse Yankee yellow cornmeal, reduce the buttermilk or yogurt slightly; the batter should just mound on a spoon.

Ingredients	For 2 servings	For 4 servings
Vegetable shortening	1 teaspoon	2 teaspoons
White cornmeal	½ cup	1 cup
Baking powder	½ teaspoon	¾ teaspoon
Baking soda	—	¼ teaspoon
Salt	⅛ teaspoon	¼ teaspoon
Egg	1 yolk or white	1 large
Nonfat buttermilk or plain yogurt	½ cup	1 cup

Preheat the oven to 425°.

Place the shortening in a 5″ (or 8″) ovenproof cast-iron skillet and heat the pan in the oven for 5 minutes, or until the shortening is sizzling hot.

While the pan is heating, make the cornbread batter: In a medium mixing bowl, stir together the cornmeal, baking powder, baking soda (if using) and salt.

In a large measuring cup, beat the egg until foamy. Add the buttermilk or yogurt and beat until well-blended. Stir into the cornmeal mixture.

Remove the skillet from the oven. (Remember, the handle will be hot — protect your hands.) Quickly pour the batter into the hot skillet and bake the cornbread on the middle shelf of the oven for 20 to 25 minutes, or until it is well-browned and pulls away from the sides of the pan.

Turn the cornbread onto a serving plate, cut into wedges and serve piping hot.

Per serving: 196 calories, 4.1 g. total fat, 1.4 g. saturated fat, 56 mg. cholesterol, 307 mg. sodium, 7.7 g. protein, 31.4 g. carbohydrates, 1.8 g. dietary fiber.

Cornbread Basics

There's a big difference between cornmeals available in different parts of the country. South of the Mason-Dixon line and east of the Mississippi, you'll find white "water-ground" or "stone-ground" meal so finely ground, it's almost floury. Elsewhere, cornmeal is uniformly yellow and generally coarser; it absorbs less liquid than the fine stuff. You can make good cornbread with either variety. Subtract a tablespoon or two of liquid when you're using yellow cornmeal in a recipe that calls for fine, white cornmeal.

To reheat cornbread, wrap it loosely in aluminum foil and heat it in a 350° oven until it is warmed through. To microwave, wrap it loosely in a paper towel.

Steamed Boston Brown Bread

Boston brown bread takes a heap of fuel for 3 hours of steaming, but it's wonderfully good and miraculously low in fat. So while you're at it, you might as well steam two loaves for the fuel costs of one. The 13-ounce coffee cans are sized right for this recipe.

Ingredients	For 1 loaf	For 2 loaves
Vegetable shortening	1 teaspoon	2 teaspoons
Whole-wheat flour, unsifted	½ cup	1 cup
Rye flour, unsifted	½ cup	1 cup
Yellow cornmeal	½ cup	1 cup
Salt	½ teaspoon	1 teaspoon
Baking soda	½ teaspoon	1 teaspoon
Nonfat buttermilk	1 cup	2 cups
Molasses	½ cup	1 cup
Raisins (optional)	½ cup	1 cup

For each loaf, grease a 13-ounce coffee can or a 4-cup Bundt pan with 1 teaspoon of the shortening; set aside.

Into a large mixing bowl, sift the whole-wheat flour, rye flour, cornmeal, salt and baking soda. Beat in the buttermilk and molasses; fold in the raisins (if using).

Fill the prepared containers no more than ¾ full with batter, cover with a double thickness of aluminum foil and secure the foil with 2 heavy rubber bands or butchers' twine.

Set a steamer rack in a stockpot or deep saucepan and place the filled containers on it. Add enough water to reach halfway up the sides of the containers. Remove the containers, bring the water to a boil over high heat, then carefully lower the containers onto the steamer rack. Cover the pot.

Reduce the heat to low and steam the bread in gently simmering water for 3 hours, adding boiling water as necessary to maintain the same level.

After 3 hours, remove the containers from the water. Unmold the bread onto a rack (if using cans, puncture the bottom of each can with a can opener; the bread should slide out easily). Cut each loaf into 12 slices. Serve warm or at room temperature.

Per slice: 118 calories, 0.7 g. total fat, 0.2 g. saturated fat, 0 mg. cholesterol, 141 mg. sodium, 2.8 g. protein, 26.3 g. carbohydrates, 1.2 g. dietary fiber.

Measuring Flour

For most recipes, it isn't necessary to sift flour before measuring it. To measure flour accurately, dip the measuring cup into the flour so that flour mounds up above the rim of the cup. Then cut off the excess and level the flour with the edge of a knife or spatula.

Spoonbread Soufflé

Next time you have company for brunch or dinner, dazzle them with spoonbread soufflés, a cross between a French soufflé and Southern cornbread. They are surprisingly easy to make, provided that you have shallow gratin or soufflé dishes that hold just 2 cups each. Serve them plain, dress them up with creamed chicken, pan-grilled ham or turkey ham, or top with mushroom marinara sauce.

Ingredients	For 1 serving	For 2 servings
Butter or margarine	½ teaspoon	1 teaspoon
Cornmeal	⅓ cup	⅔ cup
Sugar	½ teaspoon	1 teaspoon
Salt	⅛ teaspoon	¼ teaspoon
Boiling water	⅔ cup	1⅓ cups
1% low-fat milk	⅓ cup	⅔ cups
Eggs	1	2
Baking powder	½ teaspoon	1 teaspoon

Preheat the oven to 450°.

For each serving, use ½ teaspoon of the butter or margarine to grease a 2-cup baking dish, shallow gratin dish or soufflé dish; set aside.

Sift the cornmeal, sugar and salt into a heat-resistant mixing bowl. Pour in the water and stir vigorously until the mixture is smooth.

Beat in the milk, eggs and baking powder. Pour the batter into the prepared dishes. Set on a baking sheet and place the sheet on the middle shelf of the oven. Bake for 25 to 30 minutes, or until puffed and golden brown. Serve immediately (right in the baking dish or spooned onto a dinner plate).

Per serving: 303 calories, 8.5 g. total fat, 3.4 g. saturated fat, 221 mg. cholesterol, 560 mg. sodium, 12.8 g. protein, 42.6 g. carbohydrates, 2.4 g. dietary fiber.

Light Meals

and Snacks

*I*t's okay to snack; in fact, four or five or even six small meals a day can keep your metabolism up and running faster than the old three squares. But snacking can lead to weight gain in a hurry unless you're careful to keep mini-meals small—watch your daily allowance of calories and divide it by the actual number of meals you eat.

What you eat is still more important than when you eat it, so snack sensibly. Here are some suggestions.

- Stock up on plain popcorn, plain nonfat yogurt and whole-grain crackers and cereal.
- Choose naturally sweet fruits like grapes or pears instead of candy.
- When you're replacing a meal with a snack, don't skimp now to pig out later. Choose a lightweight entrée, such as a sandwich of hummus on whole-grain bread with tomato slices or a hearty salad such as Texas Caviar.
- For fiber and other nutrients, reach for fresh and dried fruits, raw and blanched vegetables and whole-grain breads and crackers to accompany dips and spreads.
- Check the new food labels for "sugars," which are listed under "total carbohydrates," so you can avoid or limit snacks high in sugar and calories.
- Back away from snacks that list a high number of calories from fat. Think in terms of lower-fat equivalents such as pretzels instead of high-fat potato chips.
- If a label reads "fruit juice," it's 100 percent juice. But fruit drinks, punches and ades contain high ratios of sugar and very little juice. Grape, orange and other flavor sodas and similar products are soft drinks. Often artificially flavored, they usually contain no real juice. Make your own low-calorie sodas by spritzing fruit juice with seltzer or club soda.

Fresh Tomato Pizza

Pizza can be a light meal. It's inexpensive, easy to make and high in carbohydrates. Stock up your freezer with potential pizza crusts: pita bread, flour tortillas and the new individual pizza crusts available at most grocery stores. This simple combination of tomato and mozzarella, herbs and olive oil given here is a favorite with most pizza-lovers.

Ingredients	For 1 serving	For 2 servings
Pita breads, flour tortillas or small pizza crusts	1	2
Olive oil	1 teaspoon	2 teaspoons
Dried or fresh basil or oregano	to taste	to taste
Thinly sliced onions	¼ cup	½ cup
Shredded part-skim mozzarella cheese	¼ cup	½ cup
Tomatoes, thinly sliced	1 medium	2 medium

Preheat the oven to 500°.

Brush the pitas, tortillas or pizza crusts with the oil on both sides; place on a baking sheet and sprinkle with the basil or oregano.

Separate the onion slices into their individual layers. Arrange the toppings in the following order: onions, mozzarella and tomatoes (which will keep the cheese from scorching).

Bake for 7 to 10 minutes, or until the tomatoes look dry and the cheese begins to brown.

Per 6" to 8" pizza: 295 calories, 11.6 g. total fat, 3.8 g. saturated fat, 16 mg. cholesterol, 500 mg. sodium, 13.9 g. protein, 36.2 g. carbohydrates, 3.3 g. dietary fiber.

Emerald Isle Pizza

Look to the salad bar at your supermarket for the greenery that characterizes this vegetarian pizza. You don't have to be too precise about measuring vegetables. Allow a total of 1 to 2 cups prepped vegetables per pizza.

For a really crisp crust, use a dark metal sheet pan and bake the pizza on the lowest shelf of your oven.

Ingredients	For 1 serving	For 2 servings
Fresh spinach, stemmed and lightly packed	1 cup	2 cups
Broccoli florets	⅓ cup	⅔ cup
Pita breads, flour tortillas or small pizza crusts	1	2
Olive or salad oil	1 teaspoon	2 teaspoons
Dried or fresh basil or oregano	to taste	to taste
Thinly sliced onions	¼ cup	½ cup
Thinly sliced zucchini	¼ cup	½ cup
Thinly sliced green peppers	6–8 slices	12–16 slices
Thinly sliced mushrooms	2 tablespoons	¼ cup
Shredded part-skim mozzarella cheese	¼ cup	½ cup
Grated Parmesan or Romano cheese	1 tablespoon	2 tablespoons

Preheat the oven to 500°.

While the oven is heating, bring 1 quart of water to a full boil in a medium saucepan; stir in the spinach and cook it just until it wilts, about 30 seconds. Using tongs or a slotted spoon, remove the spinach to a colander; drain it well.

Drop the broccoli into the boiling water and cook for 1 minute; set the pan under cold running water to stop the cooking process, then drain the broccoli and set it aside.

Brush the pitas, tortillas or pizza crusts with the oil on both sides; place on a baking sheet and sprinkle with the basil or oregano.

Separate the onion slices into their individual layers. Arrange the onions, zucchini, peppers and mushrooms over the crust. Top with the spinach and broccoli, then the mozzarella and Parmesan or Romano.

Bake for 7 to 10 minutes, or until the cheeses are melted and lightly browned. Cool slightly before serving.

Per 6" to 8" pizza: 293 calories, 11.9 g. total fat, 4.8 g. saturated fat, 21 mg. cholesterol, 518 mg. sodium, 17.1 g. protein, 31.1 g. carbohydrates, 4.4 g. dietary fiber.

Personalized Pizza

You can make really good pizza with ingredients that you probably have right now in your refrigerator, freezer and pantry. Store potential crusts like pita breads, flour tortillas and small pizza crusts, tightly wrapped, in your freezer. Keep small jars or cans of tomato sauce on hand, as well as hard cheeses like Parmesan and Romano, which keep for a long time in the refrigerator.

Here are some tips that will help you turn out perfect pizzas.

- Always bake pizza in a very hot oven, about 450° to 500°.
- Slice vegetables very thinly so they cook quickly.
- Do not stack ingredients more than ½″ to ¾″ above the crust. Vegetables release moisture as they cook. If they are stacked too high, you'll wind up with a soggy crust.
- Limit cheese to keep pizzas healthy and low in fat. Use 1 to 2 tablespoons per pizza of highly flavored salty cheeses, such as Parmesan, Romano, blue cheese, feta and goat cheese; use ¼ cup per pizza of milder cheeses, such as mozzarella, Muenster, Monterey Jack and fontina.
- Cheese shouldn't be the top layer of your pizza; it scorches easily.
- Some vegetables, such as spinach and other leafy greens, should be blanched briefly and squeezed gently to release excess moisture before they are layered onto the pizza.
- Firm vegetables, such as broccoli, carrots, peas, asparagus and cauliflower, will be more tender if they are blanched briefly before they are baked on the pizza.
- Onions, shallots, garlic and herbs can add a lot of flavor to a pizza without piling on calories and fat.
- Dried ingredients, such as sun-dried tomatoes and wild mushrooms, should be rehydrated in a little warm liquid before they are placed on the pizza.
- For a crisper crust, bake your pizza on a darker pan on the lowest shelf of your oven.

(continued)

Light Meals and Snacks

Personalized Pizza — Continued

Pizza Variations

Here are some of my favorite pizza variations. The first one, Very Personal Pizza, is really only a list of possibilities. Look in your refrigerator and pantry to see what you have on hand. If you have a few of these ingredients, including some sort of cheese, a little oil and a crust, you're in business. Follow the general instructions for Fresh Tomato Pizza, substituting the toppings that you have on hand for the ones called for in the recipe.

Very Personal Pizza
- Dried or fresh basil, thyme or oregano
- Onions
- Garlic
- Sweet red or green peppers
- Mushrooms
- Artichoke hearts
- Olives
- Crumbled feta, goat, Gorgonzola or blue cheese
- Shredded part-skim mozzarella, fontina, Muenster or Monterey Jack cheese
- Cooked and drained reduced-fat sausage
- Fresh sun-dried or canned tomatoes

New York Deli Pizza
- Smoked salmon
- Sweet onions
- Fresh tomatoes
- Neufchâtel cheese
- Fresh dill

Mushroom Pizza
- Domestic and wild mushrooms (such as crimini, shiitake, portobello or porcini), sautéed with garlic or onion and a little olive oil
- Fontina cheese
- Fresh sage

Sun-Dried Tomato-and-Goat-Cheese Pizza
- Sun-dried tomatoes
- Red onions
- Goat cheese
- Fresh or dried basil
- Crushed red-pepper flakes

Pimento Cheese Pizza
- Roasted red peppers or pimentos (available canned)
- Cheddar cheese

Tex-Mex Pizza
- Salsa
- Fresh sweet and hot peppers
- Red onions
- Monterey Jack cheese

Whole-Wheat Pizza Dough

This recipe lets you divide and conquer a family-size batch of pizza dough by freezing it in individual rounds. When you're in the mood for homemade pizza dough, pluck one or two of the dough rounds from your freezer and let them thaw on a baking sheet for 1 hour at room temperature. Top with a few oddments from the refrigerator and bake at 500° for 10 to 12 minutes, or until the crust is cooked through and the toppings are lightly browned. You'll have yourself designer pizzas as good as any you'll find in high-priced pizzerias.

To turn the dough into focaccia (Italian flatbread), thaw it and then allow it to rise until it doubles in height. Flavor it with things such as chopped olives, fresh rosemary, thinly sliced onions and a sprinkling of Parmesan cheese. Bake focaccia in a slightly cooler oven than you would use for pizza, about 400°, until it is brown and crisp, about 15 to 20 minutes.

Ingredients	For 4 crusts	For 8 crusts
Warm water	1¼ cups	2½ cups
Sugar	1 tablespoon	2 tablespoons
Active dry yeast	1 package	2 packages
Whole-wheat or unbleached flour, unsifted	3 cups	6 cups
Salt	1 teaspoon	2 teaspoons
Olive oil	2 tablespoons	¼ cup

In a large mixing bowl, combine the water with the sugar and yeast; stir to dissolve. Beat in half the flour and let the mixture stand until it gets foamy, about 10 minutes. Stir in the salt and the remaining flour to get a kneadable dough.

Turn the dough out onto a lightly floured surface and knead it for 5 minutes, or until it is smooth and elastic. Divide the dough into 4 (or 8) pieces, shape each piece into a ball, cover the balls with a clean cloth and let them rest for 10 minutes.

On a lightly floured surface, using a rocking motion of your knuckles, push each dough ball outward from the center to make a 6″ circle.

Brush the top and bottom of each circle lightly with the oil. Arrange the pizza circles in a single layer on baking sheets; freeze them just until they are firm. Transfer to heavy-duty resealable plastic freezer bags. (You can stack 4 crusts in each bag.) Store for up to 3 months.

Per crust: 381 calories, 8.4 g. total fat, 1.2 g. saturated fat, 0 mg. cholesterol, 540 mg. sodium, 13.1 g. protein, 69.1 g. carbohydrates, 11.9 g. dietary fiber.

Onion Jam

Savory onion jam lets you add the concentrated essence of caramelized onions to roast pork, chicken, baked potatoes, scrambled eggs or pan-grilled liver. It's also dynamite on pizza or steamed vegetables, with a few shavings of creamy fontina cheese.

To make onion jam, cut 1 pound of Bermuda or yellow onions into very thin slices. (I know a pound of onions sounds like a lot, but this will cook down to about 1 cup of jam. I usually double the amount and make 2 cups because it takes at least half an hour to cook down the onions, and the jam keeps very well in the refrigerator.)

Place the onions in a heavy, 10″ nonstick skillet filmed with 1½ teaspoons olive oil. Sprinkle with 1 tablespoon sugar and salt and pepper to taste. Cover the pan and cook over low heat, stirring occasionally, for 30 to 45 minutes, or until the onions have a rich brown color and are reduced to about 1 cup.

Let the onions cool and store them in a tightly covered container in the refrigerator.

Bistro Sandwich

This hearty sandwich is a big hit every time I make it. I prefer a crusty sour-dough bread, but a good whole-grain bread works well, too.

Ingredients	For 1 serving	For 2 servings
Tomato and Cheese Spread		
Thinly sliced sun-dried tomatoes	¾ tablespoon	1½ tablespoons
Red wine vinegar	1 tablespoon	2 tablespoons
Red-pepper flakes (optional)	to taste	to taste
Neufchâtel cheese, softened	1½ tablespoons	3 tablespoons
Crumbled feta cheese	2 tablespoons	¼ cup
Greek or other brine-cured olives, pitted and quartered	3	5
Garlic, crushed	½ clove	1 clove
Dried basil	⅛ teaspoon	¼ teaspoon
Bistro Sandwich		
Sweet red pepper	¼ pepper	½ pepper
Sourdough or whole-grain bread	2 slices	4 slices
Spinach, stemmed and coarsely chopped	¾ cup	1½ cups

To make the tomato and cheese spread: In a small saucepan, combine the tomatoes, vinegar and pepper flakes (if using). Heat the mixture gently over medium-low heat for 3 minutes, or until the tomatoes have absorbed the liquid.

In a small mixing bowl, beat the Neufchâtel and feta together until fluffy. Blend in the tomato-vinegar mixture, olives, garlic and basil. (Use immediately or cover the mixture and refrigerate overnight to blend the flavors.)

To make the bistro sandwich: Cut the peppers into thin strips.

Spread each slice of bread with 2 tablespoons of the tomato and cheese spread. Pat the spinach evenly over the slices; top with the pepper strips. Cut each slice of bread in half diagonally. Serve the sandwiches open-faced, with a fork and knife.

Per serving: 301 calories, 14.4 g. total fat, 6.5 g. saturated fat, 34 mg. cholesterol, 604 mg. sodium, 13 g. protein, 36.1 g. carbohydrates, 8.3 g. dietary fiber.

Basic Quesadillas

Quesadillas are the significant-other grilled cheese sandwiches for the health-conscious. They are very quick and take to a variety of embellishments. Try the plain cheese version given here topped with a spoonful of homemade or commercial salsa. Or add fresh lettuce, slivered green onions, cilantro and sliced tomatoes before you roll up the quesadillas. I like mild Monterey Jack cheese, but you can substitute Muenster, Cheddar or any cheese with good melting qualities.

Ingredients	For 1 serving	For 2 servings
Corn or flour tortillas	1	2
Shredded Monterey Jack cheese	2 tablespoons	¼ cup

Place a heavy, 5″ nonstick or cast-iron skillet over medium-low heat for 2 minutes. Lay a tortilla in the pan and sprinkle evenly with the Monterey Jack.

Cover the pan and heat the quesadilla until the Monterey Jack melts, about 1 to 2 minutes. With a broad spatula, remove the quesadilla to a plate and roll the tortilla into a cylinder to enclose the cheese.

Per serving: 122 calories, 6 g. total fat, 2.7 g. saturated fat, 17 mg. cholesterol, 167 mg. sodium, 5.8 g. protein, 13 g. carbohydrates, 1.6 g. dietary fiber.

Green Tomato Salsa

Green Tomato Salsa is especially good on oven-crisped corn chips and in quesadillas made with corn tortillas, melted Cheddar or Monterey Jack cheese and shredded lettuce. When green tomatoes aren't available, make the salsa with the hard, pale tomatoes you find in winter markets (finally—a use for them!). A squeeze of lime juice mimics the tart, slightly acidic flavor of Mexican tomatillos, distant cousins of the tomato that can be quite expensive and hard to find in many markets.

Ingredients	For 1 serving	For 2 servings
Green pepper	½ medium	1 medium
Green or hard red tomato	½ medium	1 medium
Olive oil	1 teaspoon	2 teaspoons
Onion, coarsely chopped	½ small	1 small
Garlic, crushed	1 small clove	1 clove
Red-pepper flakes	¼ teaspoon	½ teaspoon
Finely chopped fresh cilantro	1 tablespoon	2 tablespoons
Lime juice	1 tablespoon	2 tablespoons
Salt	to taste	to taste

Cut the pepper into ½" dice. Cut the tomato into ¾" cubes. Set both aside.

Place a heavy, 8" nonstick skillet over medium heat. Add the oil; stir in the onions and peppers. Cook, stirring occasionally, for 5 minutes, or until the onions are translucent.

Stir in the garlic, tomatoes and pepper flakes. Cook, stirring frequently, for 3 minutes, or until the tomatoes soften. Stir in the cilantro and lime juice. Taste for seasonings and add salt as needed.

Bring the salsa just to a simmer, then remove it from the heat. Serve it hot or cold.

Per serving: 87 calories, 4.8 g. total fat, 0.7 g. saturated fat, 0 g. cholesterol, 12 mg. sodium, 1.8 g. protein, 11.1 g. carbohydrates, 1.7 g. dietary fiber.

Salsa Rapida

Salsa means "sauce" in Spanish. Rapida means you can make this version in less than 5 minutes. Use it on everything from oven-baked tortilla chips to pizza, hamburgers and baked potatoes.

Ingredients	For 1 serving	For 2 servings
Ripe tomatoes	1 medium	2 medium
Green onions	1	2
Chopped fresh cilantro or parsley	1 tablespoon	2 tablespoons
Garlic, crushed (optional)	1 small clove	1 medium clove
Red wine vinegar	1 tablespoon	2 tablespoons
Hot-pepper sauce	¼ teaspoon	½ teaspoon
Salt	to taste	to taste

Cut the tomatoes into ½" pieces. Place in a small bowl.

Cut the onions, including the green tops, into thin slices. Add to the tomatoes. Stir in the cilantro or parsley, garlic (if using), vinegar, hot-pepper sauce and salt. Mix well.

Per serving: 34 calories, 0.4 g. total fat, 0 g. saturated fat, 0 mg. cholesterol, 18 mg. sodium, 1.3 g. protein, 8 g. carbohydrates, 1.7 g. dietary fiber.

Black Bean Pesto

You don't need bran every morning to get your daily fiber. Dietary fiber comes packaged in a wide variety of good-tasting foods, such as black beans. You can have this pesto ready in a snap; make it anytime you want it from ingredients that you keep on hand.

For parties, layer the black bean pesto in a crystal bowl with yogurt cheese or light sour cream, diced tomatoes, diced avocados and purple onions; surround the dip with oven-crisped tortilla chips. Or use the pesto as an everyday dip for raw vegetables such as carrot sticks, zucchini slices and broccoli florets.

Ingredients	For 2 servings	For 4 servings
Homemade or bottled salsa	½ cup	1 cup
Fresh cilantro sprigs (optional)	2–3	4–5
Canned black beans, rinsed and drained	¾ cup	16 ounces

Place the salsa, then the cilantro (if using) and then the beans in a blender. This order helps the machine process the ingredients more effectively. Process on medium-high speed until the pesto is smooth; stop the motor as necessary to scrape down the sides of the container.

Serve immediately or place in the refrigerator for an hour to blend the flavors.

Per serving: 117 calories, 1.4 g. total fat, 0.2 g. saturated fat, 0 g. cholesterol, 436 mg. sodium, 7.2 g. protein, 21.7 g. carbohydrates, 3.2 g. dietary fiber.

Light Meals and Snacks

Tavern-Style Carrots

Baby carrots now come polybagged by the pound for eating raw or making easy pickled carrots. You can prepare a batch in about 15 minutes, then enjoy them as a guilt-free snack with crackers. Or try them as a salad or first course on lettuce (especially red leaf lettuce) or as a relish with grilled or roasted meats, fish and poultry.

Ingredients	For 3 servings	For 6 servings
Dark beer or ale	¾ cup	12 ounces
Onion, sliced	½ small	1 small
Garlic, crushed	2 cloves	4 cloves
Olive oil	1½ teaspoons	1 tablespoon
Cumin seeds	½ teaspoon	1 teaspoon
Salt	¼ teaspoon	½ teaspoon
Ground red pepper	pinch	⅛ teaspoon
Baby carrots	½ pound	1 pound
Dijon mustard	1½ teaspoons	1 tablespoon
Chopped fresh cilantro (optional)	1 tablespoon	2 tablespoons

In a heavy 10″ skillet, combine the beer or ale, onions, garlic, oil, cumin seeds, salt and pepper. Bring to a boil over high heat, then reduce the heat to low and simmer for 5 minutes. Add the carrots and bring the mixture back to a simmer.

Cover the pan and cook the carrots for 5 minutes, or until they are crisp-tender. Remove the pan from the heat and stir in the mustard and cilantro (if using). Cool the carrots in the marinade to room temperature, then cover the mixture and refrigerate it overnight before serving.

Per serving: 41 calories, 0.3 g. total fat, 0 g. saturated fat, 0 mg. cholesterol, 212 mg. sodium, 8.8 g. carbohydrates, 1 g. protein, 2.5 g. dietary fiber.

Pesto of Sun-Dried Tomatoes & Salt-Cured Olives

You'll find all sorts of good uses for this versatile pesto. Toss it with hot spaghetti for a good dinner or spread it on bread crisps for a snack or on pizza for a meal. Blend it with nonfat yogurt or yogurt cheese for a dip for raw vegetables. Dab it on steamed or poached fish, chicken or root vegetables.

Oil-packed, sun-dried tomatoes pile on calories and fat. So look for plain sun-dried tomatoes in the produce section of your grocery store. Salt-cured olives are dry and wrinkled, with an intense flavor. If you can't find them, use Greek kalamata olives or, in a pinch, California black olives. But go easy! Olives, whatever their nationality, are relatively high in fat.

Ingredients	For 1 serving	For 2 servings
Sun-dried tomatoes, lightly packed	¼ cup	½ cup
Pitted black olives	¼ cup	½ cup
Orange juice	¼ cup	½ cup
Dried basil	½ teaspoon	1 teaspoon

In a blender, combine the tomatoes, olives, orange juice and basil. Process, stopping once or twice to scrape down the sides of the blender, until the pesto is a coarse puree. Store in a tightly covered container for up to 2 weeks.

Per serving: 139 calories, 3.2 g. total fat, 0.4 g. saturated fat, 0 g. cholesterol, 280 mg. sodium, 4.1 g. protein, 27.7 g. carbohydrates, 2.2 g. dietary fiber.

BASIL

Rainbow Hummus

This addictive spread is delicious in a sandwich with pita bread, ripe tomatoes, Greek olives, thinly sliced cucumbers, green onions and sprouts. It also makes a great dip for raw vegetables. You can prepare it with any canned beans in any color, hence the name "rainbow." Look for tahini (sesame seed paste) in health food stores or in the foreign-food section of your grocery store.

Ingredients	For 1 cup	For 2 cups
Water	2½ tablespoons	⅓ cup
Tahini	1½ tablespoons	3 tablespoons
Lemon juice	1½ tablespoons	3 tablespoons
Olive oil	1½ teaspoons	1 tablespoon
Canned Great Northern beans, rinsed and drained	¾ cup	16 ounces
Garlic, crushed	1 clove	2 cloves
Parsley sprigs (optional)	2	4
Salt	⅛ teaspoon	¼ teaspoon
Hot-pepper sauce	to taste	to taste

In a blender, combine the water, tahini, lemon juice, oil, beans, garlic, parsley, salt and hot-pepper sauce. Process the mixture on medium speed, stopping the blender as necessary to scrape down the sides of the container, until the hummus is smooth. Serve immediately or store in a covered container in the refrigerator for up to 1 week.

Per ¼ cup: 76 calories, 3.6 g. total fat, 0.5 g. saturated fat, 0 g. cholesterol, 71 mg. sodium, 3.3 g. protein, 8.5 g. carbohydrates, 2.4 g. dietary fiber.

Texas Caviar

Texas Caviar was once a favorite nibble of Texas millionaires who hung around the pool of Houston's glitzy Shamrock Hotel. Today, it's making a comeback in our nation's capital, where you need to be a millionaire to buy it!

At home, you can make four generous servings for less than a dollar—with very little effort. For the best flavor, freshly cook dried black-eyed peas. They take considerably less time than most other dried legumes and are very cheap. You can also use frozen black-eyed peas and cook them according to the package directions, as I call for in the recipe.

Serve the caviar as a snack with thin slices of French bread or as a meal with cornbread and ripe tomatoes. Since it travels well and tastes best at room temperature, it's a natural for brown-bag lunches.

Ingredients	For 2 servings	For 4 servings
Frozen black-eyed peas	1 cup	10 ounces
Green onions	1	2
Diced sweet red or green peppers	⅓ cup	⅔ cup
Red wine vinegar	2 tablespoons	¼ cup
Olive oil	1½ teaspoons	1 tablespoon
Salt	¼ teaspoon	½ teaspoon
Hot-pepper sauce	to taste	to taste
Finely chopped fresh parsley (optional)	2 tablespoons	¼ cup

Cook the peas according to the directions on the package. Drain and place them in a medium mixing bowl.

Cut the green onions, including the green tops, into thin slices. Add to the peas. Stir in the peppers, vinegar, oil, salt, hot-pepper sauce and parsley (if using); toss the ingredients well.

Cover the bowl and refrigerate for several hours or overnight to blend the flavors. Serve chilled or at room temperature.

Per serving: 127 calories, 4.1 g. total fat, 0.6 g. saturated fat, 0 mg. cholesterol, 272 mg. sodium, 7 g. protein, 17.8 g. carbohydrates, 8.5 g. dietary fiber.

Mushrooms à la Grecque

This classic French appetizer packs a lot of flavor into very few calories. Since these mushrooms taste best when they have been left to marinate overnight, make a batch before hunger strikes and keep some on hand for low-fat nibbling with whole-wheat crackers or as a salad on lettuce-lined plates.

Ingredients	For 2 servings	For 4 servings
Chopped onions	2 tablespoons	¼ cup
Olive oil	1 teaspoon	2 teaspoons
Water	¾ cup	1½ cups
Dry white wine or defatted chicken broth	¼ cup	½ cup
Lemon juice	1 tablespoon	2 tablespoons
Tomato paste	1 tablespoon	2 tablespoons
Garlic	1 clove	2 cloves
Whole peppercorns	½ teaspoon	1 teaspoon
Dried thyme	⅛ teaspoon	¼ teaspoon
Bay leaves	1	2
Button mushrooms, trimmed	12 ounces	1½ pounds

In a large heavy saucepan over medium heat, cook the onions in the oil for 3 minutes, or until they are translucent. Add the water, wine or broth, lemon juice, tomato paste, garlic, peppercorns, thyme and bay leaves.

Bring the mixture to a boil over high heat; stir in the mushrooms and return the liquid to a boil.

Reduce the heat to medium, cover the pan and cook the mushrooms for 10 minutes, or until they are tender and reduced to half their original size.

With a slotted spoon, transfer the mushrooms to a refrigerator container. Raise the heat to high, then rapidly boil down the cooking liquid until it's syrupy and reduced to about ½ cup (or 1 cup). Pour the liquid over the mushrooms, allow them to cool to room temperature, then cover and refrigerate them. Let them stand for several hours or overnight to blend flavors. Store the mushrooms for up to a week. Serve them cold or at room temperature. Remove and discard the bay leaves before serving.

Per serving: 97 calories, 2.9 g. total fat, 0.6 g. saturated fat, 0 mg. cholesterol, 101 mg. sodium, 4.1 g. protein, 11.6 g. carbohydrates, 2.6 g. dietary fiber.

Brighton Beach Eggplant

Roasted peppers and raisins add sweetness to this spicy Armenian-style eggplant dish. A friend of mine first tasted it in a restaurant in Brighton Beach, New York, and then shared the recipe with me. Try it with French bread and feta cheese for a summer lunch. Or stuff it into a pita pocket for a movable feast to take along to work.

Ingredients	For 2 servings	For 4 servings
Eggplant	12 ounces	1½ pounds
Onion	½ medium	1 medium, halved
Olive oil	1 teaspoon	2 teaspoons
Sweet red pepper	½ large	1 large, halved
Ripe tomatoes	1 medium	2 medium
Unpeeled garlic	2 cloves	4 cloves
Seedless raisins	2 tablespoons	¼ cup
Finely chopped fresh cilantro	2 tablespoons	¼ cup
Ground turmeric	½ teaspoon	1 teaspoon
Salt	to taste	to taste
Ground red pepper	to taste	to taste

Preheat the oven to 450°.

Cut the eggplant in half lengthwise. Brush the cut sides of the eggplant and onions with the oil. Arrange the eggplant and onions, cut side down, on a baking sheet. Add the sweet peppers, tomatoes and garlic.

Roast the vegetables on the top shelf of the oven for 30 minutes, or until they are tender. Transfer them to a chopping board to cool. Scrape out the pulp from the eggplant and discard the skin. Remove the skin from the tomatoes and peppers. Coarsely chop all the vegetables and place them in a medium mixing bowl.

Peel the garlic and put it through a garlic press; add it to the chopped vegetables. Stir in the raisins, cilantro, turmeric, salt and ground pepper. Mix well.

Cover and refrigerate for several hours or overnight to blend the flavors. Serve cold or at room temperature.

Per serving: 115 calories, 2.9 g. total fat, 0.4 g. saturated fat, 0 mg. cholesterol, 74 mg. sodium, 2.6 g. protein, 23.1 g. carbohydrates, 2 g. dietary fiber.

Light Meals and Snacks

Skinny Dip

When you crave a snack, you can make this creamy dill dip so fast you won't have time to fall off the diet wagon. Use it for dunking celery and carrot sticks, green onions and slices of yellow summer squash or zucchini. Spoon it onto baked potatoes or spread it on wheat crackers, Melba toast and breadsticks.

To turn this into a creamy blue cheese dip or dressing, omit the dill and add 2 tablespoons crumbled blue cheese for each cup of dip. To make creamy cucumber dressing, keep the dill and add ¼ cup finely diced cucumbers to each cup of dip.

Ingredients	For 1 cup	For 2 cups
1% low-fat cottage cheese	¾ cup	12 ounces
Nonfat buttermilk	¼ cup	½ cup
Coarsely chopped shallots or onions	1 tablespoon	2 tablespoons
Dried dill weed	½ teaspoon	1 teaspoon
Salt and pepper	to taste	to taste

In a blender, combine the cottage cheese, buttermilk, shallots or onions, dill, salt and pepper. Process on medium speed until the cottage cheese is smooth and creamy, stopping the blender as necessary to scrape down the sides. Serve immediately or refrigerate in a tightly covered container for up to 1 week.

Per ¼ cup: 41 calories, 0.5 g. total fat, 0.3 g. saturated fat, 2 mg. cholesterol, 184 mg. sodium, 6.2 g. protein, 2.7 g. carbohydrates, 0 g. dietary fiber.

Herbed Cream Cheese

Buttermilk gives this creamy cheese spread a buttery flavor without butter fat. Flavored with herbs and garlic, it's terrific with raw vegetables and crackers. Spread it over whole-grain bread for a sandwich with tomato slices, sprouts and slivers of red onion. Fines herbes is a mixture of herbs used in French cooking; look for it in the spice section of your supermarket. Or approximate the taste with a small pinch each of dried basil, thyme, tarragon and crumbled rosemary.

Ingredients	For 2 servings	For 4 servings
Neufchâtel cheese, softened	3 ounces	6 ounces
Nonfat buttermilk or plain yogurt	1 tablespoon	2 tablespoons
Garlic, crushed	1 clove	2 cloves
Dried fines herbes	¼ teaspoon	½ teaspoon
Coarsely ground black pepper	¼ teaspoon	½ teaspoon

In a small mixing bowl, cream the cheese and buttermilk or yogurt with a hand-held mixer until smooth. Blend in the garlic, herbs and pepper. Store, covered, in the refrigerator for up to 1 week.

Per serving: 110 calories, 9.3 g. total fat, 6.2 g. saturated fat, 30 mg. cholesterol, 173 mg. sodium, 4.6 g. protein, 2.2 g. carbohydrates, 0 g. dietary fiber.

Yogurt Cheese

Yogurt cheese is nothing more than thick curds of yogurt drained of the watery whey through several layers of cheesecloth. Where to buy cheesecloth? In the kitchenware or cleaning section of larger supermarkets or in hardware stores.

Plain or whisked with a little honey, versatile yogurt cheese is a dessert dip for fresh cherries, strawberries or slices of peach, mango or melon. Over chili or baked white potatoes or sweet potatoes, it's a low-fat replacement for butter or grated cheese. Mixed with thinly sliced green onions, snipped chives or minced herbs, it turns into a tangy dip for raw vegetables and crisp crackers. Blended with jam, yogurt cheese makes a healthy alternative spread for toast or muffins.

It looks like sour cream, but it doesn't behave like sour cream. You can't put yogurt cheese into cooked sauces or soups because it curdles. You can bake with yogurt cheese, however. Use it as a replacement in cake, muffin or cookie recipes that call for sour cream.

To make yogurt cheese, line a colander or large mesh strainer with four thicknesses of dampened cheesecloth. Set over a mixing bowl to catch the whey. Stir the yogurt and add to the colander or strainer. Refrigerate for four to five hours, or until the yogurt is the consistency of thick sour cream. Peel off the cheesecloth and turn the yogurt cheese into a container. Cover and refrigerate for up to one week. A 16-ounce container of yogurt makes 1 cup of yogurt cheese.

To flavor yogurt cheese, add one or more of the following:

- Strawberry jam
- Orange marmalade
- Tahini and fresh garlic
- Snipped green onions or chives
- Fresh mint, cilantro, basil or parsley
- Honey
- Fresh cherries, chopped mangoes, strawberries or peaches
- Ground cumin and orange rind

Cucumber Raita

Though raita is most often found in the company of curries, I like it as a snack with whole-wheat pita bread. It's also good as a side salad with dishes made of lentils and other legumes. It's best made and eaten right away, before the cucumber begins to weep and turn the yogurt watery.

Ingredients	For 1 serving	For 2 servings
Nonfat plain yogurt	⅓ cup	⅔ cup
Salt	⅛ teaspoon	¼ teaspoon
Ground cumin	⅛ teaspoon	¼ teaspoon
Ground red pepper	to taste	to taste
Cucumber	½ large	1 large

In a small mixing bowl, whisk the yogurt, salt, cumin and pepper until smooth.

Peel the cucumber only if it's waxed. Cut it in half lengthwise and scoop out the seeds with the tip of a teaspoon. Grate the halves coarsely and stir them into the yogurt mixture. Serve within an hour or so.

Per serving: 66 calories, 0.3 g. total fat, 0 g. saturated fat, 2 mg. cholesterol, 330 mg. sodium, 5.7 g. protein, 11.2 g. carbohydrates, 1.5 g. dietary fiber.

and Chowders

*M*arjorie Kinnan Rawlings, author of *The Yearling*, wrote in *Cross Creek Cookery* that being served a single cup of some ravishing soup was like having the Pearly Gates slam shut in your face after a brief glimpse of heaven. I couldn't agree more. I love soup and have happily kept body and soul together—and well-nourished—with a procession of the soups you're about to meet augmented with a parade of hearty peasant breads.

Here are cold soups, like Curried Bisque of Summer Squash, to keep chilled for hot-weather snacking, to carry in a thermos for enviable lunches at the office or to serve as a prelude to a fancy summer dinner. There are even more recipes for sturdy hot soups, like Old-Fashioned Mushroom-Barley Soup and Chili non Carne, that make a satisfying meal with a hunk of whole-grain bread and salad or slaw. For hurry-up suppers, help yourself to Chowder of Salmon and Green Peas, made quickly and thickly with on-hand ingredients.

Some of the best soups in this section begin with chicken broth, which may be canned but is far better and cheaper when homemade. Vegetarians may substitute diluted miso broth, cooking liquids drained from vegetables or water in recipes calling for defatted low-sodium chicken broth.

Curried Bisque of Summer Squash

This refreshing saffron-colored soup makes an elegant first course or a light summer meal. Serve it icy cold, garnished with slivered snow peas. In hot weather, I keep a pitcher of it cold and ready in the refrigerator.

Ingredients	For 2 servings	For 4 servings
Butter or margarine	2 teaspoons	4 teaspoons
Chopped onions	¼ cup	½ cup
Garlic, crushed	1 clove	2 cloves
All-purpose flour	1 tablespoon	2 tablespoons
Curry powder	1½ teaspoons	1 tablespoon
Defatted chicken broth	1½ cups	3 cups
Sliced yellow summer squash	6 ounces	12 ounces
Nonfat buttermilk	1 cup	2 cups
Lemon juice	1 tablespoon	2 tablespoons

Melt the butter or margarine in a heavy 2-quart (or 3-quart) saucepan over medium heat. Add the onions and cook, stirring frequently, for 5 minutes, or until they are soft but not brown. Stir in the garlic, then the flour and curry powder.

Add the broth and cook the mixture, stirring constantly, until it comes to a simmer and is slightly thickened. Add the squash and reduce the heat to low. Continue cooking over low heat, stirring occasionally, for 15 minutes, or until the squash is tender.

Let the soup cool to room temperature, then puree it in a blender, working in batches if necessary. Stir in the buttermilk and lemon juice. Chill the soup in a covered container for 2 hours or overnight. Serve it ice-cold in bowls or mugs.

Per serving: 135 calories, 6 g. total fat, 3.3 g. saturated fat, 17 mg. cholesterol, 252 mg. sodium, 6 g. protein, 16.2 g. carbohydrates, 0.9 g. dietary fiber.

Fire & Ice Bisque

This scarlet soup, heated with ginger and ground red pepper, is grand for cold sufferers. Because it's good steaming hot or icy cold, I recommend it for winter or summer consumption. As a health dividend, Fire and Ice Bisque packs a double dose of vitamin C in the tomatoes and orange juice.

Ingredients	For 2 servings	For 4 servings
Diced canned or fresh tomatoes (with juice)	1 cup	2 cups
Chopped onions	¼ cup	½ cup
Fresh ginger, cut into quarter-size slices	3 slices	6 slices
Orange rind	½″ × 2″ strip	½″ × 4″ strip
Ground red pepper	to taste	to taste
Orange juice	1 cup	2 cups

In a heavy 2-quart (or 3-quart) saucepan, combine the tomatoes (with juice), onions, ginger, orange rind and pepper. Bring the mixture to a boil over a medium heat; then reduce the heat to low, cover the pan and simmer the soup for 15 minutes.

Allow the tomato mixture to cool to room temperature, then puree it in a blender. Pour it into a nonreactive container (plastic, ceramic, stainless steel or glass is fine) and stir in the orange juice. Cover and chill the soup for 2 hours or overnight to blend the flavors. Serve it piping hot or ice-cold.

Per serving: 90 calories, 0.6 g. total fat, 0.1 g. saturated fat, 0 mg. cholesterol, 198 mg. sodium, 2.3 g. protein, 20.3 g. carbohydrates, 2.3 g. dietary fiber.

Easy Homemade Chicken Broth

Why bother to make your own chicken broth from scratch? Good chicken broth can be a real timesaver for people who are concerned about fat, additives and salt. Broth is very inexpensive to make, and you can eliminate almost all the fat without sacrificing flavor.

I make chicken broth by the gallon from a three-pound bag of chicken necks and backs that my friendly butcher sells for about a dollar. After skimming the fat, I freeze the broth in small containers for use in sauces, gravies and casseroles as well as soups.

Don't add salt to the broth as you're making it because the broth becomes more concentrated as it cooks. It's better to taste the finished soup, sauce or casserole and add salt, if you want it, just before serving.

> 3 pounds chicken necks, wings or backs
> 4 quarts cold water
> 1 large onion, peeled
> 2 medium carrots, cut into 2" lengths
> 2 medium celery ribs with leaves, cut into 2" lengths
> 1 teaspoon black peppercorns
> 1 teaspoon dried thyme
> 5–6 whole cloves
> 4 bay leaves
> 6 parsley sprigs (optional)

Place the chicken and water in a 6-quart saucepan or stockpot and bring to a simmer over medium heat; simmer for 30 minutes, skimming off the scum that rises to the top.

Add the onions, carrots, celery, peppercorns, thyme, cloves, bay leaves and parsley (if using); bring to a simmer.

Reduce the heat to the lowest setting and simmer the broth for 3 to 4 hours. Strain the broth and discard the solids; they will have given all their flavor to the broth. Set the container of broth in a sink full of cold water to cool quickly. Cover and refrigerate overnight.

The next day, lift off and discard the congealed chicken fat that has risen to the top.

Transfer to 1- or 2-cup containers. Store in the refrigerator for up to 3 days or in the freezer for up to 6 months. (You can also freeze some broth in ice cube trays; pop the frozen cubes into freezer bags for times when you need only a small amount of broth.)

Makes 3½ quarts.

Per cup: 14 calories, 0.7 g. total fat, 0.2 g. saturated fat, 3 mg. cholesterol, 300 mg. sodium, 0.7 g. protein, 1.2 g. carbohydrates, 0 g. dietary fiber.

Mauve Decade Borscht

Mauve has been described as pink that's trying to be purple, a description that certainly fits this easy summery soup. Make it the night before it's wanted to give it a chance to chill down and mellow. Then spoon it from a bowl, sip it from a crystal goblet or gulp it from a mug. I've made Mauve Decade Borscht with both fresh beets and canned, and honestly, there's very little difference in the taste of the soup, though there's less work when you used canned beets.

Ingredients	For 2 servings	For 4 servings
Defatted chicken broth	1¼ cups	2½ cups
Chopped onions	2 tablespoons	¼ cup
Dried dill weed	½ teaspoon	1 teaspoon
Honey	1 teaspoon	2 teaspoons
Canned beets (with juice)	1 cup	16 ounces
Red wine vinegar	1 tablespoon	2 tablespoons
Nonfat buttermilk	1 cup	2 cups

In a heavy 2-quart (or 3-quart) saucepan, combine the broth, onions, dill and honey. Bring the mixture to a simmer and cook for 10 minutes on low heat. Remove the pan from the heat and add the beets (with juice) and vinegar.

Process the mixture in a blender until smooth. Chill the borscht in a tightly covered container for 2 hours or overnight. Just before serving, stir in the buttermilk.

Per serving: 101 calories, 0.8 g. total fat, 0.3 g. saturated fat, 3 mg. cholesterol, 551 mg. sodium, 5.7 g. protein, 18.8 g. carbohydrates, 1.4 g. dietary fiber.

Cream of Asparagus Soup

In mid-April the patch outside my dining room window erupts with a profusion of tender asparagus. I blanch or steam more than I can possibly eat at a sitting so I'll have leftovers to turn into this spring-tonic soup. I think that chicken broth adds depth of flavor, but this recipe is flexible. You can make a lovely vegetarian soup by using the cooking liquid from the asparagus in place of the broth.

Ingredients	For 2 servings	For 4 servings
Fresh asparagus spears	8 ounces	1 pound
Defatted chicken broth or water	1½ cups	3 cups
1% low-fat milk	1 cup	2 cups
Butter, margarine or olive oil	1 tablespoon	2 tablespoons
Minced onions or shallots	2 tablespoons	¼ cup
All-purpose flour	1½ tablespoons	3 tablespoons
Dried tarragon (optional)	¼ teaspoon	½ teaspoon
Salt (optional)	to taste	to taste
White pepper	dash	⅛ teaspoon

Bend each asparagus spear until it snaps. Discard the cut ends, wash the spears in lukewarm water, drain and cut into 1" lengths.

Place the broth or water in a heavy, 10" nonstick skillet. Bring to a boil over high heat. Add the asparagus and reduce the heat to medium. Cover and cook for 2 to 7 minutes, or until the asparagus is tender but still bright green. Be careful not to overcook the asparagus; it will continue cooking a little when you drain it.

Place a colander over a medium heat-proof bowl. Drain the asparagus, reserving the cooking liquid.

Transfer the asparagus to a blender. Add the milk and process for 1 minute, or until the asparagus is coarsely pureed. Set the mixture aside.

Heat the butter, margarine or oil in a heavy 2-quart (or 3-quart) saucepan over medium heat. Add the onions or shallots and cook, stirring frequently, for 3 minutes, or until they are tender but not brown. Stir in the flour, tarragon (if using), salt (if using) and pepper. Add the reserved cooking liquid and cook, stirring constantly, until it comes to a boil and thickens slightly. Stir in the asparagus puree and bring the soup back to a simmer. Serve hot.

Per serving: 165 calories, 7.9 g. total fat, 4.6 g. saturated fat, 22 mg. cholesterol, 349 mg. sodium, 8.3 g. protein, 17.1 g. carbohydrates, 1.7 g. dietary fiber.

Cream of Spinach Soup

I've stripped the heavy cream from this popular soup, and I think you'll be delighted with the light, fresh-tasting results. Serve it with hot French rolls.

Ingredients	For 2 servings	For 4 servings
Butter or margarine	1 tablespoon	2 tablespoons
Finely diced carrots	¼ cup	½ cup
Finely diced onions	2½ tablespoons	⅓ cup
Finely diced celery	2½ tablespoons	⅓ cup
All-purpose flour	2 tablespoons	¼ cup
Defatted chicken broth	1½ cups	3 cups
Dried thyme	⅛ teaspoon	¼ teaspoon
Dried marjoram	⅛ teaspoon	¼ teaspoon
Frozen chopped spinach, thawed	5 ounces	10 ounces
1% low-fat milk	¾ cup	1½ cups
White wine vinegar (optional)	1½ teaspoons	1 tablespoon
Salt and pepper	to taste	to taste
Grated nutmeg	to taste	to taste

In a heavy 2-quart (or 3-quart) saucepan over medium heat, melt the butter or margarine. Add the carrots, onions and celery and cook, stirring occasionally, for 5 minutes, or until the vegetables are tender but not brown.

Stir in the flour with a wire whisk, then stir in the broth and cook the soup, stirring constantly, until it comes to a boil and thickens slightly.

Add the thyme, marjoram and spinach. Reduce the heat to low and cook the soup for 10 to 15 minutes to develop the flavors.

Stir in the milk, vinegar (if using), salt, pepper and nutmeg. Raise the heat to medium and bring the soup back to a simmer. Serve hot.

Per serving: 179 calories, 7.6 g. total fat, 4.4 g. saturated fat, 21 mg. cholesterol, 464 mg. sodium, 9.2 g. protein, 21.9 g. carbohydrates, 4.1 g. dietary fiber.

Green & White Minestrone

Traditionally, Italian minestrones are served at room temperature; they are really more like vegetable stews than soups. My version is a good choice for a brown-bag lunch—try it the Italian way: Skip the microwave and serve minestrone with a hard roll and a piece of your favorite fresh fruit. For variety, substitute Swiss chard, quartered brussels sprouts or the coarsely chopped stems and buds of broccoli for the cabbage.

Ingredients	For 2 servings	For 4 servings
Chopped onions	½ cup	1 cup
Diced green peppers	¼ cup	½ cup
Diced celery	¼ cup	½ cup
Olive oil	1½ teaspoons	1 tablespoon
Garlic, crushed	1 clove	2 cloves
Water	2 cups	4 cups
Dried sage	¾ teaspoon	1½ teaspoons
Salt and pepper	to taste	to taste
New potatoes	1 small	2 small
Shredded cabbage	1½ cups	3 cups
Zucchini, thinly sliced	1 small	1 medium
Dried elbow macaroni or rotelle	¼ cup	½ cup

In a heavy 2-quart (or 3-quart) saucepan over medium heat, cook the onions, peppers and celery in the oil, stirring occasionally, for 5 minutes, or until the vegetables are tender but not brown.

Stir in the garlic. Add the water, sage, salt and pepper; raise the heat to high and bring the soup to a boil.

Cut the potatoes into ¾" cubes and add them, with the cabbage, to the soup. Bring the soup back to a boil, reduce the heat to low and cook for 10 minutes.

Add the zucchini and macaroni or rotelle. Cook for 20 minutes, or until the vegetables and pasta are tender. Serve hot or at room temperature.

Per serving: 157 calories, 4.1 g. total fat, 0.6 g. saturated fat, 12 mg. cholesterol, 35 mg. sodium, 4.3 g. protein, 27.5 g. carbohydrates, 1 g. dietary fiber.

White Bean & Tomato Soup with Rosemary

This hearty Italian soup is inexpensive and easy to make. Great Northern beans provide protein and fiber. The vegetarian version makes a satisfying meal, but you can also add leftover chicken, turkey, cubes of ham or crumbled, cooked sausage that has been drained of all fat. Complete the meal with a slice of corn-bread and a tossed green salad.

Ingredients	For 2 servings	For 4 servings
Olive or canola oil	1 teaspoon	2 teaspoons
Chopped onions	¼ cup	½ cup
Diced celery	2 tablespoons	¼ cup
Garlic, crushed	1 clove	2 cloves
Canned tomatoes (with juice)	1 cup	16 ounces
Water	1½ cups	3 cups
Canned Great Northern beans, rinsed and drained	¾ cup	16 ounces
Diced potatoes (¾" cubes)	½ cup	1 cup
Dried rosemary, crumbled	¼ teaspoon	½ teaspoon
Salt and pepper	to taste	to taste

Add the oil to a heavy 2-quart (or 3-quart) saucepan and place over medium heat. Add the onions and celery; cook for 5 minutes, or until tender but not brown.

Stir in the garlic and cook the mixture for 1 minute. Then add the tomatoes (with juice), water, beans, potatoes and rosemary. Bring the soup to a simmer. Cover and cook for 30 minutes. Add the salt and pepper. Serve hot.

Per serving: 177 calories, 3.1 g. total fat, 0.4 g. saturated fat, 0 mg. cholesterol, 36 mg. sodium, 7.8 g. protein, 31.9 g. carbohydrates, 4.9 g. dietary fiber.

ROSEMARY

Italian Market Greens & Beans

The inspiration for this recipe came from a meal I shared with friends in Philadelphia's Italian Market. We dined inelegantly but well on a robust soup of white kidney beans and escarole wilted in garlicky chicken broth. Years later, the owner of a roadside stand in Wisconsin told me how to make Italian beans and greens. The two experiences produced this soup.

Ingredients	For 2 servings	For 4 servings
Garlic, crushed	2 cloves	4 cloves
Olive oil	1½ teaspoons	1 tablespoon
Defatted chicken broth	2 cups	4 cups
Canned Great Northern beans, rinsed and drained	16 ounces	32 ounces
Escarole, torn into 2″ pieces, loosely packed	4 cups	8 cups
Lemon juice	2 tablespoons	¼ cup
Salt and pepper	to taste	to taste

In a heavy 2-quart (or 3-quart) saucepan over medium heat, cook the garlic in the oil for 2 minutes, or until the garlic begins to color. Add the broth, increase the heat to high, and bring the soup to a boil. Stir in the beans and escarole; bring the soup back to a boil.

Reduce the heat to low and simmer the soup for 5 to 10 minutes. Stir in the lemon juice, salt and pepper.

Per serving: 292 calories, 5.9 g. total fat, 0.9 g. saturated fat, 3 mg. cholesterol, 472 mg. sodium, 17.6 g. protein, 48.9 g. carbohydrates, 15.9 g. dietary fiber.

Corn & Red Pepper Chowder

This hearty chowder is best made in summer with fresh corn scraped from the cob, though it's delicious made with frozen corn. If you're using frozen corn, puree it briefly in the blender with the milk before adding it to the soup. And for an even heartier chowder, try adding crab meat, diced cooked chicken or canned minced clams.

Ingredients	For 2 servings	For 4 servings
Butter or margarine	1 tablespoon	2 tablespoons
Diced sweet red peppers	½ cup	1 cup
Finely chopped onions	2 tablespoons	¼ cup
All-purpose flour	1 tablespoon	2 tablespoons
Dried thyme	⅛ teaspoon	¼ teaspoon
Salt and pepper	to taste	to taste
Defatted chicken broth or water	1¼ cups	2½ cups
Corn kernels, fresh or frozen	1 cup	2 cups
1% low-fat milk	⅔ cup	1⅓ cups

In a heavy 2-quart (or 3-quart) saucepan over medium heat, melt the butter or margarine. Add the red peppers and onions; cook, stirring frequently, for 5 minutes, or until the vegetables are tender but not brown.

Stir in the flour, thyme, salt and pepper; cook and stir the mixture for 1 minute.

Add the broth or water; cook the soup, stirring constantly, until it comes to a boil and thickens slightly. Add the corn and milk, bring back to a simmer and cook for 5 to 10 minutes, or until the corn is tender. Serve hot.

Per serving: 183 calories, 7.1 g. total fat, 4.2 g. saturated fat, 20 mg. cholesterol, 291 mg. sodium, 6.3 g. protein, 26.6 g. carbohydrates, 2.3 g. dietary fiber.

Chowder of Salmon & Green Peas

This hearty chowder, made with ingredients you can keep on the shelf or in the freezer, is especially good when you can't get out for groceries or when you just feel like cocooning. If you're lucky enough to have around some poached or grilled salmon, by all means flake it and use it instead of canned salmon. Serve this chowder with corn muffins or cornbread, if at all possible, and add one of the slaws in the salad section for good and healthy eating.

Ingredients	For 2 servings	For 4 servings
Canned red or pink salmon (with liquid)	6½ ounces	13 ounces
Diced celery	¼ cup	½ cup
Diced onions	2 tablespoons	¼ cup
Diced green peppers (optional)	2 tablespoons	¼ cup
All-purpose flour	2 tablespoons	¼ cup
1% low-fat milk	2 cups	4 cups
Frozen green peas	⅔ cup	1⅓ cups
Worcestershire sauce	1 teaspoon	2 teaspoons
Pepper	to taste	to taste

Pour the liquid from the salmon into a heavy 2-quart (or 3-quart) saucepan; set the salmon aside.

To the pan, add the celery, onions and green peppers. Bring the liquid to a simmer over medium heat. Reduce the heat to low, cover the pan and cook the vegetables for 5 minutes, or until crisp-tender.

Place the flour in a small mixing bowl and whisk in ½ cup of the milk until no lumps remain. Stir into the saucepan; add the remaining milk. Raise the heat to medium and cook the chowder for 5 minutes, or until it is bubbling and slightly thickened.

Add the salmon, peas, Worcestershire sauce and pepper. Simmer for 7 to 10 minutes. Serve hot.

Per serving: 295 calories, 8.4 g. total fat, 3.1 g. saturated fat, 61 mg. cholesterol, 699 mg. sodium, 29.1 g. protein, 24.9 g. carbohydrates, 0.8 g. dietary fiber.

Pumpkin-Clam Chowder

Sweet and starchy pumpkin adds a warm autumnal flavor to this clam chowder. If you don't care for clams, substitute an equal measure of diced cooked chicken or turkey. Or leave the clams out altogether and enjoy a vegetarian pumpkin chowder. If you can't find small pumpkins at your local grocery, use butternut squash instead.

Ingredients	For 2 servings	For 4 servings
Olive oil	1 teaspoon	2 teaspoons
Chopped onions	¼ cup	½ cup
Diced sweet red or green peppers	¼ cup	½ cup
Garlic, minced	1 clove	2 cloves
Canned tomatoes (with juice)	1 cup	16 ounces
Water	½ cup	1 cup
Diced pumpkin (¾" cubes)	2 cups	4 cups
Dried thyme	¼ teaspoon	½ teaspoon
Red-pepper flakes	to taste	to taste
Salt (optional)	to taste	to taste
Canned minced or chopped clams	6½ ounces	13 ounces

Place the oil in a heavy 2-quart (or 3-quart) saucepan. Add the onions and red or green peppers; cook, stirring often, over low heat, for 5 minutes, or until the vegetables are tender but not brown. Stir in the garlic and cook for 1 minute.

Pull the tomatoes into small pieces and add them with their juice to the pan. Add the water, pumpkin, thyme, pepper flakes and salt (if using).

Bring the chowder to a boil over high heat, then reduce the heat to low. Cover and cook for 30 minutes, or until the pumpkin is very tender.

Stir in the clams and bring to a simmer. Serve hot.

Per serving: 150 calories, 4.1 g. total fat, 0.7 g. saturated fat, 58 mg. cholesterol, 451 mg. sodium, 11.3 g. protein, 22.4 g. carbohydrates, 4.3 g. dietary fiber.

Orange-Scented Bisque of Acorn Squash

I'd never heard of Martha Stewart when she turned up at my Virginia restaurant some years ago; I was too busy cooking to keep up with food's who. Yet I knew from the orders placed that this party of four understood and loved good food. So after I'd filled their orders and given them a reasonable time for sampling my cooking, I went up front and immediately realized that the knockout blonde was, for all her cool good looks, a real cook. We had a delightful chat, and when she left, Martha carried a Mason jar of this soup to sustain her in North Carolina, where she was headed to promote a book.

Ingredients	For 2 servings	For 4 servings
Acorn squash	1 small (1 pound)	1 large (2 pounds)
1% low-fat milk	1 cup	2 cups
Butter or margarine	1 tablespoon	2 tablespoons
Minced onions or shallots	2 tablespoons	¼ cup
All-purpose flour	1 tablespoon	2 tablespoons
Brown sugar	1½ teaspoons	1 tablespoon
Salt	to taste	to taste
White pepper	dash	⅛ teaspoon
Grated nutmeg	dash	⅛ teaspoon
Defatted chicken broth	1 cup	2 cups
Grated orange rind	from ½ orange	from 1 orange
Orange juice	¼ cup	½ cup

Pierce the squash in several places with a fork. Place on a paper towel or microwave-safe plate. Microwave on high power for 7 to 10 (or 10 to 12) minutes.

Cut the squash in half and allow it to cool slightly. Scoop out and discard the seeds. Scrape out the flesh and place it in a blender. Add the milk and process until smooth. Set the mixture aside.

In a heavy 2-quart (or 3-quart) saucepan, melt the butter or margarine over medium heat. Add the onions or shallots and cook, stirring often, for 5 minutes, or until they are tender but not brown.

Stir in the flour, brown sugar, salt, pepper and nutmeg. Add the broth and orange rind. Cook the soup, stirring frequently, until it comes to a boil. Add the squash mixture and orange juice; bring the soup back to a simmer. Serve hot.

Per serving: 210 calories, 7.6 g. total fat, 4.5 g. saturated fat, 22 mg. cholesterol, 275 mg. sodium, 6.3 g. protein, 32 g. carbohydrates, 2.7 g. dietary fiber.

Russian Vegetable Soup

Here's a low-rent, meatless borscht for hard times in the USA. It will make you brave at very little cost. Serve this peasant soup with a spoonful of light sour cream or yogurt and a slice of coarse rye or pumpernickel bread.

Ingredients	For 2 servings	For 4 servings
Water	1½ cups	3 cups
Tomato sauce	½ cup	8 ounces
Thinly sliced new potatoes	½ cup	1 cup
Thinly sliced carrots	½ cup	1 cup
Chopped onions	½ cup	1 cup
Diced celery	¼ cup	½ cup
Caraway seeds	½ teaspoon	1 teaspoon
Dried dill weed	½ teaspoon	1 teaspoon
Shredded cabbage	1 cup	2 cups
Canned sliced beets (with juice)	1 cup	16 ounces
Brown sugar or honey	1½ teaspoons	1 tablespoon
Cider vinegar or red wine vinegar	1 tablespoon	2 tablespoons

In a heavy 2-quart (or 3-quart) saucepan, combine the water, tomato sauce, potatoes, carrots, onions, celery, caraway seeds and dill. Bring to a boil over high heat, then reduce the heat to low. Cover and cook for 30 minutes.

Add the cabbage, beets (with juice), brown sugar or honey and vinegar. Bring the soup back to a boil over high heat, reduce the heat to low and simmer for 30 minutes, or until the vegetables are tender. Serve hot.

Per serving: 124 calories, 0.5 g. total fat, 0.1 g. saturated fat, 0 mg. cholesterol, 557 mg. sodium, 3.5 g. protein, 29.5 g. carbohydrates, 3.6 g. dietary fiber.

Old-Fashioned Mushroom-Barley Soup

It's my cook's observation that soups made without appropriate chicken, beef or fish stock are thin in flavor. Yet two of my four daughters are practicing vegetarians, so it's my frequent motherly duty to compose stockless soups that taste good. I think I succeeded with this soup, thanks to the uplifting effects of plenty of dill weed.

Ingredients	For 2 servings	For 4 servings
Butter or margarine	1½ teaspoons	1 tablespoon
Chopped onions	¼ cup	½ cup
Coarsely chopped mushrooms	1½ cups	3 cups
Garlic, minced (optional)	1 clove	2 cloves
Water	2½ cups	5 cups
Pearl barley	scant 3 tablespoons	⅓ cup
Reduced-sodium soy sauce	1½ teaspoons	1 tablespoon
Carrot, thinly sliced	1 small	1 medium
Diced celery	¼ cup	½ cup
Dried dill weed	1 teaspoon	2 teaspoons
Pepper	to taste	to taste

Melt the butter or margarine in a heavy 2-quart (or 3-quart) saucepan over medium heat. Add the onions and cook, stirring occasionally, for 5 minutes, or until the onions are tender but not brown. Add the mushrooms and continue to cook, stirring occasionally, for 5 minutes, or until the mushrooms release their juices.

Stir in the garlic and cook another minute. Add the water, barley and soy sauce. Bring the soup to a boil, reduce the heat to low, cover and cook for 30 minutes.

Add the carrots, celery, dill and pepper. Cover and cook for 15 minutes, or until the barley and vegetables are tender. Serve hot.

Per serving: 136 calories, 3.4 g. total fat, 1.9 g. saturated fat, 8 mg. cholesterol, 326 mg. sodium, 4.1 g. protein, 24.1 g. carbohydrates, 5.3 g. dietary fiber.

Potato-Leek Soup

So good and yet so simple. This classic country French soup is nothing more than potatoes, leeks, water, salt and pepper. Enhance the delicate onion flavor of leeks by first cooking them gently in a bit of butter, then simmer them with the other ingredients. You can substitute chopped yellow onions for the leeks if you like. In hot weather, puree Potato-Leek Soup and turn it into summery vichyssoise by chilling it and stirring in a few tablespoons of nonfat buttermilk at serving time.

Ingredients	For 2 servings	For 4 servings
Leeks	1 large	2 large
Butter or margarine	1½ teaspoons	1 tablespoon
Peeled and sliced potatoes	1½ cups	3 cups
Water or defatted chicken broth	3 cups	6 cups
Salt and white pepper	to taste	to taste

Remove the tough outer leaves of the leeks. Cut the remaining white and tender lighter-green part of the leeks in half lengthwise and hold the halves under cold running water to make sure that any dirt hidden between the layers is removed. Trim off the root end and chop the leek coarsely. Set aside.

In a heavy 2-quart (or 3-quart) saucepan over low heat, melt the butter or margarine. Stir in the leeks. Cover and cook, stirring occasionally, for 10 minutes, or until the leeks are wilted but not brown.

Add the potatoes, water or broth, salt and pepper. Increase the heat to high and bring the soup to a boil. Reduce the heat to low and simmer for 20 to 30 minutes, or until the potatoes are tender. Serve the soup hot, or let it cool to room temperature, puree it and serve it chilled.

Per serving: 185 calories, 0.8 g. total fat, 0.1 g. saturated fat, 0 mg. cholesterol, 323 mg. sodium, 4.4 g. protein, 43.2 g. carbohydrates, 5 g. dietary fiber.

Sweet Potato Vichyssoise

In this variation of vichyssoise, I have substituted sweet potatoes for the traditional russet potatoes. I prefer this version hot. For a creamy touch, swirl in a spoonful of nonfat yogurt just before serving.

Ingredients	For 2 servings	For 4 servings
Leeks	1 medium	2 medium
Butter or margarine	1½ teaspoons	1 tablespoon
Sweet potatoes	8 ounces	1 pound
Defatted chicken broth	2 cups	4 cups
Salt	to taste	to taste
White pepper	⅛ teaspoon	¼ teaspoon
Grated nutmeg	dash	⅛ teaspoon

Remove the tough outer leaves of the leeks. Cut the remaining white and tender lighter-green part of the leeks in half lengthwise and hold the halves under cold running water to make sure that any dirt hidden between the layers is removed. Trim off the root end and slice the leeks into thin half-moons. Set aside.

In a heavy 2-quart (or 3-quart) saucepan, melt the butter or margarine over low heat. Add the leeks and cook them, stirring occasionally, for 10 minutes, or until they are tender but not brown.

Peel the sweet potatoes and cut them into thick slices. Add them to the pan. Stir in the broth, salt, pepper and nutmeg. Bring the soup to a simmer. Reduce the heat to low. Cover and cook for 30 minutes, or until the sweet potatoes are very tender.

Cool the soup to room temperature, then puree it in batches in a blender or food processor. Serve hot or cold.

Per serving: 196 calories, 4.1 g. total fat, 2.1 g. saturated fat, 10 mg. cholesterol, 622 mg. sodium, 3.5 g. protein, 37.6 g. carbohydrates, 4.6 g. dietary fiber.

Vichyssoise: Classic French Potato Soup

The mild, rustic flavor of leek (or onion) and potato soup lends itself to countless variations. In hot weather, puree Potato-Leek Soup, then chill it and turn it into summery vichyssoise by adding 2 or 3 tablespoons nonfat buttermilk for every cup of ice-cold soup.

For a hearty scallop chowder, skip the buttermilk and gently heat the pureed soup. Add 2 ounces bay scallops (or your favorite seafood) and a tablespoon dry white wine for each cup of pureed soup. Simmer the seafood in the soup for about 3 minutes, just until it is opaque. Serve the soup hot.

Portuguese Potato-Kale Soup

Kale is traditional in this classic Portuguese soup, but other aggressive greens, such as collards, turnip greens or broccoli, can stand in nicely. Like all dark green leafy vegetables, kale is rich in beta-carotene. So are sweet potatoes — for a Southern twist with a double dose of beta-carotene, substitute sweet potatoes for the boiling potatoes. You could also replace the kielbasa or chorizo with country sausage that you've cooked and drained of all fat. Serve either version with hot cornbread or French bread.

Ingredients	For 2 servings	For 4 servings
Kale, washed	8 ounces	1 pound
Cubed boiling potatoes (½" cubes)	1 cup	2 cups
Water	2 cups	4 cups
Smoked kielbasa or chorizo, sliced	2 ounces	4 ounces
Hot-pepper vinegar	1 tablespoon	2 tablespoons
Salt and pepper	to taste	to taste

Trim the thick stems from the greens, stack and roll several leaves at a time and cut them into strips about ½" wide.

Place the greens in a heavy 2-quart (or 3-quart) saucepan with the potatoes, water and kielbasa or chorizo. Bring to a simmer over medium heat. Cover and cook the soup over low heat for 30 minutes, or until the potatoes are tender.

Stir in the vinegar. Then taste the soup and add the salt and pepper to taste. Serve hot.

Per serving: 186 calories, 8.2 g. total fat, 2.9 g. saturated fat, 19 mg. cholesterol, 342 mg. sodium, 7.1 g. protein, 21.6 g. carbohydrates, 4.5 g. dietary fiber.

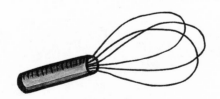

Hot-Pepper Vinegar

Hot-pepper vinegar perks up black-eyed peas and greens. It's very easy and inexpensive to make at home. Here's how:

Wash a narrow-necked glass bottle (a ketchup bottle works just fine) in hot soapy water and rinse it thoroughly with very hot water. Fill the bottle with small, whole fresh chili peppers. Any variety that can fit through the neck of the bottle will work. Serrano, tabasco, jalapeño, cayenne, fiesta and Thai chili peppers are all good choices.

Estimate how much rice or distilled white vinegar you'll need to fill the bottle and pour it into a nonreactive saucepan. Bring the vinegar to a boil over medium-high heat. Pour the hot vinegar through a funnel over the peppers to fill the bottle.

Cap the bottle and let it sit for two weeks or more before you use it. This will allow the flavor of the peppers to infuse the vinegar.

Sprinkle your hot-pepper vinegar over greens, broccoli, beans, soups, pork dishes and tomatoes—and skip the salt. When the level of the vinegar goes down, you can refill the bottle with hot vinegar one or two times to get the most flavor from your chili peppers.

CAYENNE

Baked Potato Soup
with Broccoli & Cheddar

Here is a great way to use up leftover spuds and broccoli, but this quick vegetarian soup is so good that you may want to bake a few extra potatoes to make sure you have some on hand.

Ingredients	For 2 servings	For 4 servings
Baked russet potatoes	1	2
1% low-fat milk	1½ cups	3 cups
Chopped broccoli, cooked or frozen	1 cup	2 cups
Shredded Cheddar cheese	¼ cup	½ cup
Salt and pepper	to taste	to taste

Cut the potatoes into chunks and combine them with the milk in a blender. Process the mixture until smooth. Add the broccoli and process, pulsing the motor on and off, until the broccoli is coarsely pureed. You should still be able to see tiny broccoli buds.

Transfer the mixture to a heavy 2-quart (or 3-quart) saucepan and bring to a simmer over medium heat. Remove the soup from the heat, then stir in the Cheddar, salt and pepper. Serve hot.

Per serving: 241 calories, 6.8 g. total fat, 4.2 g. saturated fat, 22 mg. cholesterol, 198 mg. sodium, 13.1 g. protein, 33.2 g. carbohydrates, 2.4 g. dietary fiber.

Almost-Instant Potatoes

You can save energy and cut potato baking time from an hour to around 20 minutes by briefly microwaving potatoes and then finishing them in a conventional oven. The microwave alone produces a disappointing baked potato; it's steamed, soggy and dense. But this two-step cooking method produces real baked potatoes—with crunchy skins and fluffy innards.

Here's how to do it. Preheat your conventional oven to 400°. Wash 2 firm, unblemished russet potatoes and microwave them on high power for 6 minutes. (Do 1 potato for 4 minutes.) Transfer the potatoes to a baking sheet and bake them in the preheated oven for 15 minutes, or until they are tender when pierced with a fork.

Cincinnati Turkey Chili

Don't be put off by the long list of ingredients. Cincinnati Turkey Chili is really quick to make once you've measured all those spices, which compensate for the blandness of ground turkey. And don't expect Cincinnati chili to taste like Tex-Mex chili; the flavor is spicy-mellow, not spicy-hot, revealing its Greek origins. Cincinnati's chili is so good that today, chili parlors outnumber hamburger joints in the Queen City, where chili-heads have a running list of embellishments for their unorthodox "bowl of red." (It's also a grand sauce for pasta.)

Served plain, Cincinnati chili is called a One Way. Over spaghetti, it's a Two Way. Add shredded mild Cheddar and it's a Three Way. Top with chopped raw onions and you've got a Four Way. All of the above, plus pinto beans heaped on top, is a Five Way. Cincinnati Turkey Chili freezes well, so you might want to double the recipe and stock your freezer.

Ingredients	For 2 servings	For 4 servings
Chili Spice Blend		
Ground cinnamon	¾ teaspoon	1½ teaspoons
Chili powder	½ teaspoon	1 teaspoon
Paprika	¼ teaspoon	½ teaspoon
Pepper	¼ teaspoon	½ teaspoon
Dried oregano	¼ teaspoon	½ teaspoon
Ground cumin	¼ teaspoon	½ teaspoon
Ground allspice	⅛ teaspoon	¼ teaspoon
Grated nutmeg	⅛ teaspoon	¼ teaspoon
Ground cloves	⅛ teaspoon	¼ teaspoon
Turkey Chili		
Ground turkey	8 ounces	1 pound
Finely chopped onions	⅓ cup	⅔ cup
Finely chopped celery	¼ cup	½ cup
Garlic, minced	1 clove	2 cloves
Bay leaf	½	1
Water or defatted chicken broth	2 cups	4 cups
Tomato paste	6 tablespoons	6 ounces

To make the chili spice blend: In a small bowl, mix the cinnamon, chili powder, paprika, pepper, oregano, cumin, allspice, nutmeg and cloves. Set aside.

To make the turkey chili: In a heavy 2-quart (or 3-quart) saucepan, combine the turkey, onions and celery. Cook over medium heat, breaking the turkey apart with a wooden spoon, until the turkey is crumbly and no longer pink. Stir in the garlic, bay leaf and the chili spice blend; cook the mixture a minute longer.

Add the water or broth and tomato paste; stir until the tomato paste is dissolved. Bring the chili to a simmer, then reduce the heat to low. Cook, stirring frequently, for 1 hour, or until the chili reaches the consistency you prefer.

Per serving: 220 calories, 9.3 g. total fat, 2.4 g. saturated fat, 83 mg. cholesterol, 471 mg. sodium, 22.2 g. protein, 13.2 g. carbohydrates, 2.8 g. dietary fiber.

Chili non Carne

The first time I made this chili for my vegetarian daughters, they insisted that I had put hamburger into the pot. I hadn't. The pebbly texture and rich flavor come from bulgur (cracked parboiled wheat), which you can find in health food stores, co-ops, Middle Eastern markets and many supermarkets. Fine or medium-grain bulgur gives the best results.

Ingredients	For 2 servings	For 4 servings
Olive or canola oil	1½ teaspoons	1 tablespoon
Chopped onions	½ cup	1 cup
Chopped celery	6 tablespoons	¾ cup
Diced carrots	6 tablespoons	¾ cup
Chopped green peppers	¼ cup	½ cup
Minced garlic	½ teaspoon	1 teaspoon
Chili powder	1½ teaspoons	1 tablespoon
Ground cumin	½ teaspoon	1 teaspoon
Canned tomatoes (with juice)	1 cup	16 ounces
Water	1 cup	2 cups
Canned pinto beans, rinsed and drained	¾ cup	16 ounces
Bulgur	2½ tablespoons	⅓ cup
Salt	to taste	to taste

Place the oil in a heavy 2-quart (or 3-quart) saucepan. Add the onions, celery, carrots and peppers. Cook over medium heat for 10 minutes, or until the vegetables are tender but not brown. Stir in the garlic, chili powder and cumin; cook for 1 minute.

Add the tomatoes (with juice) and water; bring the chili to a simmer. Cover the pan, reduce the heat to low and cook, stirring occasionally, for 1 hour.

Add the beans and bulgur. Cover and cook for 30 minutes, or until the bulgur is cooked through and the vegetables are tender. Add salt to taste. Serve hot.

Per serving: 231 calories, 4.8 g. total fat, 0.6 g. saturated fat, 0 mg. cholesterol, 267 mg. sodium, 9.4 g. protein, 41.3 g. carbohydrates, 6.7 g. dietary fiber.

Soups and Chowders

Salads

Versatile salads can start, accompany or end a good meal. Hearty salads with grains, meats and legumes make an easy meal by themselves. In this chapter you will find updated slaws and potato salads, piquant salads that blend the crisp flavors of citrus with buttery greens, hot and cold salads for every season and man-size salads with noodles, chicken, rice and beef.

Whichever salad you choose, remember that it's usually the dressing, not the salad itself, that can add fat to the meal. Regular salad dressings are made with oil, and a tablespoon of any oil—olive, canola, corn, soybean, walnut, whatever—has 14 grams of fat, more than a fifth of the daily 65 grams recommended for people with a 2,000-calorie intake. As for the new commercial bottled low- or nonfat dressings, I can honestly say that I've never tasted one I liked. (And I've tasted more than my share in the line of duty!)

Salad dressing doesn't take long to prepare. You can take advantage of the fresh flavor of citrus sections and rind, green onions, shallots, garlic, a good wine vinegar or balsamic vinegar, Dijon mustard and a tiny bit of flavorful oil such as olive or walnut oil.

With good ingredients, you won't need to bathe your salads in salt or fat to get delicious results. Allow yourself to splurge a little when you buy the oil and vinegar for your salad pantry. Remember, you won't need much for any particular salad. To create your own house dressing, follow the suggestions for the vinaigrette that accompanies Classic Green Salad with New Vinaigrette.

Classic Green Salad with New Vinaigrette

French vinaigrette is one of the best and most basic salad dressings, but normally it is quite high in fat. I've slimmed this version down by replacing a good portion of the oil with flavorful fruit or vegetable juice. Use whatever you like and don't be afraid to experiment. Orange juice and tomato juice are particularly good, but you can also substitute broth, wine, sherry or even water.

Since you will be using only a small amount of oil, treat yourself to an especially flavorful one. Extra-virgin olive oil works wonders with any green salad, as does walnut or hazelnut oil. A small amount of heavy cream can replace the oil to make a sumptuous dressing for butterleaf lettuces like Bibb and Boston.

Ingredients	For 1 serving	For 2 servings
Vinegar or lemon juice	2 teaspoons	4 teaspoons
Fruit or vegetable juice	2 teaspoons	4 teaspoons
Dijon mustard	⅛ teaspoon	¼ teaspoon
Garlic, crushed or minced	½ small clove	1 small clove
Salt and pepper	to taste	to taste
Oil	2 teaspoons	1 tablespoon
Torn salad greens	1½–2 cups	3–4 cups

In a medium salad bowl, whisk the vinegar or lemon juice, fruit or vegetable juice, mustard, garlic, salt and pepper. Gradually whisk in the oil. Add the salad greens and toss until they are well-coated with the vinaigrette dressing. Serve the salad immediately on chilled salad plates.

Per serving: 104 calories, 9.2 g. total fat, 1.8 g. saturated fat, 0 mg. cholesterol, 9.1 mg. sodium, 1.5 g. protein, 3.2 g. carbohydrates, 1.4 g. dietary fiber.

B A G U E T T E

Warm Spinach Salad Chinoise

No need to invest in a wok to enjoy the timesaving and health-enhancing benefits of stir-fries like this warm spinach salad. A heavy, 10″ nonstick skillet works well for small stir-fries and quick sautés and requires very little fat for browning. If you are thinking about buying one, choose one with outwardly sloping sides and a metal handle that can go into the oven; it will be great for dishes like frittatas.

To turn this salad into a satisfying meal, serve it over brown rice with cubes of tofu.

Ingredients	For 1 serving	For 2 servings
Spinach, stemmed and loosely packed	4 cups	8 cups
Sesame seeds (optional)	1 teaspoon	2 teaspoons
Sesame or canola oil	1½ teaspoons	1 tablespoon
Sliced mushrooms	⅓ cup	⅔ cup
Garlic, crushed	1 clove	2 cloves
Rice or distilled white vinegar	1 tablespoon	2 tablespoons
Reduced-sodium soy sauce	1½ teaspoons	1 tablespoon
Sugar	1 teaspoon	2 teaspoons
Red-pepper flakes	to taste	to taste

Wash the spinach well in cold water. Drain it well. Place it conveniently near the stove.

Sprinkle the sesame seeds (if using) into a heavy, 10″ nonstick skillet and toast them over low heat for 5 minutes, or until they turn golden; shake the skillet occasionally to toast the seeds evenly.

Add the oil to the skillet, raise the heat to medium and add the mushrooms. Cook, stirring constantly, for 2 minutes.

Stir in the garlic, vinegar, soy sauce, sugar and pepper flakes. Add the spinach and cook the mixture, turning the spinach frequently with a broad plastic or wooden spatula, until the spinach is barely wilted, about 3 minutes. Serve hot.

Per serving: 130 calories, 8.9 g. total fat, 1.3 g. saturated fat, 0 mg. cholesterol, 413 mg. sodium, 5.6 g. protein, 10.7 g. carbohydrates, 4.4 g. dietary fiber.

Moroccan Orange Salad

This colorful salad combines the sweetness of oranges with the bitterness of chicory and the piquancy of onions, olives and ground red pepper. It makes a satisfying starter—or an entire meal when topped with a sprinkle of feta cheese and accompanied by a fresh slice of crusty sourdough. Use the best grade of virgin olive oil you can find to pull all the flavors into a harmonic whole. If you can't find chicory, try arugula, endive, dandelion greens or radicchio.

Ingredients	For 1 serving	For 2 servings
Naval or seedless oranges	1 medium	2 medium
Bermuda or other mild onion	1 thin slice	2 thin slices
Olive oil	1½ teaspoons	1 tablespoon
Red-wine vinegar	1½ teaspoons	1 tablespoon
Ground red pepper	to taste	to taste
Chicory, torn into bite-size pieces	1½ cups	3 cups
Kalamata olives, pitted and chopped	2	4

Peel and section the oranges over a small bowl to catch the juice. Place the orange sections in a medium salad bowl; reserve the juice for the dressing.

Separate the onion slices into rings and add them to the oranges.

Whisk the reserved orange juice with the oil, vinegar and pepper. Pour the mixture over the orange sections and onions. Let the mixture stand for 5 to 30 minutes at room temperature to blend the flavors.

Just before serving, add the chicory and olives; toss the salad well.

Per serving: 154 calories, 6.7 g. total fat, 1 g. saturated fat, 0 mg. cholesterol, 161 mg. sodium, 5.8 g. protein, 23.4 g. carbohydrates, 6.8 g. dietary fiber.

The Chicory Family

There is a lot of good eating in the chicory family if you like the tang of bitter greens. Among the members of this versatile family are Belgian endive, escarole, curly endive and radicchio. In all cases, look for heads that have a crisp, fresh texture and no discoloration.

Belgian endive. This is the mildest and most delicate member of the chicory family. For the most part, it still comes from Belgium and can be quite expensive. Look for firm, compact heads with white leaves (a few pale yellow tips are normal). You will find Belgian endive in the produce section of your supermarket.

Escarole. Also known as broad or flat chicory, escarole has a mildly peppery flavor and firm leaves that add some texture to salads; it won't go limp after sitting in dressing for a while.

Curly endive. Called frisée by the French, this chicory is similar in flavor to escarole, but it has very lacy leaves that add pretty variety to the salad bowl.

Radicchio. This red-leaved chicory looks like a miniature head of red cabbage. It is quite expensive, but purchased in small amounts, it adds a lovely bitter flavor and color accent to salads.

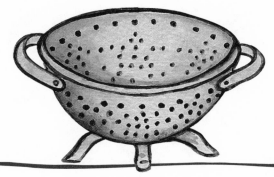

Carrots in Lemon-Walnut Vinaigrette

In France, a favorite first course is grated carrots or celery root bound with freshly made lemon-mustard mayonnaise. In this country, you're more likely to encounter grated raw carrots in carrot-raisin salad. This variation makes a good first course or accompaniment to soups and sandwiches. Walnut oil is expensive, so if you can't find it, use canola oil and toast a few walnuts to crumble over the top of the salad.

Ingredients	For 1 serving	For 2 servings
Lemon juice	1½ teaspoons	1 tablespoon
Dijon mustard	¼ teaspoon	½ teaspoon
Walnut or canola oil	1 teaspoon	2 teaspoons
Coarsely grated carrots	¾ cup	1½ cups
Salt and pepper	to taste	to taste

In a small bowl, whisk together the lemon juice and mustard until blended; then gradually whisk in the oil.

Add the carrots and toss well. Taste the salad and season it with salt and pepper as needed. Serve the salad immediately or chill it overnight.

Per serving: 78 calories, 4.7 g. total fat, 0.4 g. saturated fat, 0 mg. cholesterol, 32 mg. sodium, 0.9 g. protein, 9.1 g. carbohydrates, 2.7 g. dietary fiber.

Thin & Creamy Coleslaw

Round out your menus instead of your thighs with this lightly dressed coleslaw. It's considerably lower in fat than traditional coleslaw, which is made with lots of mayonnaise. Traditional slaw has 11 to 12 grams of fat and about 200 calories per cup. This lighter version has only 2 grams of fat and 83 calories per cup because it's made with light sour cream instead of mayonnaise.

Ingredients	For 1 serving	For 2 servings
Light sour cream	2 tablespoons	¼ cup
Sugar	1 teaspoon	2 teaspoons
Cider vinegar	1 teaspoon	2 teaspoons
Dijon mustard	¼ teaspoon	½ teaspoon
Pepper	to taste	to taste
Thinly sliced or shredded cabbage	1½ cups	3 cups
Green onion, thinly sliced	½	1

In a medium salad bowl, whisk together the sour cream, sugar, vinegar, mustard and pepper. Add the cabbage and green onions; toss well.

Chill the salad for at least 30 minutes to blend the flavors. Just before serving, toss the slaw again.

Per serving: 83 calories, 2.1 g. total fat, 1.2 g. saturated fat, 6 mg. cholesterol, 34 mg. sodium, 2.1 g. protein, 18 g. carbohydrates, 2.8 g. dietary fiber.

Broccoli Slaw

When you slightly undercook vegetables, you'll have tender-crisp leftovers for vegetable salads like this Broccoli Slaw. Lacking leftovers, make this slaw with raw broccoli. If you prefer your broccoli barely cooked, blanch it by immersing it briefly in rapidly boiling water, then run cold water into the pan to stop the cooking. This salad teams well with chili and hearty soups, with sandwiches that need a little something extra to turn them into a meal and with fish that's pan-grilled or broiled.

Ingredients	For 1 serving	For 2 servings
Light mayonnaise	1 rounded teaspoon	2 rounded teaspoons
Tarragon or cider vinegar	1½ teaspoons	1 tablespoon
Sugar	½ teaspoon	1 teaspoon
Dijon mustard	½ teaspoon	1 teaspoon
Pepper	to taste	to taste
Minced shallots or onions	1 teaspoon	2 teaspoons
Coarsely chopped barely cooked broccoli	1 cup	2 cups

In a small mixing bowl, whisk together the mayonnaise, vinegar, sugar, mustard and pepper. Stir in the shallots or onions, then add the broccoli. Toss the mixture well to coat the broccoli.

Per serving: 61 calories, 1.2 g. total fat, 0.2 g. saturated fat, 1 mg. cholesterol, 62 mg. sodium, 4.7 g. protein, 11.4 g. carbohydrates, 4 g. dietary fiber.

Vegetable Slaw with Spa Dressing

This slaw is inspired by the legendary Four Seasons in New York City. They have given a whole new meaning to slaw, by doing away with the cabbage altogether and replacing it with a vibrant mixture of barely cooked and raw vegetables that changes with the seasons. Feel free to create your own combinations with blanched asparagus, baby green peas, new and sweet potatoes, fennel and mushrooms or your favorite vegetables in season. The lemon-mustard dressing brings out the best in raw and cooked vegetables and makes a nice sauce for poached or grilled salmon. As with all dressings, please use freshly squeezed lemon juice for the best flavor.

Ingredients	For 1 serving	For 2 servings
Lemon juice	1½ teaspoons	1 tablespoon
Club soda or sparkling water	1½ teaspoons	1 tablespoon
Coarse-grain mustard	1½ teaspoons	1 tablespoon
Olive or canola oil	1 teaspoon	2 teaspoons
Grated onions	1 teaspoon	2 teaspoons
Coarsely chopped cauliflower	½ cup	1 cup
Shredded carrots	¼ cup	½ cup
Thinly sliced sweet red peppers	¼ cup	½ cup

In a salad bowl, whisk together the lemon juice, club soda or sparkling water, mustard, oil and onions. Add the cauliflower, carrots and peppers; toss the vegetables well to coat them with the dressing.

Per serving: 78 calories, 5.2 g. total fat, 0.6 g. saturated fat, 0 mg. cholesterol, 120 mg. sodium, 2 g. protein, 7.7 g. carbohydrates, 2.4 g. dietary fiber.

Shaved Fennel & Parmesan Cheese

Bulb fennel is a licorice-flavored cousin of celery. It's a late-winter vegetable that's generally available from December through April. Look for a crisp bunch with fresh-looking tops. When you get it home, wrap the fennel in a dampened paper towel and store it in the crisper of your refrigerator for up to 5 days. Snip the feathery green tops into salads or use them to garnish fish or chicken. If you like the flavor of licorice, dice or slice the bulb and use it in place of celery in all sorts of recipes.

Ingredients	For 1 serving	For 2 servings
Red or green leaf lettuce	2 leaves	4 leaves
Bulb fennel, tops trimmed and halved lengthwise	½ bulb	1 bulb
Olive oil	1½ teaspoons	1 tablespoon
Red-wine vinegar	1½ teaspoons	1 tablespoon
Parmesan cheese, thinly shaved	½ ounce	1 ounce

Arrange the lettuce on individual salad plates.

Place the fennel, cut side down, on a chopping board, and use a chef's knife to cut across the grain to make the thinnest possible half-moon slices. Arrange the fennel on the lettuce. Drizzle first with the oil, then the vinegar. Top with the Parmesan and serve immediately.

Per serving: 144 calories, 11.2 g. total fat, 3.7 g. saturated fat, 11 mg. cholesterol, 340 mg. sodium, 7.1 g. protein, 5.2 g. carbohydrates, 1.8 g. dietary fiber.

New Potato Salad with White-Wine Vinaigrette

Just about every cook I know has a favorite way to make potato salad; unfortunately, most recipes are loaded with fat. This is my favorite—and most of the fat *has* been removed. The salad is good served while it's still warm and even better after an overnight rest in the refrigerator, so make enough for now and later.

Ingredients	For 2 serving	For 4 servings
Red-skin or Yukon gold potatoes	8 ounces	1 pound
Tarragon or cider vinegar	1 tablespoon	2 tablespoons
Dry white wine	1 tablespoon	2 tablespoons
Dijon mustard	1 teaspoon	2 teaspoons
Garlic, crushed (optional)	1 clove	2 cloves
Olive or canola oil	2 teaspoons	4 teaspoons
Finely chopped shallots or onions	1 tablespoon	2 tablespoons
Salt	½ teaspoon	1 teaspoon
Pepper	to taste	to taste
Diced celery	¼ cup	½ cup
Finely chopped fresh parsley (optional)	2 tablespoons	4 tablespoons

Place the potatoes in a medium saucepan. Add enough cold water to cover. Bring to a boil and cook for 30 minutes, or until they are tender. (Because the size of the potatoes may vary, be sure to test them every 5 minutes or so with a fork. The fork should pierce the potatoes easily. Do not cook the potatoes until they are falling apart.)

When the potatoes are tender, drain them in a colander and let them cool just enough so that you can slice them without burning your fingers.

In a medium mixing bowl, whisk together the vinegar, wine, mustard and garlic (if using) until blended, then gradually whisk in the oil. Stir in the shallots or onions, salt and pepper.

Slice the warm potatoes and add them to the mixing bowl with the dressing. Toss well and let stand for 15 to 30 minutes at room temperature to absorb the dressing. Add the celery and parsley (if using) and toss the mixture well just before serving. Serve at room temperature.

Per serving: 152 calories, 4.7 g. total fat, 0.6 g. saturated fat, 0 mg. cholesterol, 292 mg. sodium, 2.5 g. protein, 25 g. carbohydrates, 2 g. dietary fiber.

Marinated Mushroom
& Celery Salad

Raw mushrooms have a delicate flavor that gets lost when mushrooms are cooked. Marinating really enhances the flavor—even the domestic white mushrooms you find in any grocery store go a little wild after they're marinated briefly in walnut oil and sherry vinegar. To get the best results, make this salad up to an hour before you plan to serve it. The combination of soft buttery mushrooms and crisp celery makes this salad an excellent first course before a fall or winter dinner—or try it as a relish with grilled beef, chicken or pork.

Ingredients	For 1 serving	For 2 servings
Walnut or olive oil	1½ teaspoons	1 tablespoon
Dry sherry or apple juice	1½ teaspoons	1 tablespoon
Lemon juice	1 teaspoon	2 teaspoons
Minced shallots or onions	1½ teaspoons	1 tablespoon
Dijon mustard	⅛ teaspoon	¼ teaspoon
Salt and pepper	to taste	to taste
Thinly sliced mushrooms	1 cup	2 cups
Finely diced celery	2 tablespoons	¼ cup
Boston or Bibb lettuce	2–3 leaves	4–6 leaves
Finely chopped fresh parsley	1½ teaspoons	1 tablespoon

In a medium salad bowl, whisk together the oil, sherry or apple juice, lemon juice, shallots or onions, mustard, salt and pepper until well-blended. Add the mushrooms and celery and toss gently to coat well. Let stand at room temperature for 30 minutes to 1 hour to develop the flavors.

Place the lettuce on individual salad plates. Spoon the mushroom salad onto the lettuce and sprinkle with the parsley.

Per serving: 92 calories, 7.2 g. total fat, 0.7 g. saturated fat, 0 mg. cholesterol, 20 mg. sodium, 2 g. protein, 5.7 g. carbohydrates, 1.5 g. dietary fiber.

Salads

Black & White Salad

This stylish salad is best in summer, when fresh white corn is widely available. Try this salad as a high-fiber entrée: Add cubes of avocado and tomato or cooked baby shrimp just before tossing the salad. Pack it as a portable lunch for the office. Or dole out half-servings as a complement to roast or barbecued chicken, pork or beef.

Ingredients	For 1 serving	For 2 servings
Canned black beans, rinsed and drained	½ cup	1 cup
Freshly cooked corn or thawed frozen corn	½ cup	1 cup
Diced sweet red or green peppers	2 tablespoons	¼ cup
Finely diced red onions	1 tablespoon	2 tablespoons
Rice or cider vinegar	1 tablespoon	2 tablespoons
Garlic, minced	½ clove	1 clove
Ground cumin	¼ teaspoon	½ teaspoon
Paprika	⅛ teaspoon	¼ teaspoon
Salt (optional)	to taste	to taste
Ground red pepper	to taste	to taste
Olive oil	1½ teaspoons	1 tablespoon

In a medium mixing bowl, combine the beans, corn, sweet peppers and onions.

In a small bowl, whisk together the vinegar, garlic, cumin, paprika, salt (if using) and ground pepper until smooth. Gradually whisk in the oil. Pour the dressing over the vegetables and toss the salad well. Cover the bowl and chill for at least 1 hour to blend the flavors.

Per serving: 256 calories, 7.5 g. total fat, 1.1 g. saturated fat, 0 mg. cholesterol, 502 mg. sodium, 8.9 g. protein, 45 g. carbohydrates, 11.7 g. dietary fiber.

Beefsteak Tomato & Sweet Onion Salad

Several years ago, I ordered a salad at one of Chicago's most popular Italian restaurants. It turned out to be thin slices of an enormous ripe tomato fanned across a plate with thin slices of an equally enormous Vidalia onion. Topped with wisps of fresh basil and sprinkled with red wine vinegar and rosemary-infused olive oil, it was a salad to remember.

You can enjoy this version as a side salad or first course — or make a double helping and add some crumbled goat cheese or feta for a sumptuous summer supper. Serve it with plenty of warm French bread for mopping up the juices.

Ingredients	For 1 serving	For 2 servings
Large sweet onion	¼	½
Large ripe tomato	½	1
Olive oil	1½ teaspoons	1 tablespoon
Red-wine vinegar	1½ teaspoons	1 tablespoon
Fresh basil leaves	3	6

Peel the onion and cut it into very thin slices. Cut the tomato into large, thin slices.

On individual salad plates, arrange the onions and tomatoes in overlapping, alternating layers. Drizzle the vegetables with the oil, then sprinkle with the vinegar.

Stack the basil leaves, then roll them into a cylinder like a tiny cigar. Slice across to form shreds and sprinkle over the salad.

Per serving: 152 calories, 7.8 g. total fat, 1.1 g. saturated fat, 0 mg. cholesterol, 29 mg. sodium, 3.5 g. protein, 21.1 g. carbohydrates, 5.1 g. dietary fiber.

Country-Style Cucumbers

These next-to-no-cal cukes are good for nibbling, for perking up summer vegetables, such as sliced tomatoes and steamed zucchini, and for garnishing grilled fish or chicken.

Ingredients	For 1 serving	For 2 servings
Large cucumber	½	1
Red onion slices	2	4
Rice or white-wine vinegar	1 tablespoon	2 tablespoons
Water	1 tablespoon	2 tablespoons
Sugar	½ teaspoon	1 teaspoon
Salt	pinch	⅛ teaspoon
Hot-pepper sauce or ground red pepper	to taste	to taste

If the cucumber is waxed, peel it; otherwise leave the skin intact. Cut the cucumber in half lengthwise, scoop out the seeds with the tip of a teaspoon and slice the cucumber into ¼" crescents. Place the slices in a small mixing bowl.

Separate the onion slices into rings and add them to the bowl.

In a measuring cup, stir together the vinegar, water, sugar, salt and hot-pepper sauce or pepper. Pour the dressing over the cucumbers and onions.

Let the salad stand for at least 30 minutes at room temperature before serving, or cover and chill overnight. Serve cold or at room temperature.

Per serving: 21 calories, 2.8 g. total fat, 0 g. saturated fat, 0 mg. cholesterol, 130 mg. sodium, 0.5 g. protein, 6.1 g. carbohydrates, 0.9 g. dietary fiber.

Gazpacho Salad

This recipe is surprisingly similar to one from America's first truly regional cookbook, *The Virginia House-Wife*, self-published in 1824 by Mary Randolph of Richmond. Related by blood and marriage to Thomas Jefferson, Mrs. Randolph knew her way around the very best kitchens of those times. This salad is improved by an overnight sojourn in the refrigerator and looks especially elegant layered in a glass bowl.

Ingredients	For 2 servings	For 4 servings
Ripe tomatoes, thickly sliced	8 ounces	1 pound
Peeled and thinly sliced cucumbers	¼ cup	½ cup
Thinly sliced green pepper rings	¼ cup	½ cup
Thinly sliced onions	¼ cup	½ cup
Coarse fresh bread crumbs	2 tablespoons	¼ cup
Tomato juice	¼ cup	½ cup
Olive oil	1½ teaspoons	1 tablespoon
Red-wine vinegar	1 teaspoon	2 teaspoons
Sugar	¼ teaspoon	½ teaspoon
Dry mustard	¼ teaspoon	½ teaspoon
Salt and pepper	to taste	to taste

In a medium salad bowl, arrange the tomatoes, cucumbers, green peppers, onions and bread crumbs in alternating layers.

In a small bowl, whisk together the tomato juice, oil, vinegar, sugar, mustard, salt and pepper; pour the dressing evenly over the vegetables.

Cover the bowl and chill for 2 hours or overnight before serving.

Per serving: 97 calories, 4.2 g. total fat, 0.6 g. saturated fat, 0 mg. cholesterol, 169 mg. sodium, 2.4 g. protein, 14.5 g. carbohydrates, 2.7 g. dietary fiber.

Salads

Waldorf Salad
with Creamy Lime Dressing

The original Waldorf Salad was created by Oscar Tschirky, maître d' of New York City's glittering Waldorf-Astoria Hotel at the turn of this century. His original recipe was nothing more than tart unpeeled apples and celery bound with freshly made mayonnaise. The walnuts that are now indispensable came after Oscar and were added by no-one-knows-whom. Here, freshly made creamy lime dressing replaces the mayonnaise and thereby subtracts 20 to 30 grams of fat. Try the dressing on salads with fresh fruit, such as red leaf lettuce with red seedless grapes or endive with pears and toasted walnuts.

Ingredients	For 1 serving	For 2 servings
Creamy Lime Dressing		
Light sour cream	2 tablespoons	¼ cup
Grated lime rind	¼ teaspoon	½ teaspoon
Lime juice	1 tablespoon	2 tablespoons
Sugar	1 teaspoon	2 teaspoons
Waldorf Salad		
Tart apples	1 medium	2 medium
Diced celery	¼ cup	½ cup
Leaf lettuce	1 large leaf	2 large leaves
Toasted walnut pieces (optional)	1 tablespoon	2 tablespoons

To make the creamy lime dressing: In a small bowl, whisk together the sour cream, lime rind, lime juice and sugar; set aside.

To make the Waldorf salad: Core the apples and cut them into ½" cubes; place in a medium salad bowl. Add the celery. Pour in the dressing and mix well.

Line salad plates with the lettuce leaves and spoon the salad onto the lettuce. Sprinkle with the walnuts (if using) and serve.

Per serving: 212 calories, 8.8 g. total fat, 2.7 g. saturated fat, 12 mg. cholesterol, 40 mg. sodium, 2.6 g. protein, 35.7 g. carbohydrates, 3.9 g. dietary fiber.

Creamy Peanut Dressing

This dressing is easily whisked together in a minute or less from ingredients that you probably have in your kitchen right now. It's especially good tossed with shredded cabbage for a nutty coleslaw or spooned over sliced tomatoes and sprouts for an open-faced sandwich on whole-grain bread.

To turn the dressing into creamy tahini dressing, substitute tahini (sesame seed paste) for the peanut butter and add a dash of cumin. Serve it with diced cooked chicken, celery and sweet red peppers for an unusually good chicken salad.

Ingredients	For 1 serving	For 2 servings
Nonfat plain yogurt	2 tablespoons	¼ cup
Creamy peanut butter	2 teaspoons	4 teaspoons
Lemon juice	1 teaspoon	2 teaspoons
Hot-pepper sauce	to taste	to taste

In a small bowl using a table fork, blend the yogurt with the peanut butter and lemon juice until smooth. Stir in the hot-pepper sauce.

Per serving: 79 calories, 5.3 g. total fat, 1 g. saturated fat, 1 mg. cholesterol, 74 mg. sodium, 4.3 g. protein, 4.9 g. carbohydrates, 0.7 g. dietary fiber.

York County Dutch Dressing

This is an old-fashioned boiled dressing that adds a lot of flavor to raw and cooked vegetables. Make this low-fat version of the traditional dressing to toss with thinly shredded cabbage for Dutch-style coleslaw. Stir it, straight from the refrigerator, into steaming hot vegetables like cabbage to make hot Dutch slaw. Add it to diced cooked potatoes for warm German potato salad. Toss it with cooked brussels sprouts and carrots for a warm winter vegetable salad. If I were you, I'd make at least a cup to keep handy.

Ingredients	For ½ cup	For 1 cup
Sugar	1 tablespoon	2 tablespoons
All-purpose flour	1½ teaspoons	1 tablespoon
Salt	¼ teaspoon	½ teaspoon
Pepper	⅛ teaspoon	¼ teaspoon
Paprika	⅛ teaspoon	¼ teaspoon
Evaporated skim milk	⅓ cup	5 ounces
Prepared mustard	1 teaspoon	2 teaspoons
Cider vinegar	2 tablespoons	¼ cup
Egg, well-beaten	1 yolk	1 whole egg

In a small heavy saucepan, stir the sugar, flour, salt, pepper and paprika until the mixture is free of lumps. Whisk in the milk and mustard. Bring the dressing to a simmer over medium heat, stirring constantly.

Reduce the heat to low and stir in the vinegar. Bring the dressing back to a simmer and rapidly whisk in the egg. Cook the dressing for 1 minute longer, stirring constantly, then pour it into a heat-resistant container.

Cool the dressing to room temperature in the uncovered container; then cover the container, chill the dressing and store it for up to 1 week in the refrigerator. Stir it well before each use.

Per ¼ cup: 79 calories, 1.4 g. total fat, 0.4 g. saturated fat, 55 mg. cholesterol, 356 mg. sodium, 4.5 g. protein, 12.8 g. carbohydrates, 0.1 g. dietary fiber.

Red French Dressing

This tart-sweet dressing is good on a salad of grapefruit sections tossed with bite-size greens, shrimp or crab and avocado.

Ingredients	For ¼ cup	For ½ cup
Canola or olive oil	1 tablespoon	2 tablespoons
Apple juice	1 tablespoon	2 tablespoons
Ketchup	1 tablespoon	2 tablespoons
Cider vinegar	1½ teaspoons	1 tablespoon
Sugar or honey	½ teaspoon	1 teaspoon
Grated onions	½ teaspoon	1 teaspoon
Worcestershire sauce	¼ teaspoon	½ teaspoon
Hot-pepper sauce	to taste	to taste

Place the oil, apple juice, ketchup, vinegar, sugar or honey, onions, Worcestershire sauce and hot-pepper sauce in a half-pint jar with a screw-top lid. Cover the jar and shake the dressing vigorously until it is smooth. Use it immediately or store it in the refrigerator for up to 1 week.

Per 2 tablespoons: 76 calories, 6.8 g. total fat, 0.9 g. saturated fat, 0 mg. cholesterol, 86 mg. sodium, 0 g. protein, 4.4 g. carbohydrates, 0 g. dietary fiber.

Pink Grapefruit Vinaigrette

This vinaigrette is especially pretty made with pink grapefruit juice, but use white grapefruit if that's what you have. Whatever the color, freshly squeezed juice gives maximum flavor. A good salad combination for this dressing is Bibb or Boston lettuce with grapefruit sections, slivers of mango and sweet red peppers or unpeeled red apples. Or try it with watercress, Belgian endive and thin slices of red onions and avocado.

Ingredients	For ¼ cup	For ½ cup
Grapefruit juice	2 tablespoons	¼ cup
Olive or canola oil	1 tablespoon	2 tablespoons
White- or red-wine vinegar	1½ teaspoons	1 tablespoon
Honey	½ teaspoon	1 teaspoon
Finely chopped cilantro, chives or parsley	1½ teaspoons	1 tablespoon

In a small bowl, whisk together the grapefruit juice, oil, vinegar and honey. Stir in the cilantro, chives or parsley.

Per 2 tablespoons: 71 calories, 6.8 g. total fat, 0.9 g. saturated fat, 0 mg. cholesterol, 0 mg. sodium, 0.1 g. protein, 3.1 g. carbohydrates, 0.1 g. dietary fiber.

Smoked Turkey & Fruit Salad

Buy a thick slice of smoked or roast turkey breast at the deli department of your supermarket to cut into cubes for this bountiful supper salad. Or use leftover roast turkey, either dark or white meat, as long as it's skinless. When you're using smoked or roast turkey from a deli in this salad or any other recipe, go easy on the salt. You probably won't need to add any since there's enough for most tastes in commercially cooked turkey.

Ingredients	For 1 serving	For 2 servings
Slivered almonds (optional)	1 tablespoon	2 tablespoons
Nonfat plain yogurt	2 tablespoons	¼ cup
Prepared mustard	1 tablespoon	2 tablespoons
Dried tarragon (optional)	⅛ teaspoon	¼ teaspoon
Pepper	to taste	to taste
Diced smoked or roast turkey breast	½ cup	1 cup
Diced celery	¼ cup	½ cup
Seedless red or green grapes	½ cup	1 cup
Finely chopped fresh parsley	1 tablespoon	2 tablespoons

Place the almonds (if using) in a microwave-safe custard cup or small bowl. Microwave on high power for 1 minute; stir, then cook for another minute on high. (Alternatively, preheat the oven to 350°. Spread the almonds in a small baking pan and bake them for 5 minutes, or until lightly browned.) Set the almonds aside.

In a medium mixing bowl, whisk together the yogurt, mustard, tarragon (if using) and pepper. Add the turkey, celery, grapes and parsley; toss well. Sprinkle with the almonds.

Cover the salad and chill for several hours to blend the flavors.

Per serving: 209 calories, 6.6 g. total fat, 1 g. saturated fat, 61 mg. cholesterol, 663 mg. sodium, 25 g. protein, 14.6 g. carbohydrates, 1.6 g. dietary fiber.

PARSLEY

Spicing Up Fruit Salads

Baltimore is so backward it's ahead of New York when it comes to farmers' markets. For while natives of the Big Apple take pride in the Union Square Farmers' Market that debuted in 1989, Baltimorians have been patronizing *their* farmers' markets continuously since 1751. By 6:00 A.M., from the first Sunday in June until the Sunday before Thanksgiving, those of us who live in or around Charm City buy things such as sweet black and sour red cherries, blueberries, Carroll County strawberries, cantaloupe, white peaches, golden nectarines and apricots, blackberries, raspberries, slip-skin grapes, figs and antique varieties of apples and pears, all in season.

Invariably, I buy too much, so I've learned to deal with an abundance of fresh fruit as soon as I get it home. I turn some of the fruit into jam or homemade fruit liqueur. I turn more fruit into fruit salad for spontaneous refreshment, plain or with honey-spiced yogurt.

You can whisk up honey-spiced yogurt in about 2 minutes. Put ½ cup nonfat plain yogurt into a small bowl and add 1 teaspoon frozen orange juice concentrate, 1 tablespoon honey and a healthy dash of cinnamon. Whisk everything together until the dressing is smooth and spoon it over your favorite fresh fruit. The dressing will keep for up to a week in the refrigerator. Store it in a tightly closed container.

Bulgur: A Healthy Grain from the Middle East

Bulgur is basically parboiled broken pieces of whole wheat. Middle Eastern cooks have developed a unique way of processing their wheat, which makes this grain cook quickly and retain essential nutrients. Whole kernels of wheat are steamed or parboiled and then cracked into small pieces. This process softens the wheat without removing the fiber-rich bran or the nutrient-rich germ.

Bulgur has a pleasantly mild, nutty flavor. It is the chief ingredient in Middle Eastern tabbouleh and makes an excellent quick-cooking replacement for rice in pilafs and casseroles. Here are a few tips for using bulgur.

- Look for bulgur at health food stores, Middle Eastern groceries and some supermarkets.
- Check the package or bin; fine-grain bulgur and medium-grain bulgur cook quickly and can be used in the recipes in this book. Avoid coarse-grain bulgur, since it must be cooked for a long time.
- Cracked wheat is not a good substitute for bulgur.
- Try cooked bulgur as a side dish in place of rice or pasta. Its mild flavor goes well with stir-fries and curries.

Curried Chicken & Bulgur Salad

Attention vegetarians: Transform this colorful chicken salad into a vegetarian main dish by substituting an equal amount of cooked lentils for the chicken. The recipe calls for chutney, and you can buy it or make a quick chutney at home: Thin your favorite plum or peach jam with an equal amount of cider vinegar.

This cool curry salad lends itself to a variety of accompaniments. Serve it on crisp lettuce with one or more of the following garnishes: diced tomatoes, sliced bananas, sliced avocados or cucumbers, chopped hard-cooked egg or dry-roasted peanuts.

Ingredients	For 2 servings	For 4 servings
Medium-grain bulgur	¼ cup	½ cup
Water	½ cup	1 cup
Salt	to taste	to taste
Mango chutney	2 tablespoons	¼ cup
Nonfat plain yogurt	2 tablespoons	¼ cup
Curry powder	1 teaspoon	2 teaspoons
Green onions	1	2
Cubed cooked chicken	½ cup	1 cup
Currants or seedless raisins	1 tablespoon	2 tablespoons
Canned Mandarin orange segments, drained	½ cup	1 cup

In a small saucepan, combine the bulgur, water and salt; bring the mixture to a boil over medium heat. Simmer for 10 to 15 minutes, or until the bulgur is tender and the water is absorbed. Fluff the bulgur with a fork and turn it into a mixing bowl to cool.

If there are large pieces of mango in the chutney, dice them; then place the chutney in a medium bowl with the yogurt and curry powder. Mix well with a table fork. Add the bulgur and toss everything until the bulgur grains are well-coated.

Cut the green onions, including the tender green parts, into fine slices. Add the green onions, chicken, currants or raisins and oranges to the bulgur mixture and toss again. If desired, cover the bowl and chill the salad for 30 minutes or overnight to blend the flavors.

Per serving: 195 calories, 1.2 g. total fat, 0.3 g. saturated fat, 17 mg. cholesterol, 35 mg. sodium, 9.9 g. protein, 38.5 g. carbohydrates, 4.7 g. dietary fiber.

Downsized Tabbouleh

Here's a one-dish hot-weather meal based on nutritious, inexpensive bulgur. Though the number of ingredients seems a little high, the prep work goes fast—all you need are a chopping board and a sharp knife.

Ingredients	For 1 serving	For 2 servings
Medium-grain bulgur	⅓ cup	⅔ cup
Water	½ cup	1 cup
Salt	pinch	⅛ teaspoon
Lemon juice	1 tablespoon	2 tablespoons
Olive oil	1½ teaspoons	1 tablespoon
Finely chopped fresh parsley	¼ cup	½ cup
Finely chopped fresh mint	1½ teaspoons	1 tablespoon
Garlic, crushed (optional)	½ clove	1 clove
Green onion	½	1
Tomato, cubed	½ medium	1 medium
Cubed cucumbers	¼ cup	½ cup
Crumbled feta cheese	2 tablespoons	¼ cup

In a small saucepan, combine the bulgur, water and salt; bring the mixture to a boil over medium heat. Simmer for 10 to 15 minutes, or until the bulgur is tender and the water is absorbed. Fluff the bulgur with a fork and turn it into a mixing bowl to cool for 10 minutes.

Add the lemon juice, oil, parsley, mint and garlic (if using). Toss well.

Cut the green onion, including the tender green part, into thin slices. Add the tomatoes, green onions and cucumbers to the bulgur and toss well.

Cover the tabbouleh and chill for several hours or overnight to blend the flavors. Serve sprinkled with the feta.

Per serving: 321 calories, 13.8 g. total fat, 5.3 g. saturated fat, 25 mg. cholesterol, 468 mg. sodium, 10.9 g. protein, 42.8 g. carbohydrates, 12.4 g. dietary fiber.

Big Easy Salad of Red Beans & Rice

For the best flavor, make this Cajun-inspired salad a day ahead; the beans absorb more flavor when they are allowed to rest overnight. Enjoy the salad as a hearty main dish or team it with baked ham, grilled meats or fish—it makes an excellent change of taste from potato salad. For a satisfying meal, add salad greens and thick slices of ripe tomato.

Ingredients	For 1 serving	For 2 servings
Brown or white long-grain rice	⅓ cup	⅔ cups
Water	¾ cup	1½ cups
Green onions	1	2
Carrot (optional)	½ small	1 small
Canned red kidney beans, rinsed and drained	¾ cup	16 ounces
Chopped celery	¼ cup	½ cup
Diced green peppers	2 tablespoons	¼ cup
Olive oil	1½ teaspoons	1 tablespoon
Vinegar	1 tablespoon	2 tablespoons
Minced garlic	½ teaspoon	1 teaspoon
Salt	¼ teaspoon	½ teaspoon
Dried thyme	⅛ teaspoon	¼ teaspoon
Hot-pepper sauce	to taste	to taste

Cook the rice in the water according to the directions on the package.

While the rice is cooking, cut the green onions, including the tender green parts, into thin slices. Coarsely shred the carrot (if using).

Turn the cooked rice into a medium mixing bowl and combine it with the beans, celery, green peppers, green onions and carrots.

In a small bowl, whisk together the oil, vinegar, garlic, salt, thyme and hot-pepper sauce; pour the dressing over the rice and beans and toss the mixture well. Cover the bowl and chill the salad for 2 hours or overnight to blend the flavors.

Per serving: 487 calories, 9.4 g. total fat, 1.4 g. saturated fat, 0 mg. cholesterol, 583 mg. sodium, 17.5 g. protein, 85.3 g. carbohydrates, 5.5 g. dietary fiber.

Sweet Onions

Sweet onions are usually large onions that have a mild, sweet flavor and are excellent for salads that call for raw onion. If you decide to pay a little extra for sweet onions, be sure that your onions came from the region that is noted for producing them. Mild onions are associated with mild climates, and a Vidalia that doesn't hail from temperate Georgia may not be sweet enough to justify the extra expense. Here are some varieties to look for.

- Vidalia onions (from Vidalia, Georgia)
- Walla Walla onions (from Washington state)
- Texas Sweet 10/15 onions (from Texas)
- Maui onions (from Hawaii)

Epicurean Roast Beef Salad

Rare roast beef from the deli makes this he-man salad a fast one-dish meal for hot summer nights. Treat yourself to a big tasty sweet onion; look for Vidalias, Walla Wallas or Texas Sweet onions. For a satisfying dinner, enjoy the salad with crusty French or Italian bread and fresh tomato wedges. For dessert, help yourself to some fresh black cherries, nectarines or peaches.

Ingredients	For 1 serving	For 2 servings
Nonfat plain yogurt or light sour cream	¼ cup	½ cup
Dijon mustard	2 teaspoons	4 teaspoons
Prepared horseradish	1½ teaspoons	1 tablespoon
Rare roast beef, thinly sliced	3 ounces	6 ounces
Thinly sliced sweet onions	½ cup	1 cup
Torn romaine or iceberg lettuce	2 cups	4 cups
Salt and pepper	to taste	to taste

In a medium salad bowl, whisk together the yogurt or sour cream, mustard and horseradish.

Stack the slices of beef on a chopping board and cut them across the grain into ½″ × 2″ strips. Add to the salad bowl.

Separate the onion slices into rings and add them to the bowl along with the lettuce. Toss the salad well. Season to taste with the salt and pepper.

Per serving: 237 calories, 4.6 g. total fat, 1.5 g. saturated fat, 77 mg. cholesterol, 197 mg. sodium, 36.7 g. protein, 11 g. carbohydrates, 2.8 g. dietary fiber.

Tuna Salad Monterey

Keep a few cans of water-packed tuna on the shelf to turn into quick and healthy main dishes like this tuna salad, which actually has more vegetables than tuna. Other add-ons and garnishes that will increase your dining pleasure are half a hard-cooked egg, cherry tomatoes, asparagus spears, tender green beans and whole-grain bread. If you can't find cooked mustard dressing at your store (it's sold as Durkee Famous Sauce), substitute a mixture of equal parts nonfat plain yogurt and prepared Dijon mustard.

Ingredients	For 2 servings	For 4 servings
Nonfat plain yogurt	2 tablespoons	¼ cup
Cooked mustard dressing	1 tablespoon	2 tablespoons
Lemon juice	1 tablespoon	2 tablespoons
Canned water-packed tuna	3¼ ounces	6¼ ounces
Diced celery	½ cup	1 cup
Diced cucumbers	¼ cup	½ cup
Diced sweet red peppers	¼ cup	½ cup
Finely diced red onions	1 tablespoon	2 tablespoons
Kalamata olives, pitted and quartered (optional)	3	6

In a medium mixing bowl, whisk together the yogurt, mustard dressing and lemon juice.

Drain the tuna and add it to the bowl. Stir in the celery, cucumbers, peppers, onions and olives (if using). Serve immediately.

Per serving: 99 calories, 3.2 g. total fat, 0.6 g. saturated fat, 21 mg. cholesterol, 268 mg. sodium, 13.7 g. protein, 5.1 g. carbohydrates, 0.9 g. dietary fiber.

Salads

Shrimp Salad Rémoulade

Shrimp rémoulade is a favorite New Orleans first course that features small whole shrimp in a garlicky mustard sauce. It's especially appealing in hot weather. Four ounces of raw shrimp will give you 2½ ounces of shrimp after cooking and shelling. Leave the shrimp whole for this salad and serve it on leaf lettuce with cherry tomatoes or tomato wedges and whole-wheat melba toast or crackers.

Ingredients	For 1 serving	For 2 servings
Dijon mustard	1 tablespoon	2 tablespoons
Water or white wine	1½ teaspoons	1 tablespoon
Olive or canola oil	1½ teaspoons	1 tablespoon
Lemon juice or vinegar	1½ teaspoons	1 tablespoon
Garlic, minced	½ clove	1 clove
Dried tarragon (optional)	⅛ teaspoon	¼ teaspoon
Ground red pepper	to taste	to taste
Hard-cooked egg, mashed	½ large	1 large
Finely chopped fresh parsley	1½ teaspoons	1 tablespoon
Thinly sliced green onion tops or chives	1 tablespoon	2 tablespoons
Whole cooked shrimp	2½ ounces	5 ounces
Diced celery	⅓ cup	⅔ cup

In a medium salad bowl, stir the mustard with the water or wine until smooth. Stir in the oil, lemon juice or vinegar, garlic, tarragon (if using) and pepper. Then add the egg, parsley and green onions or chives.

Add the shrimp and celery and toss well. Serve the salad immediately or cover the bowl and chill the salad overnight to blend the flavors.

Per serving: 182 calories, 10.3 g. total fat, 2 g. saturated fat, 245 mg. cholesterol, 262 mg. sodium, 18.6 g. protein, 3.2 g. carbohydrates, 0.8 g. dietary fiber.

Spicy Sesame Noodles

Tahini, a paste of ground sesame seeds that looks like peanut butter, gives these spicy noodles their distinctive flavor. Tahini is available in the foreign-food section of most large grocery stores and in the peanut butter section of health food stores. At my Virginia restaurant, we served this noodle salad garnished with strips of snow peas, slivered carrots and options of julienned ham or cooked shrimp.

Ingredients	For 2 servings	For 4 servings
Linguine or spaghetti	4 ounces	8 ounces
Water	2 tablespoons	¼ cup
Reduced-sodium soy sauce	1 tablespoon	2 tablespoons
Tahini	1 tablespoon	2 tablespoons
Rice or distilled white vinegar	1½ teaspoons	1 tablespoon
Red-pepper flakes (optional)	⅛ teaspoon	¼ teaspoon
Canola oil	1½ teaspoons	1 tablespoon
Sliced mushrooms	⅓ cup	¾ cup
Diced sweet red or green peppers	⅓ cup	⅔ cup
Sliced celery	¼ cup	½ cup
Coarsely chopped onions	¼ cup	½ cup
Minced fresh ginger	1 tablespoon	2 tablespoons
Garlic, crushed	1 clove	2 cloves

Cook the linguine or spaghetti in boiling water, without salt, according to the directions on the package. Drain the pasta well and turn it into a medium bowl.

While the pasta is cooking, combine the water, soy sauce, tahini, vinegar and pepper flakes (if using) in a measuring cup; stir until the mixture is smooth and well-blended. Set aside.

Place the oil in a heavy, 10″ nonstick skillet. Add the mushrooms, red or green peppers, celery, onions and ginger. Cook and stir the vegetables over medium-high heat for 3 minutes. Add the garlic and continue cooking and stirring for another minute. Add the dressing mixture. Cook, stirring constantly, until the sauce begins to bubble and becomes smooth.

Pour the sauce over the pasta and toss well. Serve the noodles warm or cold.

Per serving: 296 calories, 6.7 g. total fat, 0.4 g. saturated fat, 0 mg. cholesterol, 322 mg. sodium, 9.9 g. protein, 42.5 g. carbohydrates, 1 g. dietary fiber.

Beet & Endive Salad with Goat Cheese Toasts

Make this classic salad with (shhh!) canned baby beets, as I do. (If you scorn canned vegetables, roast, steam or microwave some fresh beets.) For intense flavor, marinate the beets, briefly or overnight, in the raspberry vinegar and walnut oil with a little minced shallot. Stop right there and enjoy the world's best pickled beets or continue and make this elegant salad. If you can't find Belgian endive, replace it with 3 cups torn curly endive, also known as chicory, per serving.

Ingredients	For 1 serving	For 2 servings
Raspberry vinegar	1 tablespoon	2 tablespoons
Dijon mustard	¼ teaspoon	½ teaspoon
Pepper	to taste	to taste
Walnut or canola oil	1½ teaspoons	1 tablespoon
Shallot, minced	½ small	1 small
Canned whole baby beets, drained and quartered	¾ cup	16 ounces
Belgian endive	1 small head	2 small heads
Walnut pieces, toasted	1 tablespoon	2 tablespoons
Sliced French bread	2 slices	4 slices
Goat cheese	1 ounce	2 ounces

In a medium salad bowl, whisk together the vinegar, mustard and pepper until smooth; gradually whisk in the oil to form an emulsion. Stir in the shallots, add the beets and toss to coat them evenly with the raspberry vinaigrette. Let the beets stand in the vinaigrette for 30 minutes or overnight to blend the flavors.

Preheat the broiler.

Cut the endive into ¼" cross sections. Add the endive to the bowl with the beets and toss well. Arrange the salad on dinner plates, sprinkle it with the walnuts and set it aside.

Arrange the bread in a single layer on a baking sheet and toast it on one side, about 6" from the heat. Turn the bread and lightly toast the other side, then spread the toast with the goat cheese and return it to the broiler until the cheese begins to brown, about 2 to 3 minutes. Serve with the salad.

Per serving: 357 calories, 19.2 g. total fat, 5.6 g. saturated fat, 25 mg. cholesterol, 885 mg. sodium, 10.9 g. protein, 37.4 g. carbohydrates, 3.3 g. dietary fiber.

Meatless

*T*wo of my four daughters are veteran vegetarians, ovolacto division. That means they'll eat eggs, milk and other dairy products but no meat, poultry or fish. Cooking vegetarian can become complicated when the whole household isn't vegetarian. Personally, I don't think I'll ever be a vegetarian, but because I do my best to be a good mother, I've had plenty of practice cooking entrées that are mainly meatless for my vegetarians, whose ranks now include Baby Jules and little Ivy and her dad.

It makes sense to include vegetarian meals in a well-rounded diet. It's a great way to get more variety, take advantage of the best of the season, reduce your food costs and break the meat-and-potatoes habit.

In this chapter I've included many of my family's favorites—in downsized versions, of course. Even if you're a confirmed carnivore, I think you'll enjoy these meatless main dishes so much that you'll have three or four or more meatless meals every week—it's a healthier way of eating.

Salad Bar Pasta Primavera

My Virginia restaurant boasted a magnificent primavera, with a dozen fresh vegetables, ¾ cup of golden heavy Guernsey cream and a mixture of Gruyère, Parmesan and Cheddar cheeses. Unfortunately, it contained over 90 grams of fat and over 1,400 calories per serving—not including the plate.

My current pasta primavera is considerably lighter; white wine or broth takes the place of cream, and the prep time is cut down by using ready-to-cook fresh vegetables from the supermarket salad bar. How many different vegetables to include is up to you; use as few as 2 varieties or as many as 12. Allow a total of 1½ to 2 cups of vegetables per serving of pasta.

Ingredients	For 1 serving	For 2 servings
Linguine or fettuccine	3 ounces	6 ounces
Olive oil	1½ teaspoons	1 tablespoon
Broccoli or cauliflower florets	¼ cup	½ cup
Sliced zucchini or yellow summer squash	¼ cup	½ cup
Sliced mushrooms	¼ cup	½ cup
Thinly sliced carrots	2 tablespoons	¼ cup
Thinly sliced red or yellow onions	2 tablespoons	¼ cup
Sliced red or green peppers	2 tablespoons	¼ cup
Sliced celery	2 tablespoons	¼ cup
Minced garlic	½ teaspoon	1 teaspoon
Salt and pepper	to taste	to taste
Dry white wine or defatted chicken broth	¼ cup	½ cup
Spinach leaves, loosely packed	1½ cups	3 cups
Frozen green peas, thawed	2 tablespoons	¼ cup
Grated Parmesan or Romano cheese	2 tablespoons	¼ cup

Cook the linguine or fettuccine according to the directions on the package but without salt.

While the pasta is cooking, place a heavy, 10″ nonstick skillet over medium heat for 1 minute. Add the oil and stir in the broccoli or cauliflower, zucchini or squash, mushrooms, carrots, red or yellow onions, red or green peppers and celery.

Cook the vegetables, stirring frequently, for 3 minutes. Stir in the garlic and cook for 1 minute longer. Sprinkle with the salt and pepper, then add the wine or broth. Stir in the spinach and peas, cover the skillet and cook for 1 minute, or just until the spinach is wilted.

Mainly Meatless

Drain the pasta well. Serve topped with the vegetables and sprinkled with the Parmesan or Romano.

Per serving: 548 calories, 12.6 g. total fat, 3.6 g. saturated fat, 10 mg. cholesterol, 344 mg. sodium, 21.9 g. protein, 79.5 g. carbohydrates, 5 g. dietary fiber.

Carbohydrates: A Complex Tale

In olden days, when starchy foods were off-limits, those who would be slim yearned for bread and pasta and rice with unfulfilled passion. Now that we are urged to eat 6 to 11 servings of starchy foods every day, we complain that it's just too much starch. Go figure.

Aside from dutifully polishing off a breakfast bowl of cereal, can a normal human being actually put away 6 to 11 servings of grain-based complex carbohydrates in the course of a day? Yes, because a serving really isn't all that much. It's half a bagel, English muffin or hamburger bun or one slice of bread. It's an airy ounce of ready-to-eat cereal or a modest half-cup of cooked grits, oatmeal, rice or pasta.

Hong Kong Primavera with Spicy Peanut Sauce

For oriental flavor, toss steaming hot thin spaghetti with spicy peanut sauce and vegetables that you've stir-fried in very little sesame oil. This dish is good hot, cold or at room temperature and lends itself to further embellishment. Try stir-frying raw peeled and deveined shrimp or diced chicken pieces in the sesame oil for a minute before adding the carrots and peas. Or add cooked shrimp or diced cooked chicken at the end of cooking.

Ingredients	For 1 serving	For 2 servings
Vermicelli or thin spaghetti	1½ ounces	3 ounces
Green onions, thinly sliced	1	2
Water	2 tablespoons	¼ cup
Creamy peanut butter	1 tablespoon	2 tablespoons
Reduced-sodium soy sauce	1½ teaspoons	1 tablespoon
Rice or distilled white vinegar	1 teaspoon	2 teaspoons
Sugar	½ teaspoon	1 teaspoon
Red-pepper flakes	¼ teaspoon	½ teaspoon
Sesame oil	1 teaspoon	2 teaspoons
Coarsely grated carrots	⅓ cup	⅔ cup
Frozen green peas	2 tablespoons	¼ cup
Minced fresh ginger	1½ teaspoons	1 tablespoon
Garlic, crushed	1 clove	2 cloves
Thinly sliced napa (Chinese) cabbage	2 cups	4 cups

Cook the vermicelli or spaghetti according to the directions on the package but without salt. Drain and toss with the green onions; keep warm.

While the pasta cooks, combine the water, peanut butter, soy sauce, vinegar and sugar in a blender container. Cover and process until smooth. Add the pepper flakes and set aside.

Place the oil in a heavy, 10″ nonstick skillet; stir in the carrots, peas, ginger and garlic. Cook over medium-high heat, stirring constantly, for 30 seconds. Stir in the cabbage and peanut sauce. Cook, stirring constantly, for 1 minute, or until the cabbage is wilted. Add to the pasta and toss well. Serve hot, cold or at room temperature.

Per serving: 353 calories, 13.5 g. total fat, 2.3 g. saturated fat, 0 mg. cholesterol, 631 mg. sodium, 12.3 g. protein, 48.3 g. carbohydrates, 3.6 g. dietary fiber.

Fettuccine with Spinach & Feta

You can prepare the uncooked sauce used for this dish in less time than it takes to cook the pasta. For a real treat, use fresh spinach fettuccine instead of regular dry fettuccine. If you do that, increase the portion to 3 ounces per serving. You won't need to add any salt to the sauce or the pasta cooking water when making this entrée since there's more than enough for flavoring in the feta cheese.

Ingredients	For 1 serving	For 2 servings
Spinach leaves, loosely packed	4 cups	8 cups
Green onion	½	1
Crumbled feta cheese	⅓ cup	⅔ cup
Olive oil	1½ teaspoons	1 tablespoon
Lemon juice (optional)	1½ teaspoons	1 tablespoon
Dried dill weed	¼ teaspoon	½ teaspoon
Pepper	to taste	to taste
Fettuccine	2 ounces	4 ounces

Pick over and stem the spinach, discarding any withered or yellowed leaves. Wash the spinach well in several changes of water until no trace of sand or dirt is left behind. Drain the spinach in a colander and set it aside.

Thinly slice the green onion, including the tender green part, and place in a medium mixing bowl. Add the feta, oil, lemon juice (if using), dill and pepper.

Cook the fettuccine according to the directions on the package but without salt. For the last 30 seconds of cooking, stir the spinach into the water with the fettuccine and push it under the water to wilt it. Drain.

Add the fettuccine and spinach to the bowl and toss with the cheese mixture. Serve the pasta hot or at room temperature.

Per serving: 449 calories, 20.1 g. total fat, 9.6 g. saturated fat, 50 mg. cholesterol, 727 mg. sodium, 18.7 g. protein, 49.8 g. carbohydrates, 3.1 g. dietary fiber.

Braised Broccoli with Whole-Wheat Spaghetti

Whole-wheat spaghetti has a rustic, earthy flavor that pairs well with strong flavors like broccoli and garlic. You can dine inexpensively and well on this one-dish dinner that's nutritionally balanced and deliciously satisfying.

Ingredients	For 1 serving	For 2 servings
Garlic, minced	1 clove	2 cloves
Olive oil	1½ teaspoons	1 tablespoon
Coarsely chopped broccoli	2 cups	4 cups
Dry white wine or water	¼ cup	½ cup
Salt and pepper	to taste	to taste
Whole-wheat spaghetti	3 ounces	6 ounces

In a heavy, 10″ nonstick skillet over medium heat, sauté the garlic in the oil for 1 to 2 minutes, or until the garlic begins to color. Stir in the broccoli, wine or water, salt and pepper. Bring the liquid quickly to a boil, then reduce the heat to low. Cover the skillet and cook, stirring occasionally, for 10 to 15 minutes, or until the broccoli is tender (if necessary to prevent sticking, add a little water from time to time).

Meanwhile, cook the spaghetti according to the directions on the package but without salt. Drain and toss with the broccoli. Serve hot.

Per serving: 417 calories, 8.5 g. total fat, 1.2 g. saturated fat, 0 mg. cholesterol, 70 mg. sodium, 16.8 g. protein, 62.7 g. carbohydrates, 6.2 g. dietary fiber.

Vermicelli with Herbed Mushrooms

Whenever friends ask me what to make for a quick dinner, the word "pasta" falls instinctively from my lips. Keep at least two kinds of pasta on the shelf: quick-cooking thin noodles like angel hair, vermicelli or spaghetti and fat tubular pasta like macaroni or shells, which stand up to heavier sauces. You can have a sauce ready for your pasta in less time than it takes to cook the pasta.

This dish is very simple—freshly cooked pasta with domestic mushrooms that are quickly sautéed with shallots, lemon juice, lots of fresh parsley and a little olive oil. But oh, does this dish taste good when you're hungry and in a hurry.

Ingredients	For 1 serving	For 2 servings
Vermicelli	3 ounces	6 ounces
Olive oil	1½ teaspoons	1 tablespoon
Sliced mushrooms	3 cups	6 cups
Minced shallots or onions	2 tablespoons	¼ cup
Lemon	½	1
Chopped fresh parsley or cilantro	2 tablespoons	¼ cup
Salt and pepper	to taste	to taste

Cook the vermicelli according to the directions on the package but without salt.

While the pasta cooks, place the oil in a heavy, 10″ nonstick skillet and warm it for 1 to 2 minutes over medium-high heat. Add the mushrooms and shallots or onions and cook the mixture, stirring frequently, for 2 to 3 minutes, or just until the mushrooms are piping hot throughout.

Squeeze the juice from the lemon and add the juice to the pan along with the parsley or cilantro, salt and pepper.

Drain the pasta and place it in a large bowl. Toss the pasta with the mushroom mixture. Serve immediately.

Per serving: 442 calories, 8.9 g. total fat, 1.2 g. saturated fat, 0 mg. cholesterol, 23 mg. sodium, 15.2 g. protein, 78.1 g. carbohydrates, 2.7 g. dietary fiber.

Braised Mushrooms & Plum Tomatoes over Pan-Grilled Polenta

Not so long ago, a few ounces of "exotic" mushrooms such as shiitakes, criminis or portobellos cost more than caviar. But as supplies of these richly flavored brown mushrooms have increased, prices have fallen precipitately. You won't be gambling with your grocery money when you buy a carton to turn into an elegant vegetarian entrée like this one.

Ingredients	For 1 serving	For 2 servings
Plum tomatoes	1	2
Mushrooms	4 ounces	8 ounces
Olive oil	2 teaspoons	4 teaspoons
Cold cooked polenta, cut into ½″ squares	2 pieces	4 pieces
Finely chopped onions	2 tablespoons	¼ cup
Garlic, crushed	1 clove	2 cloves
Port or Madeira wine	¼ cup	½ cup
Salt and pepper	to taste	to taste

Cut a shallow × in the blossom end of each tomato and drop the tomatoes into rapidly boiling water. Slowly count to 10, then pour off the water; rinse the tomatoes under cold running water. Strip the skin from the tomatoes, cut them in half and set them aside.

Rinse the mushrooms briefly in lukewarm water, brushing off clinging dirt with a soft pastry brush or your fingertips. Drain them well. If the mushrooms are large, cut them into ½″ cubes. Cut smaller mushrooms into thick slices. Set them aside.

Coat a heavy, 10″ nonstick skillet with half the oil. Place the pan over medium-high heat for 1 minute. Add the polenta and cook for 2 to 3 minutes on each side, or until crispy and brown. Transfer the polenta to a warm plate and keep warm.

Add the remaining oil to the skillet. Raise the heat to high and cook the tomatoes, turning as necessary, for 2 to 3 minutes, or until they're browned. Top each slice of polenta with a tomato half.

Reduce the heat to medium and add the mushrooms and onions to the skillet. Cook and stir the mixture for 3 minutes, or until the mushrooms begin to give up their juices.

Stir in the garlic, then add the wine. Raise the heat to high and cook the

Mainly Meatless

mixture rapidly until the wine is reduced by half. Pour over the polenta and tomato halves. Season with the salt and pepper; serve immediately.

Per serving: 373 calories, 10.2 g. total fat, 1.4 g. saturated fat, 0 mg. cholesterol, 292 mg. sodium, 5.6 g. protein, 53.4 g. carbohydrates, 3.7 g. dietary fiber.

Polenta from the Microwave

You can rustle up polenta without fuss in your microwave. Or you can stand there and stir one or two servings of polenta for 25 to 30 minutes, as per stove-top directions given by authoritarian authors of authentic Italian cookbooks. It's your choice. For my money, the microwave wins.

Either way, polenta is a comforting main dish and a welcome change from pasta—served with your favorite sauce. You can also pan-sizzle it as suggested in my recipe for Braised Mushrooms and Plum Tomatoes over Pan-Grilled Polenta.

Coarsely ground yellow cornmeal works best here and can be found in most health food stores, but packaged cornmeal from your supermarket is quite acceptable.

> 2 cups water
> ½ cup cornmeal
> ¼ teaspoon salt

In a 4-cup microwave-safe casserole or glass measure, whisk together the water, cornmeal and salt until smooth. Microwave on high power for 5 minutes; stir well.

Microwave on medium power (70%) for a total of 8 minutes; stop and stir every 3 minutes during this time. The polenta is ready when it pulls away from the sides of the casserole when stirred. Let stand for 5 minutes before serving. (Or, spoon the hot polenta into a miniature foil loaf pan that you've rinsed with cold water and cool to room temperature. Cover with plastic wrap and refrigerate several hours or overnight.)

Makes 2 servings

Per serving: 126 calories, 0.6 g. total fat, 0.1 g. saturated fat, 0 mg. cholesterol, 275 mg. sodium, 2.9 g. protein, 26.8 g. carbohydrates, 1.8 g. dietary fiber.

Fried Green Tomatoes with Country Gravy

In my grandmother's house in Rome, Georgia, we didn't eat fried green tomatoes as a side dish at dinner; we ate them by the bushel for breakfast, with country-cured bacon and cream gravy sluiced over outsized biscuits. I've overhauled my grandmother's recipe with results that still taste pretty much like the olden days to me, provided that you use a nonstick skillet. And if you're not a vegetarian, sizzle some wafer-thin slices of boiled ham or prosciutto in the skillet next to the tomatoes. Serve fried green tomatoes with biscuits.

Ingredients	For 1 serving	For 2 servings
Green or hard pink tomatoes	1 medium	2 medium
All-purpose flour	1 tablespoon	2 tablespoons
Salt	pinch	¼ teaspoon
Pepper	to taste	to taste
Butter or olive oil	2 teaspoons	4 teaspoons
1% low-fat milk	⅓ cup	⅔ cup

Slice the top and bottom from each tomato; cut the tomato into 3 thick slices.

On a plate, mix the flour, salt and pepper. Set aside 1 teaspoon (or 2 teaspoons) of the seasoned flour to make the gravy. Coat the tomato slices with the remaining flour.

Heat a heavy, 8″ (or 10″) nonstick skillet for 1 minute over medium-high heat. Add the butter or oil and when it sizzles, add the tomatoes in a single layer. Fry the tomatoes until they are browned and crisp, about 2 to 3 minutes per side. Transfer the tomatoes to a warm plate and keep them warm while you make the gravy.

In a small bowl, whisk the reserved flour with the milk and stir the mixture into the skillet in which the tomatoes were fried. Cook the gravy, stirring constantly, until it comes to a boil and is slightly thickened. Pour it into a small pitcher and serve with the tomatoes.

Per serving: 158 calories, 8.8 g. total fat, 5.3 g. saturated fat, 24 mg. cholesterol, 401 mg. sodium, 5 g. protein, 16.1 g. carbohydrates, 0.8 g. dietary fiber.

Roasted Eggplant Parmesan

Let Aunt Fran show you how to strip almost 600 calories and 50 grams of fat from old-fashioned eggplant Parmesan. My recipe mimics the flavor of standard recipes. But by roasting the eggplant instead of frying it, skipping the usual breading and topping the eggplant with paper-thin slices of skim-milk mozzarella instead of thick layers of whole-milk cheese, you can enjoy an old favorite without guilt.

For a change, turn this into roasted Mexican eggplant: Use salsa instead of marinara sauce and Monterey Jack instead of mozzarella. To get really thin slices of cheese, try using a cheese plane instead of a knife.

Ingredients	For 2 servings	For 4 servings
Eggplants	1 medium	2 medium
Olive oil	2 teaspoons	4 teaspoons
Marinara sauce	1 cup	2 cups
Part-skim mozzarella cheese, thinly sliced	2 ounces	4 ounces

Preheat the oven to 400°.

Trim both ends from each eggplant and slice them crosswise into 8 circles of equal thickness. Brush a baking sheet with half the oil, arrange the slices on it in a single layer and bake for 20 to 25 minutes, or until the slices are browned on top and tender in the center.

Reduce the oven temperature to 375°.

Brush an 8″ × 8″ (or 9″ × 13″) baking pan with the remaining oil and arrange 4 (or 8) eggplant slices in a single layer in the bottom of the pan. Spoon half the marinara sauce evenly over the eggplant and top with half the mozzarella. Add a second layer of eggplant slices directly over the first to form sandwiches. Top with the remaining sauce and cheese.

Bake for 20 to 25 minutes, or until the cheese is browned and bubbling. Serve immediately.

Per serving: 248 calories, 13.6 g. total fat, 4.2 g. saturated fat, 16 mg. cholesterol, 924 mg. sodium, 10.4 g. protein, 25.7 g. carbohydrates, 4.9 g. dietary fiber.

Potato Pancakes with Apple Puree

The microwave oven is one of the most useful appliances in one- or two-person kitchens. Here it is used in conjunction with a conventional oven to speed up the cooking process. Crispy potato pancakes are great for brunch and can be frozen and reheated in a toaster oven, microwave or oven for a satisfying snack or light supper. Tart cooking apples such as Granny Smith and Rome Beauty make a flavorful puree.

Ingredients	For 1 serving	For 2 servings
Apple puree		
Tart apples	1 large	2 large
Water	2 tablespoons	¼ cup
Potato pancakes		
Baking potatoes	1 medium	2 medium
Egg whites	1 large	2 large
Coarsely grated onions	1 tablespoon	2 tablespoons
Salt	¼ teaspoon	½ teaspoon
Pepper	to taste	to taste
All-purpose flour	1 tablespoon	2 tablespoons
Canola oil	1 teaspoon	2 teaspoons

To make the apple puree: Peel the apples and cut them in half from stem to blossom end; trim out the seeds and cut the apples into chunks. Put the apple chunks in a 2-cup (or 4-cup) microwave-safe container with the water. Cover and microwave on high power for 3 to 6 minutes, or until the apples are mushy.

With a table fork, press the apples against the sides of the container until they're coarsely pureed. Set them aside to cool slightly while you make the potato pancakes.

To make the potato pancakes: Peel the potatoes and coarsely shred them with a grater onto 2 paper towels. Gently twist the towels and the potatoes over the sink to wring out excess liquid, then place the potatoes in a mixing bowl.

Beat the egg whites in a small bowl until foamy and add to the potatoes along with the onions, salt and pepper. Toss gently to blend, sprinkle with the flour and toss again.

Brush a heavy, 10″ nonstick skillet with 1 teaspoon of the oil and preheat for 1 to 2 minutes on medium heat. Drop in the potato mixture by ½-cup measures to form 3 pancakes; press each gently with a broad spatula to flatten slightly.

Mainly Meatless

Reduce the heat to medium-low and cook the pancakes for 6 to 7 minutes, or until they're crisp and browned on both sides.

Transfer the cooked pancakes to a warm plate. (If you are making the larger portion, keep the finished pancakes warm in a 275° oven as you cook the rest. Repeat to use the remaining oil and potato mixture.)

Serve the pancakes hot with the apple puree.

Per serving: 162 calories, 5 g. total fat, 0.4 g. saturated fat, 0 mg. cholesterol, 589 mg. sodium, 4.6 g. protein, 26.2 g. carbohydrates, 2.8 g. dietary fiber.

Garlic-Baked Mushrooms

For easy casserole entrées like this one, invest in a set of individual glazed earthenware casseroles with lids, the kind intended for baked beans or onion soup. I found 4 such matching casseroles, with their lids intact, in a junk store for literally pennies. Accompany the mushrooms with your favorite green salad and plenty of good French bread for soaking up the luxurious juices. For a fancy dinner, bake half-portions to serve as a first course.

Ingredients	For 1 serving	For 2 servings
Mushrooms	5 ounces	10 ounces
Unpeeled garlic	3–4 cloves	6–8 cloves
Salt	¼ teaspoon	½ teaspoon
Pepper	to taste	to taste
Olive oil	1 tablespoon	2 tablespoons
Sherry vinegar or white wine vinegar	1 teaspoon	2 teaspoons

Preheat the oven to 400°.

Wash and drain the mushrooms. Leave small button mushrooms whole but cut larger ones into halves or quarters, depending on their size.

For each serving, place the mushrooms and garlic in a deep individual 3-cup casserole. Sprinkle with the salt and pepper, then drizzle with the oil and vinegar.

Cover the casseroles with lids or heavy foil and bake for 30 minutes, until the mushrooms have shrunk to half their original size and the garlic is tender. Serve piping hot; squeeze the garlic from its peel to eat.

Per serving: 198 calories, 14.1 g. total fat, 1.9 g. saturated fat, 0 mg. cholesterol, 545 mg. sodium, 3.2 g. protein, 16.9 g. carbohydrates, 1.8 g. dietary fiber.

Hopping John Risotto

It is tradition in the South to sit down to a bowl of rice and black-eyed peas to celebrate the New Year. In this recipe that traditional dish is updated for the microwave and borrows a hint of flavor from classic Italian risottos. For the best flavor, use frozen black-eyed peas cooked according to the directions on the package. If you do use canned peas, rinse them and drain them to get rid of excess salt and the packing liquid they come in. For a heartier entrée, add ¼ to ½ cup diced trimmed ham toward the end of cooking. I prefer to use bacon drippings for this recipe to give it authentic flavor, but you may substitute olive oil.

Ingredients	For 2 servings	For 4 servings
Water	2 cups	4 cups
Shredded cabbage	3 cups	6 cups
Olive oil or bacon drippings	1 tablespoon	2 tablespoons
Chopped onions	¼ cup	½ cup
Long-grain white rice	⅓ cup	⅔ cup
Dried thyme	½ teaspoon	1 teaspoon
Salt	½ teaspoon	1 teaspoon
Red-pepper flakes	¼ teaspoon	½ teaspoon
Cooked black-eyed peas	1 cup	2 cups

In a 2-quart (or 3-quart) saucepan over high heat, bring the water to a boil. Carefully add the cabbage, bring the water back to a boil and cook for 5 minutes. Drain, saving the liquid.

Place the oil or bacon drippings in a microwave-safe 8″ × 8″ (or 11″ × 7″) baking dish. Microwave on high power for 1 minute. Stir in the onions and microwave on high for 2 minutes. Stir in the rice and microwave on high for 2 minutes.

Measure the reserved cabbage water. Stir 1½ cups (or 3 cups) of the water into the dish. Add the thyme, salt and pepper flakes. Stir in the cabbage. Microwave on high for 8 (or 10) minutes. Stir the mixture well and microwave on high for another 3 (or 5) minutes.

Add the black-eyed peas and microwave on high for 3 to 4 minutes, or until the rice is just tender. Let stand for 5 minutes before serving.

Per serving: 306 calories, 7.6 g. total fat, 2.8 g. saturated fat, 6 mg. cholesterol, 567 mg. sodium, 10.8 g. protein, 50.1 g. carbohydrates, 10.9 g. dietary fiber.

Spanish Pilaf

I could tell you that Spanish pilaf is really an Italian risotto, but that would be a lie. Cooking authorities are very strict about what constitutes a risotto; they insist that the rice must be imported short-grain Arborio and must be stirred constantly for 20 to 30 minutes. Well, I'm not standing here stirring a tiny pot of rice for more than 5 minutes, so I might as well confess that Spanish Pilaf is plain old Spanish rice from the 1950s. It's comfort food par excellence.

Topped with a little shredded Cheddar, it becomes a vegetarian entrée. Turn it into snappy shrimp Creole by cooking 2 or 3 ounces of raw cleaned and deveined shrimp per serving with the rice. Or reheat leftover roast chicken and some frozen green peas with the pilaf to create easy arroz con pollo.

Ingredients	For 2 servings	For 4 servings
Olive oil	1½ teaspoons	1 tablespoon
Chopped onions	⅓ cup	⅔ cup
Chopped sweet red or green peppers	⅓ cup	⅔ cup
Garlic, minced	1 clove	2 cloves
Long-grain white rice	½ cup	1 cup
Canned tomatoes (with juice)	1 cup	16 ounces
Defatted chicken broth or water	¾ cup	1½ cups
Salt	¼ teaspoon	½ teaspoon
Dried thyme	¼ teaspoon	½ teaspoon
Red-pepper flakes	¼ teaspoon	½ teaspoon
Bay leaves	1	2

Place the oil in a heavy, 8″ (or 10″) nonstick skillet over medium heat. Stir in the onions and red or green peppers; cook, stirring frequently, for 3 minutes, or until the vegetables are soft.

Stir in the garlic and rice; cook for 1 minute. Use a fork to break up the tomatoes right in the can; add to the skillet (with juice). Stir in the broth or water, salt, thyme, pepper flakes and bay leaves.

Bring the rice to a simmer, stir it well and reduce the heat to low. Cover the skillet and cook for 15 to 20 minutes, or until the rice is tender and the liquid is absorbed. During cooking, stir the rice once or twice and add a little extra liquid if necessary to prevent sticking. Remove and discard the bay leaves.

Per serving: 246 calories, 4.3 g. total fat, 0.7 g. saturated fat, 1 mg. cholesterol, 578 mg. sodium, 2.2 g. protein, 46.8 g. carbohydrates, 6.8 g. dietary fiber.

Esau's Pottage of Lentils & Leeks

A pottage is a very thick sustaining soup, almost a stew. I've named this one after Esau, the famous biblical brother who offered to swap his birthright for a bowl of lentils. Clearly, the red lentils that Jacob cooked up to tempt his brother must have been pretty darned good.

You may not want to swap anything for this pottage, but you will probably appreciate an inexpensive rib-sticking meal that cooks up in about 45 minutes and reheats well. Today's thin-skinned lentils, unlike ancient lentils, require no soaking and cook quickly.

While the pottage cooks, toss a salad of finely shredded romaine, diced tomatoes and raw sweet onions with olive oil and red wine vinegar. Put the salad in shallow bowls, then ladle the hot pottage over the cold salad. The contrast of flavors and temperatures is wonderful, though messy. Have leftover pottage cold or hot for lunch with French bread, feta cheese and black Greek olives.

Ingredients	For 2 servings	For 4 servings
Olive oil	1½ teaspoons	1 tablespoon
Sliced leeks (white and tender green parts), rinsed well	1½ cups	3 cups
Garlic, minced	2 cloves	4 cloves
Brown rice	½ cup	1 cup
Water	2 cups	4 cups
Salt	½ teaspoon	1 teaspoon
Pepper	¼ teaspoon	½ teaspoon
Lentils	½ cup	1 cup

Place the oil in a heavy 2-quart (or 3-quart) saucepan over medium heat. Stir in the leeks and cook, stirring frequently, for 3 to 5 minutes, or until soft.

Stir in the garlic and rice; sauté the mixture for 1 to 2 minutes, or until the rice looks opaque.

Add the water, salt and pepper. Raise the heat to high and bring the mixture quickly to a simmer. Reduce the heat to low, cover the pan and cook for 10 minutes.

While the rice cooks, pick over the lentils and rinse them in cold water; drain well. Stir the lentils into the pan and cook the pottage for 20 to 25 minutes, or until the rice and lentils are tender and the water is absorbed. If the pottage sticks during cooking, add a little more water; the finished dish should be dry, not soupy.

Per serving: 421 calories, 5.6 g. total fat, 0.8 g. saturated fat, 0 mg. cholesterol, 571 mg. sodium, 16.7 g. protein, 78.3 g. carbohydrates, 11.3 g. dietary fiber.

Skillet Casserole of Bulgur & Crimini Mushrooms

Crimini mushrooms look much like standard white mushrooms, except that their rough caps are brown and their flavor is earthier. If you can't find criminis, use white mushrooms. Good last-minute additions for stirring into this stove-top casserole include crumbled feta, yogurt cheese, nonfat yogurt and light sour cream.

Ingredients	For 1 serving	For 2 servings
Butter or margarine	1½ teaspoons	1 tablespoon
Sliced crimini mushrooms	1 cup	2 cups
Finely chopped onions or shallots	1 tablespoon	2 tablespoons
Defatted chicken broth or water	1 cup	2 cups
Bulgur	¼ cup	½ cup
Dried thyme	¼ teaspoon	½ teaspoon
Salt	⅛ teaspoon	¼ teaspoon
Pepper	to taste	to taste

Place a heavy, 8″ (or 10″) nonstick skillet over medium heat. Add the butter or margarine and allow it to melt. Add the mushrooms and onions or shallots; cook, stirring frequently, for 3 to 5 minutes, or until the mushrooms release their juices.

Stir in the broth or water, raise the heat and bring the mixture quickly to a boil. Then stir in the bulgur, thyme, salt and pepper. Reduce the heat to low and cover the skillet. Cook for 15 minutes, or until the liquid is absorbed and the bulgur is tender.

Per serving: 128 calories, 6.8 g. total fat, 3.8 g. saturated fat, 18 mg. cholesterol, 631 mg. sodium, 3.9 g. protein, 14.8 g. carbohydrates, 2.6 g. dietary fiber.

Couscous with Sweet Potatoes & Yellow Squash

Here's an East Baltimore cousin of the classic North African dish. My version is packed with vegetables in a spicy gravy that is ladled over quick-cooking couscous. This is a meal in itself. You won't even need a salad, but you may want to follow the meal with a strong cup of sweet spearmint tea garnished with a few pine nuts—a traditional North African beverage.

Ingredients	For 1 serving	For 2 servings
Canned tomatoes (with juice)	1 cup	16 ounces
Sweet potato	1 small	1 medium
Carrot	1 small	1 medium
Yellow summer squash	½ small	1 small
Olive oil	1½ teaspoons	1 tablespoon
Onion, coarsely chopped	½ small	1 small
Garlic, minced (optional)	½ clove	1 clove
Water	½ cup	1 cup
Ground cinnamon	½ teaspoon	½ teaspoon
Turmeric	½ teaspoon	½ teaspoon
Ground cumin	½ teaspoon	½ teaspoon
Salt	⅛ teaspoon	¼ teaspoon
Ground red pepper	to taste	to taste
Cooked or rinsed and drained canned chick-peas	½ cup	1 cup
Couscous	½ cup	1 cup

Use a fork to break up the tomatoes right in the can and set them aside. Cut the sweet potato into 1″ cubes. Peel the carrot and cut it diagonally into 1″ lengths. Cut the squash into thick slices. Set the vegetables aside.

Place the oil in a large saucepan over medium heat for 30 seconds. Stir in the onions and cook them, stirring frequently, until they begin to brown. Stir in the garlic (if using), then the tomatoes (with juice), water, cinnamon, turmeric, cumin, salt and pepper.

Add the sweet potatoes and carrots. Raise the heat and bring the vegetables quickly to a boil. Reduce the heat to low, cover the pan and cook the mixture for 15 minutes.

Add the squash and chick-peas; cook for 15 minutes, or until the sweet potatoes are tender.

Mainly Meatless

While the vegetables are simmering, cook the couscous according to the directions on the package.

Fluff the couscous with a fork and place it in shallow bowls. Ladle the vegetables and broth over the couscous.

Per serving: 668 calories, 10.4 g. total fat, 1.4 g. saturated fat, 0 mg. cholesterol, 799 mg. sodium, 21.5 g. protein, 124.5 g. carbohydrates, 13.9 g. dietary fiber.

Couscous

Couscous is often mistaken for bulgur, but it's quite different. For one thing, bulgur is a form of whole-wheat kernels and is rightly considered a grain. Couscous could be considered its refined cousin. It's really a granular form of pasta, which is traditionally served with spicy stews and harissa, a very hot chili paste popular in North Africa.

Couscous is made from wheat semolina, the same ingredient used in high-quality dried Italian pastas. It cooks very quickly and has a mild, nutty flavor. Many supermarkets sell prepackaged couscous in the rice section or the international foods section. Look for it in the bulk section of health food stores.

Follow the directions on the package for preparing it. But if no directions exist, you can pretty much count on using equal parts water or broth and couscous. Bring the liquid to a boil, stir in the couscous and cover the pan. Remove it from the heat and let it stand about 5 minutes, or until all the liquid has been absorbed. Fluff the couscous with a fork before serving.

Autumn Vegetables with Balsamic Sauce

For a vegetarian supper that will leave you absolutely bursting with vitamins and well-being, have this mixture with a small wedge of fontina or Gruyère cheese and some whole-wheat French bread. Sweet-tart balsamic vinegar brings out the earthy best of root vegetables and offsets the slight bitterness of brussels sprouts and radicchio. To get a company dinner off to a fine start, serve half-portions of this warm salad.

Ingredients	For 1 serving	For 2 servings
Carrots	1 small	2 small
Turnips	1 small	2 small
Red-skinned potatoes	1 small	2 small
Brussels sprouts	4–5	8–10
Balsamic vinegar	1 tablespoon	2 tablespoons
Dijon mustard	½ teaspoon	1 teaspoon
Walnut or olive oil	1½ teaspoons	1 tablespoon
Salt and pepper	to taste	to taste
Minced shallots or onions	1 tablespoon	2 tablespoons
Radicchio leaves	3	6

Peel the carrots and cut them diagonally into 1″ pieces. Peel the turnips only if tough and cut them into quarters. Scrub the potatoes and quarter them. Cut the brussels sprouts in half. Arrange the vegetables in a collapsible metal steamer. Place the steamer in a large saucepan and add water to a depth of 1″. Bring the water to a boil, cover the pan and steam the vegetables for 10 minutes, or until tender.

In a small bowl, whisk together the vinegar and mustard until smooth. Gradually whisk in the oil. Stir in the salt, pepper and shallots or onions.

Arrange the radicchio on individual plates. Top with the hot vegetables and spoon the dressing over the vegetables.

Per serving: 254 calories, 7.5 g. total fat, 0.8 g. saturated fat, 0 mg. cholesterol, 103 mg. sodium, 10 g. protein, 44.9 g. carbohydrates, 6.8 g. dietary fiber.

Mainly Meatless

Balsamic Vinegar

Balsamic vinegar is a wine vinegar with a sweet-sour taste quite unlike that of any other vinegar. This highly prized vinegar begins as the juice of white Trebbiano grapes (the grapes that go into white Chianti and Soave wines). The juice is then boiled down to a sweet syrup with a high sugar content. By contrast, other wine vinegars begin with dry wines that have little or no sugar.

Natural yeasts convert the balsamic's grape syrup into alcohol, and then other yeasts turn it into vinegar. The characteristic rich brown color of this distinctive vinegar comes from the wooden kegs in which it is aged. The best balsamic vinegar ages for several years—or several generations. During the aging process, the vinegar is further concentrated by evaporation. Production and long aging make it expensive, but the complex flavor makes it worth the cost. And as with so many high-cost, high-flavor ingredients, a little goes a long way.

Rapid Ratatouille

This may not be the ratatouille for purists, but it's definitely the one for busy people. It has no eggplant, it's missing the traditional large dose of olive oil and it takes 30 minutes to prepare instead of 2 hours. It's wonderful spooned over pasta or polenta and sprinkled with a spoonful of shredded mozzarella or crumbled feta cheese. It's also good as a vegetable side dish with grilled fish, chicken or lamb.

Ingredients	For 1 serving	For 2 servings
Onion	½ small	1 small
Sweet red or green pepper	¼ medium	½ medium
Zucchini	1 small	2 small
Olive oil	1½ teaspoons	1 tablespoon
Garlic, crushed	1 clove	2 cloves
Fresh or canned diced tomatoes	1 cup	2 cups
Dried basil	¼ teaspoon	½ teaspoon
Salt	⅛ teaspoon	¼ teaspoon
Pepper	to taste	to taste

Cut the onion into ¼″ slices. Dice the red or green pepper. Cut the zucchini into ¼″-thick slices. Set the vegetables aside.

Place the oil in a heavy, 8″ (or 10″) nonstick skillet over medium heat. Stir in the onions and peppers; cook, stirring occasionally, for 5 minutes, or until the onions are tender but not brown.

Stir in the garlic, then the zucchini, tomatoes, basil, salt and pepper. Raise the heat to high and bring the mixture quickly to a boil; reduce the heat to low. Cover and cook the vegetables for 10 minutes, or until the zucchini is just tender.

Remove the cover and rapidly cook down the mixture until almost all the liquid has been absorbed.

Per serving: 168 calories, 7.7 g. total fat, 1.1 g. saturated fat, 0 mg. cholesterol, 664 mg. sodium, 5.1 g. protein, 23.9 g. carbohydrates, 5.3 g. dietary fiber.

BASIL

Mainly Meatless

New Boston Baked Beans

This simple recipe will surprise and delight you with its rib-sticking good taste—as I discovered one Christmas eve. Next to the baked ham, I set out a huge casserole of these porkless baked beans for my vegetarian kin. The meat-eaters helped polish off every last bean but pretty much ignored the ham.

You won't need to add salt if you're using canned beans because they contain salt, as does the ketchup. You may need to add salt to taste, however, when you use beans that you cook yourself. Make a meal of baked beans with a slice of Boston brown bread and a side dish of coleslaw.

Ingredients	For 2 servings	For 4 servings
Onion	½ small	1 small
Canned Great Northern beans, rinsed and drained	16 ounces	32 ounces
Water	¼ cup	½ cup
Molasses	2 tablespoons	¼ cup
Ketchup	2 tablespoons	¼ cup
Dry mustard	½ teaspoon	1 teaspoon
Pepper	to taste	to taste

Preheat the oven to 300°.

Put the onion in a deep 3-cup (or 1½-quart) casserole and cover it with the beans.

In a small saucepan, combine the water, molasses, ketchup, mustard and pepper. Bring to a boil over medium heat. Pour the mixture over the beans.

Set the casserole on the middle shelf of the oven and bake for 1 hour without stirring, until the beans are glazed on top and most of the liquid has been absorbed. Serve hot or lukewarm.

Per serving: 248 calories, 1 g. total fat, 0 g. saturated fat, 0 mg. cholesterol, 171 mg. sodium, 11.8 g. protein, 49.6 g. carbohydrates, 7.4 g. dietary fiber.

Mexican Lasagna

Mexican lasagna is a quick-fix casserole of popular ready-to-eat ingredients: corn tortillas, canned pinto or kidney beans, cheeses, salsa and yogurt—all layered in a casserole that you can bake while you make a green salad. (You could also microwave the casserole on high power for 2 minutes to heat the ingredients through.)

Ingredients	For 2 servings	For 4 servings
Green onions	1	2
Canned diced tomatoes (with juice)	1 cup	16 ounces
Finely chopped fresh cilantro (optional)	1 tablespoon	2 tablespoons
Chili powder	1 teaspoon	2 teaspoons
Ground cumin	1 teaspoon	2 teaspoons
Garlic, minced	1 clove	2 cloves
Corn tortillas	6	12
Rinsed and drained canned pinto or kidney beans	¾ cup	16 ounces
Coarsely shredded part-skim mozzarella cheese	½ cup	1 cup
Nonfat plain yogurt	¼ cup	½ cup
Coarsely shredded Cheddar cheese	¼ cup	½ cup

Preheat the oven to 400°.

Thinly slice the green onions, including the tender green part. Place the green onions in a small bowl or glass measure. Add the tomatoes (with juice), cilantro (if using), chili powder, cumin and garlic.

Spread half the mixture evenly in an 8″ pie pan (or an 11″ × 7″ baking pan). Top with half the tortillas and all the beans. Sprinkle with the mozzarella. Top with the remaining tortillas and tomato mixture. Whisk the yogurt briefly and spread it over the tomato mixture. Sprinkle the Cheddar over the top.

Bake for 15 to 20 minutes, or until the casserole is bubbling hot throughout and the cheese is melted. Let stand for 5 to 10 minutes before cutting and serving.

Per serving: 470 calories, 13.8 g. total fat, 6 g. saturated fat, 31 mg. cholesterol, 614 mg. sodium, 25.4 g. protein, 65.1 g. carbohydrates, 6.2 g. dietary fiber.

Chili-Corn Custard

This spicy custard is basically a no-crust quiche. If fresh corn is available, cut it off the cob and add it to the custard—there's no need to cook it first. You can scramble everything together in 5 minutes and let the custard bake while you make a green salad with avocado and tomato.

It's easy to vary this custard.

To make *chili-cheese corn custard*, spread 2 tablespoons shredded Cheddar with the corn in the bottom of each buttered casserole.

For *Southern corn pudding*, omit the chili powder, hot-pepper sauce, onions and pimentos; beat in ½ teaspoon sugar per serving and serve the pudding with grilled ham or Canadian bacon.

For *Carolina shrimp and corn pie*, omit the chili powder and pimentos; put 4 or 5 cooked peeled shrimp in each casserole along with the corn.

Ingredients	For 1 serving	For 2 servings
Butter or margarine	½ teaspoon	1 teaspoon
Fresh or thawed frozen corn	¾ cup	1½ cups
Eggs	1	2
Chili powder	½ teaspoon	1 teaspoon
Salt	¼ teaspoon	½ teaspoon
Hot-pepper sauce	to taste	to taste
1% low-fat milk	½ cup	1 cup
Minced onions	1 tablespoon	2 tablespoons
Finely chopped pimentos or roasted red peppers (optional)	1 tablespoon	2 tablespoons

Preheat the oven to 350°.

For each serving, grease a shallow 2-cup casserole or gratin dish with ½ teaspoon butter or margarine. Spread ¾ cup corn in the bottom of each casserole.

Beat the eggs, chili powder, salt and hot-pepper sauce until foamy. Beat in the milk, onions and pimentos or red peppers. Pour the egg mixture over the corn.

Bake the casseroles on the middle shelf of the oven for 25 to 30 minutes, or until the custards are puffed but barely set in the center. Let stand for 5 to 10 minutes before serving.

Per serving: 255 calories, 8.6 g. total fat, 3.6 g. saturated fat, 223 mg. cholesterol, 698 mg. sodium, 14.5 g. protein, 34.3 g. carbohydrates, 3.3 g. dietary fiber.

Greengrocer's Frittata

You can improvise frittatas with leftover or cooked-to-order vegetables. Allow about ½ cup cooked vegetables for every egg. And until you get the hang of such improvisational cooking, practice on this open-textured, delicate frittata, with its measured amounts of vegetables.

Ingredients	For 1 serving	For 2 servings
Fresh spinach, stemmed and lightly packed	2 cups	4 cups
Olive oil	1½ teaspoons	1 tablespoon
Coarsely grated zucchini	1 cup	2 cups
Thinly sliced green peppers	¼ cup	½ cup
Thinly sliced onions	¼ cup	½ cup
Eggs	2	4
Salt	⅛ teaspoon	¼ teaspoon
Pepper	to taste	to taste
Grated Parmesan cheese	1 tablespoon	2 tablespoons

Wash the spinach in cold water to remove any sand and grit. Shake off the excess water but don't dry the spinach.

Place the spinach in a heavy, 8″ (or 10″) nonstick skillet with just the water left clinging to the leaves. Cook over medium heat until just wilted. Coarsely chop the spinach and set it aside.

Dry the skillet with a paper towel and place over medium heat for a minute or two. Add the oil, then stir in the zucchini, green peppers and onions. Cook the vegetables, stirring frequently, for 5 minutes, or until the liquid released from the zucchini has evaporated and the vegetables have cooked down to about half their original volume. Stir in the spinach and remove the skillet from the heat.

In a small mixing bowl, beat the eggs, salt and pepper until foamy. Return the skillet to the heat and pour the eggs evenly over the vegetables. Reduce the heat to low, cover the pan and cook for 4 to 5 minutes, or until the eggs are set.

Run a knife around the edge of the frittata to loosen it; then carefully invert it onto a plate. Sprinkle with the Parmesan. Cut into wedges and serve.

Per serving: 305 calories, 19.3 g. total fat, 5.3 g. saturated fat, 431 mg. cholesterol, 602 mg. sodium, 20.5 g. protein, 14.9 g. carbohydrates, 6 g. dietary fiber.

Mainly Meatless

Improvised Frittata

One of the best frittatas I ever made was by chance. The recipe is lost forever, never to be duplicated because it was improvised one June noon from seasonal leftovers: a few stalks of barely cooked asparagus cut into pieces, a scant half cup of green peas, another of barely cooked spinach, some chopped parsley, plenty of sweet Vidalia onions, eggs and some Parmesan cheese. It tidied up my refrigerator nicely.

You too can improvise frittatas with leftover or cooked-to-order vegetables. Allow about ½ cup cooked vegetables for every egg and briefly blanch raw vegetables (except tomatoes and onions). Potential ingredients, in addition to those I found in my refrigerator, include escarole, green beans, zucchini, summer squash, leeks, sweet red or green peppers, cooked potatoes, artichoke quarters or hearts, mushrooms, cauliflower, tomatoes and broccoli.

The Egg & You

In late 1989, the U.S. Department of Agriculture quietly released new data on the cholesterol content of eggs. Turns out that instead of the 274 milligrams of cholesterol per large egg previously believed, there are only 213 milligrams. That's 23 percent less. Suddenly, instead of the three or four eggs per week formerly allotted for healthy diets, four or five eggs are permissible.

This is very good news for people who hate to cook, because eggs make such easy suppers. You can scramble, fry, poach or boil them in minutes. Or you can whip them into omelets, frittatas, soufflés, quiches and custards.

Spanish Potato Cake

In Spain, an oil-soaked version of this potato cake is called tortilla espagnole and traditionally served in small wedges at room temperature as an appetizer. I've cut back sharply on the oil and rearranged cooking methods to come up with a low-fat, rib-sticking entrée.

Ingredients	For 1 serving	For 2 servings
Boiling potatoes	8 ounces	1 pound
Water or beef broth	¼ cup	½ cup
Eggs	1	2
Salt	¼ teaspoon	½ teaspoon
Pepper	to taste	to taste
Chopped onions	¼ cup	½ cup
Olive oil	1 teaspoon	2 teaspoons

Peel and slice the potatoes. Place them in a saucepan with the water or broth. Cook, covered, for 15 to 20 minutes, or until tender. Remove the pan from the heat.

Preheat the oven to 375°.

With a slotted spoon, remove half the potatoes to a mixing bowl and set them aside. Using a hand-held mixer, briefly beat the remaining potatoes right in the saucepan with the cooking liquid, then beat in the eggs, salt and pepper.

In a 5″ (or 8″) cast-iron or other ovenproof skillet over high heat, cook the onions in half the oil until tender. Fold the onions into the beaten potato mixture. Stir in the reserved potatoes.

Heat the remaining oil in the skillet over high heat until the oil is rippling hot; quickly add the potato mixture and spread it evenly in the skillet.

Bake the potato cake on the middle shelf of the oven for 15 minutes, or until it is set and firm in the center. Cut it into wedges and serve.

Per serving: 325 calories, 9.8 g. total fat, 2.2 g. saturated fat, 213 mg. cholesterol, 291 mg. sodium, 10.6 g. protein, 49.5 g. carbohydrates, 3.2 g. dietary fiber.

chicken

and Turkey

A chicken (or turkey) in every pot can apply to small-size households every bit as much as large ones. Supermarkets are stocking many cuts that appeal to single cooks. Turkey cutlets, turkey half-breasts, turkey thighs, skinless and bone-less chicken breasts or thighs and ground turkey or chicken can be purchased in smaller amounts and cooked with little waste. The mild flavor of poultry makes it one of the most versatile foods. And the fact that it's low in fat doesn't hurt one bit.

Of course, to keep poultry dishes low-fat and flavorful, it's important to deal with the skin properly. By the simple expedient of stripping the skin from the chicken, you can unload a goodly amount of fat from your diet. But do you strip the skin before or after you cook the chicken? The answer is before — or after. It all depends on how you cook the chicken; the same rules apply to turkey.

When you roast, broil or grill chicken without sauce or coating, leave the skin on. It helps keep the meat moist during cooking. Leave the skin intact for poaching too; it will yield a more flavorful broth and a more flavorful bird. The trick is to remove the cooked skin before serving the bird.

On the other hand, strip the skin off before you bake, grill or roast poultry that's sauced or coated before or during cooking. Do likewise for chicken used in stir-fries, pan-sautés and dishes such as cacciatore and fricassee, in which the chicken is cooked in the sauce. If you don't remove the skin in those cases, fat from it will melt into the sauce and be very difficult to remove.

Parmesan-Glazed Chicken

When I rejoined the labor force in the 1960s, my four small daughters were all under age 6. During that busy time, I invented this easy meal. The recipe was fast and good. I could have the chicken breasts in the oven 10 minutes after I got home, and while they baked, I made real mashed potatoes and a green vegetable for a sit-down family dinner with my girls. If you like, prepare a double batch of this chicken so that you can enjoy it tonight with mashed sweet potatoes and a green salad and serve the leftovers cold tomorrow for lunch or dinner with a fresh fruit salad.

Ingredients	For 2 servings	For 4 servings
Bone-in chicken breast halves (about 10 ounces each)	2	4
Salt and pepper	to taste	to taste
Grated Parmesan or Romano cheese	2 tablespoons	4 tablespoons
Dry white wine or sherry	2 tablespoons	4 tablespoons

Preheat the oven to 375°. Line a baking pan with heavy foil.

Remove the skin from the chicken. Arrange the breasts, rib side down, in a single layer on the baking pan. Sprinkle them with the salt and pepper.

In a small bowl, make a paste of the Parmesan or Romano and wine or sherry; spread it evenly over the tops of the chicken.

Bake the breasts on the top shelf of the oven for 35 to 45 minutes, or until the chicken is glazed and browned and the juices are clear when the breast is pierced with a fork. Serve hot or cold.

Per serving: 261 calories, 6.7 g. total fat, 2.6 g. saturated fat, 119 mg. cholesterol, 216 mg. sodium, 44.4 g. protein, 0.4 g. carbohydrates, 0 g. dietary fiber.

Poaching Chicken Breasts

The next time chicken breasts are on sale, buy a family-size package to enjoy in sandwiches, salads, soups and entrées. You can poach the breasts in a flavorful broth and keep them for several days in the refrigerator or up to three months in the freezer. When you poach the breasts yourself, you control sodium and fat. And you'll save money by buying in quantity. Further, the flavorful chicken broth that you produce during poaching can be used for soups and other dishes.

You can start with boneless, skinless breasts, but I don't. They cost more than bone-in pieces, and the bones add flavor to the broth. Chill the poaching liquid and skim off any fat.

For each chicken breast you will need about ½ small onion, ½ celery rib (celery leaves are fine, too), ½ medium carrot, a sprig of fresh parsley, ¼ teaspoon dried tarragon or thyme, 3 or 4 whole peppercorns and salt to taste.

Cut the vegetables into 1″ pieces. Select a nonstick skillet that will comfortably hold the chicken in a single layer. Place the chicken, skin side down, and vegetables and seasonings in the pan. Add enough cold water to barely cover the chicken. Then bring the mixture to a boil over a high heat.

Reduce the heat to low, cover the skillet and cook the chicken until there is no sign of pink in the center part of the breast when it's pierced with a thin paring knife. Allow about 15 minutes for small breasts averaging 8 ounces or less each; 20 minutes for larger breasts weighing over 8 ounces. For juicy chicken, resist the temptation to overcook.

For maximum flavor, allow the chicken to cool in the broth, then remove and discard the skin and bones. The chicken is ready to use for salads, entrées and sandwiches. Freeze or refrigerate the poached chicken breasts in individual plastic bags for future meals. Strain the cooled broth and refrigerate it until the fat contained in it congeals. Skim it off and then refrigerate or freeze the liquid.

One poached chicken breast yields ⅔ to 1 cup bite-size pieces or enough sliced chicken to make an overstuffed sandwich.

Carolina Casserole

From the late seventeenth century until the Civil War, rice was the major crop of the coastal Carolinas. Georgetown, South Carolina, exported more rice than any seaport except Calcutta. Though the Carolinas no longer grow rice commercially, you can still buy Carolina rice. It's a generic long-grain, all-purpose rice that works well in most rice recipes. Carolina Rice (with a capital R) is also a registered brand name. This simple rice casserole makes a great brunch or lunch; it's also a good way to use up leftover cooked chicken or turkey.

Ingredients	For 1 serving	For 2 servings
Long-grain white rice	¼ cup	½ cup
Water or defatted chicken broth	¾ cup	1½ cups
Salt	⅛ teaspoon	¼ teaspoon
Dried thyme	⅛ teaspoon	¼ teaspoon
1% low-fat milk	⅓ cup	⅔ cup
Diced cooked chicken or turkey	⅓ cup	⅔ cup
Mushrooms, thinly sliced	2	4
Worcestershire sauce	dash	¼ teaspoon
Frozen green peas	¼ cup	½ cup
Coarsely shredded Cheddar cheese	2 tablespoons	¼ cup

Combine the rice, water or broth, salt and thyme in a 1-quart (or 2-quart) microwave-safe casserole. Microwave on high power for 5 minutes. Stir well.

Microwave on medium power (70%) for a total of 10 minutes; stop and stir after 5 minutes.

Stir in the milk, chicken or turkey, mushrooms and Worcestershire sauce. Cover and microwave on medium for a total of 3 (or 5) minutes; stop and give the casserole a quarter turn after 1½ (or 2½) minutes.

Stir in the peas and sprinkle with the Cheddar; cover and microwave on medium for 2 (or 3) minutes, or until the peas are tender. Let the casserole stand for 5 minutes before serving.

Per serving: 387 calories, 8 g. total fat, 4.2 g. saturated fat, 66 mg. cholesterol, 485 mg. sodium, 29.3 g. protein, 47.3 g. carbohydrates, 2.1 g. dietary fiber.

Bachelor's-Prize Chicken

This recipe is so-named because it's made with two ingredients found in most single kitchens—yogurt and peanut butter—and because it's so easy to make even noncooking bachelors are assured of success. The sauce is inspired by the yogurt marinade traditionally used for Indian tandoori chicken and the ground peanuts found in Indonesian satays. After brushing chicken pieces with this quickly made glazing sauce, bake them in the oven as directed below. For variety, grill them. Either way, serve them hot with rice, green peas and a fresh peach half-filled with chutney. If you make enough for cold leftovers, serve them with a tomato and cucumber salad and whole-wheat pita.

Ingredients	For 2 servings	For 4 servings
Bone-in chicken breast halves (about 10 ounces each)	2	4
Nonfat plain yogurt	½ cup	1 cup
Creamy peanut butter	2 tablespoons	4 tablespoons
Ground red pepper	⅛ teaspoon	¼ teaspoon

Preheat the oven to 375°. Line a baking pan with heavy foil.

Remove the skin from the chicken.

In a small bowl, blend the yogurt, peanut butter and pepper until smooth. Dip the chicken in the mixture to coat evenly and arrange the pieces, rib side down, in a single layer on the prepared pan.

Bake on the top shelf of the oven for 35 to 45 minutes, or until the chicken is richly browned and the juices are clear when the breast is pierced with a fork. Serve hot or cold.

Per serving: 350 calories, 12.8 g. total fat, 2.9 g. saturated fat, 116 mg. cholesterol, 220 mg. sodium, 49.4 g. protein, 8.4 g. carbohydrates, 1 g. dietary fiber.

THYME

Roast Chicken & Encore Treatments

Though I'm the only one here (unless you count the dog), I wouldn't dream of roasting less than a whole chicken. Roast chicken is good (my veteran vegetarian daughters swear that if ever again they eat flesh, that flesh will be roast chicken). It's easy (put the chicken in a pan and put the pan in the oven). It's cheap (especially when on sale). And I can feast for several well-spaced days on one bird, then simmer up the salvaged skin and bones, neck and giblets for a quart or so of good and cheap chicken stock. I advise you to do the same.

Roast an entire frying chicken, weighing from 3 to 4 pounds, then enjoy it with new potatoes or corn on the cob and your favorite green vegetable. Next day for lunch, slice some of the white meat to make a sandwich with whole-wheat bread, mustard and leaf lettuce. Day three, use some of the cooked chicken in Carolina Casserole or Curried Chicken and Bulgur Salad. And while you're at it, finish stripping the meat from the carcass, cut it into neat slices or cubes and freeze it for use in recipes calling for cooked chicken.

For a change of taste, try *Lemon-Rosemary Roasted Chicken*. Prepare the chicken as directed below, but sprinkle the cavity with crumbled dried rose-mary instead of thyme. With a table fork, poke holes in a washed lemon until the lemon is mushy, then tuck the lemon in the cavity of the chicken. To make *Orange-Roasted Chicken*, thinly slice an orange and insert half of the slices in the cavity. With your fingers, loosen the skin over the breast and slide the remaining orange slices under the skin, along with optional fresh or dried rosemary.

> 1 frying chicken (3 to 4 pounds)
> ½ teaspoon dried thyme
> Salt and pepper (to taste)
> 1 small onion, halved

Preheat the oven to 350°.

Remove the neck and giblets from the cavity of the chicken. Wash the chicken under cold running water; pat it dry with paper towels. Sprinkle the cavity of the chicken with the thyme, salt and pepper. Insert half the onion in the cavity and the other half under the skin over the breast at the neck opening.

Place the chicken, breast side down, in a small roasting pan or casserole. Bake on the middle shelf of the oven for 30 minutes. Turn the chicken breast side up. Baste with the pan juices.

Bake for 45 minutes, or until the juices run clear yellow when you pierce the thickest part of the thigh with a fork. Let stand at room temperature for 15 minutes before carving.

Makes 8 to 10 servings

Per 3 ounces light meat (without skin): 140 calories, 3 g. total fat, 0.9 g. saturated fat, 72 mg. cholesterol, 62 mg. sodium, 26.4 g. protein, 0 g. carbohydrates, 0 g. dietary fiber.

Per 3 ounces dark meat (without skin): 173 calories, 8.3 g. total fat, 2.3 g. saturated fat, 79 mg. cholesterol, 79 mg. sodium, 23.3 g. protein, 0 g. carbohydrates, 0 g. dietary fiber.

Deviled Chicken Breasts

These crispy, oven-fried chicken breasts are good for people who love fried chicken but want to cut down on fat. The "devil" comes from the traditional French mixture of mustard and hot pepper. Chicken breasts baked in this mustard-crumb coating are as good cold as hot, so make double the amount you need for tonight in order to have enough for lunch tomorrow. They're great travel and picnic food; serve them with your favorite potato salad or crusty French bread and a green salad.

Ingredients	For 2 servings	For 4 servings
Bone-in chicken breast halves (about 10 ounces each)	2	4
Dijon mustard	2 tablespoons	¼ cup
Dry white wine or apple juice	2 tablespoons	¼ cup
Olive oil	1½ teaspoons	1 tablespoon
Dried thyme	¼ teaspoon	½ teaspoon
Hot-pepper sauce	to taste	to taste
Minced shallots or onions	2 tablespoons	¼ cup
Soft white bread crumbs	½ cup	1 cup

Preheat the oven to 375°. Line a baking pan with heavy foil.

Remove the skin from the chicken breasts.

In a small bowl, whisk together the mustard, wine or apple juice, oil, thyme and hot-pepper sauce. Stir in the shallots or onions.

Place the bread crumbs in a shallow dish or on a piece of wax paper.

Roll the chicken in the mustard mixture, then in the bread crumbs to coat. Arrange in a single layer in the prepared pan and bake on the top shelf of the oven for 35 to 45 minutes, or until the crumb coating is browned and the juices are clear when the breast is pierced with a fork. Serve hot or cold.

Per serving: 301 calories, 8.7 g. total fat, 1.9 g. saturated fat, 114 mg. cholesterol, 196 mg. sodium, 43.1 g. protein, 7.4 g. carbohydrates, 0.3 g. dietary fiber.

B A G U E T T E

Szechuan Chicken in Lettuce Bundles

These spicy packages will remind you of egg rolls; they're fun for guests and surprisingly low in fat. Crunchy peanuts add contrast to a simple, gingery stir-fry that is rolled in crispy leaves of fresh iceberg lettuce. To make stir-frying easier, arrange all the ingredients conveniently at hand by the range top.

Ingredients	For 1 serving	For 2 servings
Canola or peanut oil	1½ teaspoons	1 tablespoon
Boneless, skinless chicken breasts, cut into 1″ strips	4 ounces	8 ounces
Medium sweet red or green pepper, cut into ½″ squares	¼	½
Celery, cut into ⅓″ slices	½ cup	1 cup
Minced fresh ginger	1 teaspoon	2 teaspoons
Garlic, minced	1 clove	2 cloves
Sugar	½ teaspoon	1 teaspoon
Low-sodium soy sauce	1½ teaspoons	1 tablespoon
Rice or distilled white vinegar	1½ teaspoons	1 tablespoon
Red-pepper flakes	¼ teaspoon	½ teaspoon
Unsalted dry-roasted peanuts	1 tablespoon	2 tablespoons
Green onions, thinly sliced	1	2
Large iceberg lettuce leaves	2	4

Place a heavy, 10″ nonstick skillet over medium heat for 3 minutes. Add the oil and swirl the pan to coat it evenly. Add the chicken, red or green peppers, celery and ginger. Cook and stir for 3 minutes, or until the chicken is opaque.

Stir in the garlic and sugar. Add the soy sauce, vinegar and pepper flakes; continue to cook and stir the mixture for 1 minute.

Stir in the peanuts and green onions. Remove the pan from the heat.

Divide the mixture among the lettuce leaves, spooning it into the center of each. Roll the lettuce around the mixture as you would roll a burrito.

Per serving: 161 calories, 8.5 g. total fat, 0.9 g. saturated fat, 34 mg. cholesterol, 388 mg. sodium, 14.5 g. protein, 7 g. carbohydrates, 2 g. dietary fiber.

Chicken in Red Wine

It takes the better part of 2 days to make authentic French coq au vin. Chicken, usually a tough old rooster, is simmered to succulence in red wine with button mushrooms and tiny onions. Save considerable time with this microwave recipe. It takes a mere 30 minutes to produce, including the time it takes you to prep the vegetables. Serve it with steamed or microwaved new potatoes and green peas or a green salad.

Ingredients	For 1 serving	For 2 servings
Bone-in chicken legs and thighs	1	2
Bacon, diced	½ slice	1 slice
Carrots, thinly sliced	1 small	2 small
Small white boiling onions, peeled	4	8
Button mushrooms	4	8
Garlic, crushed	½ clove	1 clove
Dry red wine	⅓ cup	⅔ cup
Tomato paste	1½ teaspoons	1 tablespoon
Dried thyme	⅛ teaspoon	¼ teaspoon
Salt	pinch	⅛ teaspoon
Pepper	to taste	to taste
Cornstarch	1 teaspoon	2 teaspoons
Water	1 tablespoon	2 tablespoons

Remove the skin from the chicken. Sever the joint between the leg and thigh. Set the pieces aside.

Spread the bacon in a microwave-safe 1-quart casserole (or 8″ × 8″ baking dish). Cover with a paper towel and microwave on high power for 1 minute. Remove the paper towel.

Add the carrots, onions and mushrooms to the casserole. Cover with plastic wrap and cut vents in the plastic. Microwave on high for a total of 2 (or 3) minutes; stop and stir halfway through. Stir in the garlic. Arrange the chicken over the vegetables, with the meaty portions facing the outside of the dish.

In a small bowl, mix the wine, tomato paste, thyme, salt and pepper; pour over the chicken and vegetables. Cover again with the plastic wrap and microwave on high for a total of 6 (or 8) minutes, or until the chicken shows no trace of pink near the thighbone when pierced with a sharp knife; rotate the casserole and flip the chicken pieces after 3 (or 4) minutes.

Chicken and Turkey

Transfer the chicken to a serving dish and keep it warm.

In a cup, whisk the cornstarch with the water until the mixture is smooth; stir it into the casserole. Microwave on high, uncovered, for 2 (or 3) minutes, or until the sauce is bubbling and slightly thickened. Pour the sauce and vegetables over the cooked chicken and let stand for 5 minutes before serving.

Per serving: 395 calories, 15.8 g. total fat, 5 g. saturated fat, 99 mg. cholesterol, 624 mg. sodium, 30.6 g. protein, 19.4 g. carbohydrates, 3.1 g. dietary fiber.

Your Grocery Store Pantry

In most restaurant kitchens there's a section called the cold pantry. It's where appetizers, salads and side dishes are quickly made to order from a wide selection of raw and cooked vegetables, fruits, relishes and cheeses conveniently arranged in a refrigerated counter.

You, too, have a cold pantry. You call it the salad bar at your supermarket. When you're in a hurry—or don't feel like washing and chopping whole vegetables and then dealing with the leftovers—use it as your source for prepped raw ingredients. You'll pay more per pound than you would if you bought each vegetable separately. But you'll pay less in the long run because you buy only those vegetables you need and in the amounts you want.

Stir-Fry of Chicken
& Salad Bar Fixings

When I make this stir-fry, I generally choose salad bar fixings of broccoli and cauliflower buds, slivers of red onion and green pepper, sliced mushrooms, celery crescents and long shreds of carrots. And sometimes I substitute boneless lean pork chops for chicken breast. Serve the stir-fry over hot rice.

Ingredients	For 1 serving	For 2 servings
Boneless, skinless chicken breasts	8 ounces	1 pound
Defatted chicken broth	½ cup	1 cup
Reduced-sodium soy sauce	2 teaspoons	4 teaspoons
Cornstarch	1 teaspoon	2 teaspoons
Sugar	1 teaspoon	2 teaspoons
Canola or sesame oil	1½ teaspoons	1 tablespoon
Minced fresh ginger	1 teaspoon	2 teaspoons
Garlic, crushed	1 clove	2 cloves
Sliced fresh vegetables	2–3 cups	4–6 cups

Cut the chicken into strips about 1½″ × ½″.

In a measuring cup, stir together the broth, soy sauce, cornstarch and sugar; set aside.

Place a heavy, 10″ nonstick skillet over high heat for 1 minute. Add the oil and swirl the pan to coat it evenly. Add the chicken and cook, stirring constantly, for 1 minute.

Push the chicken to the side of the skillet and add the ginger, garlic and vegetables. Cook and stir for 1 minute. Reduce the heat to medium and stir in the broth mixture. Cover the pan and cook, stirring every 30 seconds, for 1 to 2 minutes longer, or until the vegetables are crisp-tender.

Per serving: 307 calories, 9.1 g. total fat, 0.8 g. saturated fat, 66 mg. cholesterol, 747 mg. sodium, 34.9 g. protein, 26.8 g. carbohydrates, 6.5 g. dietary fiber.

Chicken & Rice Veracruz

A preponderance of low-fat chicken recipes call for high-priced boneless chicken breasts, but not this sunny sauté made with inexpensive drumsticks. Stripped of their skins, which contain most of the fat, the drumsticks add a rich, meaty flavor to this easy skillet dinner. Extra helpings taste great the next day, so make a double batch. Add a green salad and some crusty French or Italian bread to complete the meal.

Ingredients	For 2 servings	For 4 servings
Bone-in chicken drumsticks	4	8
Olive oil	1 teaspoon	2 teaspoons
Diced green peppers	½ cup	1 cup
Chopped onions	¼ cup	½ cup
Garlic, minced	1 clove	2 cloves
Orange juice	1 cup	2 cups
Chili powder	1 teaspoon	2 teaspoons
Ground cumin	½ teaspoon	1 teaspoon
Salt	to taste	to taste
Ground red pepper	to taste	to taste
Medium-grain white rice	⅓ cup	⅔ cup
Sliced stuffed green olives	1 tablespoon	2 tablespoons

Remove the skin from the chicken and set the drumsticks aside.

Briefly heat the oil in a heavy, 10″ nonstick skillet over medium heat. Add the green peppers and onions. Cook, stirring frequently, for 3 minutes, or until the vegetables begin to brown.

Stir in the garlic; then add the orange juice, chili powder, cumin, salt and red pepper. Add the rice, stir the mixture and arrange the chicken over the rice.

Bring the liquid to a simmer, then reduce the heat to low. Cover the pan and cook for 45 minutes, or until the rice is tender, the liquid has been absorbed and the chicken shows no trace of pink near the bone when pierced with a sharp knife. Scatter the olives over the chicken and rice and serve.

Per serving: 393 calories, 10.1 g. total fat, 2 g. saturated fat, 91 mg. cholesterol, 353 mg. sodium, 31.8 g. protein, 43.4 g. carbohydrates, 2.4 g. dietary fiber.

Oven-Barbecued Chicken

In the Midwest, barbecue sauce is generally sweet enough to induce a toothache in North Carolinians, who like their barbecue sauce with plenty of vinegar for pucker. I've tried to appeal to both camps with this quick sauce that gets its sweetness and spice from ketchup and its tang from grated lemon rind and lemon juice.

Serve the chicken hot from the oven (or grill) with corn on the cob and thick slices of ripe tomato. Serve cold barbecued chicken with potato, pasta or rice salad or salads of marinated beans or peas. Either way, try wedges of watermelon or cantaloupe for dessert.

Ingredients	For 2 servings	For 4 servings
Bone-in chicken legs with thighs	2	4
Ketchup	2 tablespoons	¼ cup
Brown sugar	1½ teaspoons	1 tablespoon
Dijon mustard	1 teaspoon	2 teaspoons
Grated lemon rind	½ teaspoon	1 teaspoon
Lemon juice	1 tablespoon	2 tablespoons

Preheat the oven to 350°. Line a baking pan with heavy foil.

Remove the skin from the chicken and set the legs aside.

In a small bowl, whisk together the ketchup, brown sugar, mustard, lemon rind and lemon juice.

Arrange the chicken in a single layer on the prepared pan, brush it with the sauce mixture and bake it on the middle shelf of the oven for 45 minutes, or until the chicken shows no trace of pink near the thighbone when pierced with a sharp knife. Serve hot or cold.

Per serving: 212 calories, 8 g. total fat, 2.2 g. saturated fat, 89 mg. cholesterol, 250 mg. sodium, 25.8 g. protein, 8.1 g. carbohydrates, 0 g. dietary fiber.

Florida Dirty Rice

If you are one of those people who tosses out the giblets when you buy a whole chicken because you don't know what to do with them, try this flavorful, inexpensive dish from Florida. Even if you think you won't like chicken livers, gizzards and hearts, this down-home dish of rice, chicken and herbs may change your mind. You can buy gizzards at the store or save and freeze them for this dish the next time you prepare a whole chicken.

Ingredients	For 1 serving	For 2 servings
Chopped onions	2 tablespoons	¼ cup
Chopped celery	2 tablespoons	¼ cup
Chopped green peppers	2 tablespoons	¼ cup
Garlic, crushed (optional)	½ clove	1 clove
Olive or canola oil	1½ teaspoons	1 tablespoon
Giblets (liver, gizzard and heart)	1 each	2 each
Long-grain white rice	¼ cup	½ cup
Defatted chicken broth	1 cup	2 cups
Dried thyme	¼ teaspoon	½ teaspoon
Salt	⅛ teaspoon	¼ teaspoon
Pepper	⅛ teaspoon	¼ teaspoon

In a 1-quart (or 1½-quart) microwave-safe casserole, stir together the onions, celery, green peppers, garlic (if using) and oil.

Cut the chicken livers and gizzards in half. Add the giblets to the casserole. Cover and microwave on high power for 2 (or 3) minutes.

Remove the giblets from the casserole and set aside.

Stir the rice, broth, thyme, salt and pepper into the casserole and microwave on high, uncovered, for a total of 10 minutes; stop and stir after 5 minutes.

Finely chop the giblets. Stir them into the casserole. Microwave on high for 5 minutes, or until the rice is tender, the giblets show no trace of pink and most of the liquid has been absorbed. Let stand for 5 minutes before serving.

Per serving: 372 calories, 11.1 g. total fat, 2.2 g. saturated fat, 270 mg. cholesterol, 624 mg. sodium, 22.4 g. protein, 44.1 g. carbohydrates, 1.5 g. dietary fiber.

Bronzed Cornish Hen

Here's an elegant dinner that's suitable for company. If you're making it for just yourself, keep the leftovers for a splendid picnic tomorrow. Skim the fat from the soy-and-honey juices left in the roasting pan and use the juices as a glaze for steamed baby carrots, brussels sprouts, baby onions or cubed sweet potatoes that will make an excellent accompaniment to this dish. Serve the hen with Thai Peach Salsa and plenty of hot rice. If you are using a frozen hen, remember to thaw it overnight in the refrigerator before starting this dish.

Ingredients	For 2 servings	For 4 servings
Cornish hens (20–24 ounces each)	1	2
Green onions, white part only	2	4
Garlic, crushed	1 clove	2 cloves
Honey	2 tablespoons	¼ cup
Reduced-sodium soy sauce	1 tablespoon	2 tablespoons

Preheat the oven to 350°.

Remove the neck and giblets from the hens; wash and freeze them for future use in broth and gravy.

Wash the hens under cold running water; drain and pat dry with paper towels. Tuck the wing tips under the back to secure them and place the hens, breast side up, in a small baking pan or loaf pan. Place the green onions and garlic in the cavity.

In a small bowl, whisk together the honey and soy sauce; brush or drizzle the glaze evenly over the hens.

Roast, basting occasionally with pan juices, for 1 hour, or until the juice runs clear when you pierce the thickest part of the thigh with a sharp knife. Transfer the hens to a warm plate and let stand for 10 minutes. Cut each hen in half through the breastbone and back, using kitchen shears or a boning knife. Serve hot or at room temperature.

Per serving: 369 calories, 13.4 g. total fat, 3.9 g. saturated fat, 135 mg. cholesterol, 375 mg. sodium, 40.5 g. protein, 18.4 g. carbohydrates 0.2 g. dietary fiber.

Thai Peach Salsa

Salsa can be made with all sorts of fruits and vegetables other than tomatoes. This one uses typically Thai ingredients of ginger, cilantro and lime juice. If fresh chili peppers are available, substitute 1 teaspoon finely minced serrano or jalapeño peppers for the pepper flakes. This salsa is spicy; you may want to use less hot pepper than I do. (Remember to wear plastic or rubber gloves when working with hot peppers.)

If you have access to ripe mangoes, try making the salsa with mango instead of peaches. Either way, enjoy it with grilled or roasted fish, chicken and pork. It is especially good with Bronzed Cornish Hen. Or serve it over melba toast rounds spread with light cream cheese as a snack.

2 large unpeeled peaches
2 tablespoons lime juice
2 tablespoons finely diced red onions
2 tablespoons chopped fresh cilantro
1 tablespoon minced fresh ginger
½ teaspoon crushed red-pepper flakes

CAYENNE

Pit the peaches and cut into ½" dice. Place in a medium bowl. Add the lime juice, onions, cilantro, ginger and pepper flakes. Stir well and let stand at room temperature for 30 minutes to blend the flavors.

Makes 2 servings

Per serving: 49 calories, 0.1 g. total fat, 0 g. saturated fat, 0 mg. cholesterol, 6 mg. sodium, 0.9 g. protein, 12.8 g. carbohydrates, 1.7 g. dietary fiber.

Downsized Roast Turkey

Even though there's just one or two of you, buy a 3- to 5-pound bone-in turkey breast, fresh or frozen, next time you see it on sale. Roast your purchase according to the recipe that follows, but avoid menu fatigue and food poisoning by carving and freezing leftovers within a couple of days *for use within three months*. (Nothing is forever, including foods stowed in freezer compartments of small refrigerators.)

For tender, juicy turkey, be careful not to overcook. Cover and refrigerate leftover turkey within 2 hours of roasting. Next day, strip off the skin, then slice and dice the meat. Refrigerate it for use within the 2 days or freeze it with a little low-fat gravy for later use. For cold sandwiches, freeze turkey slices in a single layer on a baking sheet just until stiff. Transfer the pieces to resealable plastic bags in 1- or 2-serving sizes and return them to the freezer.

1 medium onion, coarsely chopped

1 medium carrot, thinly sliced

1 celery rib, thinly sliced

1 bone-in turkey breast (3–5 pounds), fresh or thawed frozen

Salt and pepper

½ teaspoon canola oil

Preheat the oven to 325°.

Spread the onions, carrots and celery in a 9″ × 9″ baking pan. Place the turkey breast, skin side up, on top of the vegetables. Sprinkle with the salt and pepper.

Brush one side of a 12″ to 18″ square of foil with the oil and gently press the oiled side of the foil around the turkey to cover it without sealing. Don't let edges of foil hang over the outside of the pan, or it will collect steaming juices, which will condense and drip onto the oven floor.

Roast the turkey on the middle shelf of the oven for 1 hour, then remove the foil and brush the turkey with pan drippings. Continue roasting the turkey for another 1 to 2 hours, or until a meat thermometer reads 170° to 175° when inserted into the thickest part of the breast (or until the built-in timer, if present, pops and the juices run clear when you pierce the thickest part of the turkey with a cooking fork).

Let the turkey rest for 10 minutes. Remove the skin before slicing and serving.

Makes 9 to 15 servings

Per 3 ounces: 115 calories, 0.6 g. total fat, 0.2 g. saturated fat, 71 mg. cholesterol, 44 mg. sodium, 25.6 g. protein, 0 mg. carbohydrates, 0 g. dietary fiber.

Turkey Tostadas

Turn leftover roast turkey into this informal supper that's best cooked to order and eaten in the kitchen as each tortilla is heated.

Ingredients	For 1 serving	For 2 servings
Corn tortillas	2	4
Diced cooked turkey	⅓ cup	⅔ cup
Shredded iceberg or leaf lettuce	⅔ cup	1⅓ cups
Diced ripe tomatoes	1 small	2 small
Green onions, thinly sliced	1	2
Shredded Cheddar or Monterey Jack cheese	2 tablespoons	¼ cup

Preheat a heavy, 5" nonstick or cast-iron skillet for 2 minutes over low heat. Add the tortillas, one at a time, and heat each for 1 minute, turning once. (Or heat according to the package directions in the microwave.)

Top the tortillas with the turkey, lettuce, tomatoes, green onions and Cheddar or Monterey Jack. Serve immediately.

Per serving: 317 calories, 11.6 g. total fat, 4.1 g. saturated fat, 55 mg. cholesterol, 243 mg. sodium, 23.4 g. protein, 32.5 g. carbohydrates, 5.2 g. dietary fiber.

Turkey Medallions Seared in Thai Butter

Veal piccata is a classic Italian entrée of thin veal cutlets, oozing with butter and lemon juice and sharpened with a garnish of paper-thin lemon slices. Instead of veal piccata, treat yourself to this elegant entrée—boneless cutlets of turkey breast seared in very little butter and enhanced with minced ginger and lime juice. For a cross-cultural feast with Italian overtones, serve the turkey cutlets over a microwaved risotto with sautéed zucchini.

Ingredients	For 1 serving	For 2 servings
Lime juice	2 tablespoons	¼ cup
Minced fresh ginger	1 teaspoon	2 teaspoons
Sugar	½ teaspoon	1 teaspoon
Boneless turkey breast cutlets (¼" thick)	4 ounces	8 ounces
Salt	to taste	to taste
Butter or margarine	2 teaspoons	4 teaspoons
Thinly cut lime slices	3	6
Finely chopped fresh cilantro	1 tablespoon	2 tablespoons

In a small bowl, stir together the lime juice, ginger and sugar until the sugar dissolves; set aside.

Dry the turkey pieces with a paper towel and sprinkle them with the salt.

Place a heavy, 8" (or 10") nonstick skillet over high heat for 1 minute. Swirl in the butter or margarine. Quickly add the turkey. Cook for 3 minutes, turning as necessary, until the turkey is firm to the touch and browned on both sides, with no trace of pink in the thickest part.

Transfer the turkey to a warm serving plate. Pour the lime juice mixture into the skillet and cook for 30 seconds, or until it becomes syrupy and is reduced by half. Pour over the turkey. Garnish with the lime slices and cilantro. Serve immediately.

Per serving: 200 calories, 8.3 g. total fat, 4.9 g. saturated fat, 91 mg. cholesterol, 390 mg. sodium, 25.9 g. protein, 5.4 g. carbohydrates, 0.2 g. dietary fiber.

Turkey Florentine

In cookery, the term "Florentine" indicates food served on a bed of spinach—and usually blended with a rich cheese sauce. The spinach in this rich-tasting dish gets a flavor boost not from cheese sauce but from dry white wine (or apple juice), which provides just enough liquid to cook the spinach quickly without scorching. Judicious additions of shallots, nutmeg and butter or margarine further enhance the flavor, making this a fine dish to set before company. This is a quick-cooking entrée, so make sure that you have all the ingredients prepped and assembled next to the stove before you begin.

Ingredients	For 1 serving	For 2 servings
Boneless turkey breast cutlets (¼" thick)	4 ounces	8 ounces
Salt and pepper	to taste	to taste
Butter or margarine	1 teaspoon	2 teaspoons
Minced shallots or onions	2 teaspoons	4 teaspoons
Dry white wine or apple juice	2 tablespoons	¼ cup
Spinach, loosely packed	4 cups	8 cups
Grated nutmeg (optional)	dash	⅛ teaspoon

Dry the turkey pieces with a paper towel, then sprinkle them with the salt and pepper.

Place a heavy, 8" (or 10") nonstick skillet over high heat for 1 minute. Swirl in the butter or margarine and add the turkey. Cook, turning as necessary, for 3 minutes, or until the turkey is browned and firm to the touch, with no trace of pink in the center. Transfer to a plate and keep warm.

To the skillet, add the shallots or onions, wine or apple juice and spinach. Reduce the heat to medium and cook for 1 minute, or until the spinach is barely wilted. Sprinkle with the nutmeg (if using). Place the spinach on a serving plate, top with the turkey and serve.

Per serving: 198 calories, 4.8 g. total fat, 2.6 g. saturated fat, 81 mg. cholesterol, 175 mg. sodium, 29.1 g. protein, 5.3 g. carbohydrates, 3 g. dietary fiber.

Luau Turkey Loaf

Substituting lean ground turkey (7 to 12 percent fat) for ground beef (10 to 34 percent fat) or ground pork (18 to 50 percent fat) is a good way to cut down on dietary fat in many of your favorite recipes. To compensate for turkey's rather bland flavor, you may need to increase the amount of herbs and spices. And because turkey tends to dry out, don't overcook it.

With hot Luau Turkey Loaf, have mashed sweet potatoes and a green vegetable or salad. With cold leftovers, serve a fresh fruit salad and whole-wheat bread. Either way, Pineapple Chutney is a nice and easy accompaniment.

Ingredients	For 2 servings	For 4 servings
Pineapple or orange juice	1 tablespoon	2 tablespoons
Reduced-sodium soy sauce	1½ teaspoons	1 tablespoon
Coarsely chopped onions	1 tablespoon	2 tablespoons
Sweet red or green pepper, chopped	⅛ small	¼ small
Sliced fresh ginger	2 quarter-size slices	4 quarter-size slices
Lean ground turkey	6 ounces	12 ounces
Fresh bread crumbs	¼ cup	½ cup
Egg	1 large white or yolk	1 large

Preheat the oven to 350°.

In a blender, combine the pineapple or orange juice, soy sauce, onions, peppers and ginger. Process on medium speed until the vegetables are finely pureed. Pour into a medium mixing bowl. Add the turkey, bread crumbs and egg.

Lightly coat a small baking sheet with no-stick spray. Blend everything well with your hands and pat the mixture into a loaf shape on the baking sheet. Bake on the middle shelf of the oven for 25 to 30 (or 45 to 50) minutes, until the loaf is brown on top with no trace of pink in the center when you pierce it with a sharp knife.

Let the loaf stand for 5 to 10 minutes before slicing. Serve hot or cold.

Per serving: 211 calories, 12.3 g. total fat, 0.5 g. saturated fat, 75 mg. cholesterol, 405 mg. sodium, 22.8 g. protein, 5.3 g. carbohydrates, 0.4 g. dietary fiber.

Pineapple Chutney

first made this chutney with fresh pineapple. It took a lot of peeling, dicing, chopping, stirring and so forth. The results weren't nearly as good as this version, made painlessly with canned crushed pineapple. This chutney is made quickly in the microwave and zips up the flavor of grilled chicken, fish, ham or pork chops. It's especially good with Luau Turkey Loaf.

1 can (8 ounces) juice-packed canned crushed pineapple (with juice)

2 tablespoons sugar

2 tablespoons vinegar

2 tablespoons chopped onions

2 tablespoons chopped red or green peppers

1 tablespoon minced fresh ginger

¼ teaspoon crushed red-pepper flakes

2 tablespoons golden raisins

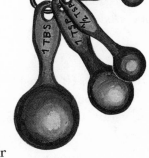

In a 4-cup microwave-safe glass measure, combine the pineapple (with juice), sugar, vinegar, onions, red or green peppers, ginger and pepper flakes. Microwave on high power for 3 minutes. Stir in the raisins and microwave on high for 1 minute.

Let the chutney stand at least 5 minutes before serving. Serve warm or cold.

Makes about 1⅓ cups

Per ⅓ cup: 72 calories, 0.1 g. total fat, 0 g. saturated fat, 0 mg. cholesterol, 19 mg. sodium, 0.6 g. protein, 19.3 g. carbohydrates, 1 g. dietary fiber.

Turkey in the Straw

This is just meat sauce made with ground turkey instead of ground beef. It's especially good over spaghetti squash or pasta.

Ingredients	For 2 servings	For 4 servings
Lean ground turkey	8 ounces	1 pound
Chopped onions	½ cup	1 cup
Diced green peppers	½ cup	1 cup
Garlic, crushed	1 clove	2 cloves
Canned tomatoes (with juice)	1 cup	16 ounces
Dried basil	½ teaspoon	1 teaspoon
Dried oregano	½ teaspoon	1 teaspoon
Fennel seeds	½ teaspoon	1 teaspoon
Salt	⅛ teaspoon	¼ teaspoon
Pepper	pinch	⅛ teaspoon

In a heavy, 10" nonstick skillet over medium heat, sauté the turkey, onions and green peppers for 5 minutes, or until the turkey is crumbly and the vegetables are tender but not brown. Stir in the garlic, tomatoes (with juice), basil, oregano, fennel seeds, salt and pepper.

Bring the sauce to a simmer, cover and reduce the heat. Cook over low heat for 30 minutes, or until most of the liquid has evaporated.

Per serving: 252 calories, 13.1 g. total fat, 0.2 g. saturated fat, 75 mg. cholesterol, 430 mg. sodium, 23.5 g. protein, 16.3 g. carbohydrates, 4.8 g. dietary fiber.

Chicken and Turkey

Cooking Spaghetti Squash

Spaghetti squash is a winter squash that separates after cooking into strands that look like a pile of golden straw. Its mild, sweet flavor and lovely color make it an ideal companion for poultry and a versatile side dish. Portion and freeze extra spaghetti squash in resealable plastic bags or plastic containers for future meals.

You can serve spaghetti squash as a simple side dish seasoned with a little salt and pepper. Or you can fancy it up by stirring it into pan-glazed apple slices to go with chicken or pork. For an easy main dish, heat the squash in the microwave or a skillet with a little shredded Cheddar. For an unusually good salad or appetizer, toss cold spaghetti squash with honey-mustard dressing.

To cook spaghetti squash, place a small (2 or 3 pounds) squash in a large saucepan or Dutch oven. Add enough cold water to cover the squash, then bring it to a boil over high heat. Cover the pan, reduce the heat to medium and cook the squash for 25 to 30 minutes, or until you can easily pierce it with a knife.

Remove the squash from the water and carefully cut it in half lengthwise, protecting your fingers from the heat with a folded dish towel. Scrape out and discard the seeds. Using a table fork, scrape the squash in one direction to separate it into spaghetti-like strands.

Tipsy Turkey Hash

Dark-meat turkey parts, like thighs and drumsticks, are usually a bargain compared with turkey breasts. This recipe lets you cash in on such savings in an easy, oven-baked stew. Have it over rice, pasta or cornbread or beside new potatoes or warm French bread. Refrigerate or freeze extras to reheat in the microwave or on the stovetop in a covered saucepan over low heat. If you have the time, you can marinate the turkey overnight before cooking it.

Ingredients	For 2 servings	For 4 servings
Bone-in turkey drumsticks (12–14 ounces each)	1	2
Thinly sliced onions	½ cup	1 cup
Garlic	2 cloves	4 cloves
Dry white or red wine	1 cup	2 cups
Dried rosemary, crumbled	½ teaspoon	1 teaspoon
Salt	¼ teaspoon	½ teaspoon
Pepper	to taste	to taste
All-purpose flour	2 teaspoons	4 teaspoons
Water	2 tablespoons	¼ cup
Chopped fresh parsley (optional)	2 tablespoons	¼ cup

Remove the skin from the turkey and arrange the drumsticks in a glass or plastic lidded container. Sprinkle with the onions and garlic. In a small bowl, combine the wine, rosemary, salt and pepper and pour over the turkey. Cover and refrigerate for several hours or overnight, turning the turkey several times as it marinates.

Preheat the oven to 325°.

Transfer the turkey and marinade to a loaf pan or casserole. Cover and bake the turkey for 2 hours; turn the pieces after 1 hour. Remove from the oven and let stand until the turkey is cool enough to handle.

Pull the bones and tendons from the meat. Cut the meat into bite-size pieces.

Strain the cooking juices into a small saucepan. In a cup, whisk the flour and water until smooth. Whisk the mixture into the cooking juices. Bring the sauce to a simmer and cook, stirring constantly, until it is bubbling and slightly thickened.

Add the turkey to the pan. Heat until the turkey is piping hot. Serve hot, sprinkled with the parsley (if using).

Per serving: 222 calories, 3.8 g. total fat, 1.1 g. saturated fat, 47 mg. cholesterol, 330 mg. sodium, 20.1 g. protein, 7.2 g. carbohydrates, 0.9 g. dietary fiber.

Good Gravy

Never, never throw away the pan drippings from any roast, be it turkey, chicken, beef, lamb, pork, ham or veal. By adding a little water or wine to the roasting pan, you can transform pan drippings into flavorful *jus* (French for juice) to go with your roast. Or you can make very good gravy with the addition of a little flour, salt and pepper. Here's how.

Remove the roast from the pan and add about ½" of water (or a combination of water and wine) to the roasting pan. Set the pan over medium-high heat on the stovetop and bring the liquid to a simmer; stir and scrape the bottom of the pan to loosen the crusty drippings. Cook the liquid rapidly for 5 to 10 minutes, until you have 1½ to 3 cups *jus*, to reduce the liquid and concentrate the flavors.

Strain the liquid into a heatproof container, then skim off as much fat as possible. If you have the time, chill the liquid for several hours or overnight, during which time the fat will rise to the top and solidify for easy removal. Use the *jus* as is or turn it into gravy as below. (If you don't have any fat reserved from the roast as specified in the directions, substitute an equal amount of butter, margarine or olive oil.)

> 1½ teaspoons fat reserved from roast
> 1 tablespoon all-purpose flour
> Salt and pepper
> 1 cup *jus*

Melt the fat in a small saucepan over medium heat. Add the flour, salt and pepper and stir the mixture until no lumps remain. Stir in the *jus* and cook, stirring constantly, until the liquid comes to a boil and is slightly thickened.

Makes 1 cup

Per ¼ cup: 25 calories, 1.8 g. total fat, 0.5 g. saturated fat, 2 mg. cholesterol, 75 mg. sodium, 0.4 g. protein, 1.8 g. carbohydrates, 0.1 g. dietary fiber.

and Shellfish

*D*on't, whatever you do, be intimidated about cooking fish. It couldn't be easier! The only hard thing is resisting the urge to overcook it. Fish cooks to succulent tenderness in a very short time because it doesn't have the same kind of connective tissue found in meat and poultry. Overcooking makes fish tough and dry, so learn to snatch it from the heat the instant that the thickest part loses its translucence.

You needn't thaw frozen fish before you cook it. In fact, it's better when cooked without thawing. Whether fish is fresh or frozen, for best results, calculate the cooking time according to thickness. Measure the thickest part of whole finfish or fillets with a ruler.

🐟 For fresh or thawed fish, allow 8 to 10 minutes per inch of thickness.

🐟 For frozen fish, allow 20 minutes per inch of thickness, or about 10 to 12 minutes for ½ inch thickness.

Delicately flavored, white-fleshed fish like cod and flounder are, almost without exception, very low in fat, averaging only one gram of fat in every 3½ ounces of raw fish. Other low-fat fish include hake, pollock, skate, sole, whiting, sea bass, cusk, grouper, haddock, snapper, tilefish, tilapia and monkfish. For any of the preceding delicate fish, choose moist-heat methods, such as poaching, steaming and microwaving. Delicate fish tends to dry out with dry-heat cooking methods, such as broiling and grilling.

Fuller-flavored fish, such as bluefish, mullet, salmon, catfish and herring, are higher in fat. It's the fat that keeps them from drying out and makes them a good choice for dry-heat methods like broiling, grilling, baking and pan-grilling. The fat in fatty fish is actually desirable, since it's loaded with omega-3 fatty acids, which are credited with helping lower blood cholesterol levels in people who eat these types of fish regularly. Other fatty fish include tuna, rainbow trout, pompano, swordfish, whitefish and mackerel.

Pan-Fried Catfish

Pan-fried catfish makes a great poor-boy sandwich — on a French roll with spicy mustard, finely shredded cabbage and fresh tomatoes. Or turn it into a classic Southern dinner by serving it with greens, black-eyed peas and a slice of watermelon for dessert.

Ingredients	For 1 serving	For 2 servings
Egg white	1	1
Catfish fillets (5 ounces each)	1	2
Cornmeal	1 tablespoon	2 tablespoons
Salt and pepper	to taste	to taste
Olive or canola oil	2 tablespoons	¼ cup
Lemon wedges	2	4

In a shallow bowl, beat the egg white until foamy. Dip the catfish in the egg white; then roll it in the cornmeal and sprinkle it with the salt and pepper.

Set a heavy, 8″ (or 10″) nonstick skillet over medium heat and add the oil. Heat the oil until it is very hot but not smoking, about 3 to 4 minutes. Lay the catfish in the pan and cook for 2 to 3 minutes. Turn it and cook for another 2 to 3 minutes, or until the catfish is golden brown outside and firm to the touch.

Transfer the catfish to a paper towel–lined plate to absorb all excess oil. Transfer to individual dinner plates and serve with the lemon wedges.

Per serving: 253 calories, 10.8 g. total fat, 2 g. saturated fat, 82 mg. cholesterol, 118 mg. sodium, 28.5 g. protein, 9.6 g. carbohydrates, 0.7 g. dietary fiber.

Fear of Frying

The health benefits of a low-fat diet have been proven conclusively, but the fear of frying has been grossly overrated in many instances, as I'm about to prove to you anecdotally. My grandmotherly research was inspired by some choice catfish at a very attractive price.

I dipped the fillets in beaten egg white, then cornmeal, and fried them in $1/8$" of sizzling hot olive oil. To see how much grease the fish absorbed, I poured off and carefully measured the oil left in the skillet. Guess what! In each of four test fries, each fillet absorbed slightly less than a teaspoon of oil.

Fish is a good choice when you get a craving for fried foods. Because it cooks in a shorter time than chicken or meat, it has less time to absorb oil. So if you love fried fish, here are some things you can do to ensure that your pan-fried fish comes out crispy and delicious without soaking up unnecessary oil.

- Use an egg white dip instead of whole eggs and milk. This cuts some of the fat from the recipe.
- A cornmeal coating absorbs less oil than flour, crumbs or batter.
- Pan-fry fish in a small amount of oil; don't deep-fry it.
- Make sure the oil is rippling hot before the fish hits the pan; when cooking oil isn't hot enough, foods tend to absorb more grease.

So if you love fried fish, enjoy it occasionally. Just don't make a habit of eating fried fish or, for that matter, any fried foods.

Poached Cod
with Creamy Cucumber Sauce

David Letterman, king of the late-night talk-show hosts, usually reduces celebrity cooks to impotent rage by playing with their food. That didn't work with Julia Child. She is unflappable during her on-camera ordeals with Dave, probably because she invariably chooses to cook something simple. One night, using a portable electric unit, she poached cod fillets in water tinged with white wine, chopped vegetables and a pinch of herbs. Then she dabbed the poached fish with a quick and easy cucumber sauce. On tasting the combination, Letterman pronounced that simple dish the best ever cooked on his show. Without Dave around to hassle you, there's no reason you can't master Poached Cod with Creamy Cucumber Sauce.

Here is a downsized variation of that simple dish. Add some boiled potatoes and a fresh tomato salad to round out the meal. If you like, you can replace the cod with any other firm-fleshed white fish.

Ingredients	For 1 serving	For 2 servings
Sour cream	2 tablespoons	$\frac{1}{4}$ cup
Thinly sliced cucumbers	$\frac{1}{4}$ cup	$\frac{1}{2}$ cup
Minced shallots	1 teaspoon	2 teaspoons
Dried dill weed	$\frac{1}{4}$ teaspoon	$\frac{1}{2}$ teaspoon
Dry white wine	$\frac{1}{2}$ cup	$\frac{1}{2}$ cup
Carrot, sliced	1 small	1 small
Celery rib, sliced	$\frac{1}{2}$	$\frac{1}{2}$
Onion slice	1	1
Dried thyme	$\frac{1}{4}$ teaspoon	$\frac{1}{2}$ teaspoon
Salt	$\frac{1}{4}$ teaspoon	$\frac{1}{4}$ teaspoon
White pepper	$\frac{1}{4}$ teaspoon	$\frac{1}{4}$ teaspoon
Cod fillets (5 ounces each)	1	2

In a small mixing bowl, combine the sour cream, cucumbers, shallots and dill. Mix well and set aside.

Place the wine, carrots, celery, onion, thyme, salt and pepper in a heavy, 8" (or 10") nonstick skillet. Add about 1" cold water to the skillet. Bring to a boil over high heat. Reduce the heat to low and simmer the liquid for 10 minutes.

Using a broad spatula, carefully lower the fish into the simmering liquid. Cook for 5 to 8 minutes, or until the fish is opaque and firm to the touch.

Transfer the fish to a warm serving plate and top it with the cucumber sauce.

Per serving: 180 calories, 7 g. total fat, 4 g. saturated fat, 74 mg. cholesterol, 359 mg. sodium, 26.1 g. protein, 1.5 g. carbohydrates, 0.1 g. dietary fiber.

Flounder with New Potatoes & Onions

In this healthy version of a French country recipe, wafer-thin potatoes and onions are first oven-poached in cider. The fish fillets are then placed over the vegetables, sprinkled with lightly buttered crumbs and baked until golden.

Ingredients	For 1 serving	For 2 servings
Butter or margarine	2 teaspoons	4 teaspoons
Soft white bread crumbs	2 tablespoons	¼ cup
Small new potatoes	4 ounces	8 ounces
Small yellow onion	½	1
Cider or apple juice	¼ cup	½ cup
Salt and pepper	to taste	to taste
Flounder fillets (5 ounces each)	1	2

Preheat the oven to 425°.

For each serving, grease a shallow 2-cup baking dish or gratin dish with ½ teaspoon of the butter or margarine.

In a small saucepan over medium-low heat, melt the remaining butter or margarine; stir in the bread crumbs and set aside.

Slice the potatoes and onion as thinly as possible and arrange them in alternating layers in the prepared dishes. Pour the cider or apple juice over the vegetables and sprinkle with the salt and pepper. Bake for 20 minutes.

Reduce the oven temperature to 350°.

Spoon the liquid in the baking dishes over the vegetables to baste them, then arrange the fish over the vegetables, folding the tips of any long, thin fillets under if necessary to fit them into the baking dishes. Sprinkle the buttered crumbs over the fish and bake for 10 to 15 minutes, or until the fish is opaque and firm to the touch and the crumb topping is golden brown.

Per serving: 379 calories, 9.7 g. total fat, 5.2 g. saturated fat, 89 mg. cholesterol, 233 mg. sodium, 30.7 g. protein, 41.7 g. carbohydrates, 1.1 g. dietary fiber.

Microwave Cod
in Fresh Tomato Sauce

I wouldn't dream of making 1 or 2 servings of fresh tomato sauce on the stove; it takes just about as much time as making sauce for a mob. But with a microwave, one or two servings is a zap. This sauce lifts ordinary fish into the realm of something special. For a fast but stylish dinner, add rice and a green salad.

Ingredients	For 1 serving	For 2 servings
Olive or canola oil	1½ teaspoons	1 tablespoon
Chopped onions	2 tablespoons	¼ cup
Garlic, crushed	1 small clove	1 clove
Tomatoes, peeled and coarsely chopped	1 medium	2 medium
Dried thyme or basil	pinch	⅛ teaspoon
Salt	to taste	to taste
Ground red pepper	to taste	to taste
Cod fillets (5 ounces each)	1	2
Finely chopped fresh parsley (optional)	1½ teaspoons	1 tablespoon

In a 2-cup (or 1-quart) microwave-safe casserole, stir together the oil and onions. Microwave on high power for 2 (or 3) minutes.

Stir in the garlic, tomatoes, thyme or basil, salt and pepper. Cover the casserole with a paper towel to prevent splatters and microwave on high for a total of 3 (or 5) minutes; stop and stir after 2 minutes.

Arrange the fish on the tomato sauce, folding thin portions under to make a uniform thickness. Cover the casserole with a lid or vented plastic wrap. Microwave on high for 1½ to 2 (or 3 to 4) minutes, or until the fish is opaque and firm to the touch. Sprinkle with the parsley (if using) and let stand for 3 minutes before serving.

Per serving: 215 calories, 8.2 g. total fat, 1.2 g. saturated fat, 62 mg. cholesterol, 90 mg. sodium, 26.7 g. protein, 8.6 g. carbohydrates, 2 g. dietary fiber.

BASIL

Red Snapper Panned with Pink Grapefruit

The hardest part of this recipe—in fact, the only hard part—is sectioning the grapefruit, a kitchen routine that buffaloes many people. But sectioning grapefruit, as well as oranges, is a snap when you have a sharp paring knife.

Holding the fruit over a bowl to catch the precious juices, slice off the top to expose the juicy innards. Peel around and down as you would an apple, cutting away the inner white membrane along with the outer peel. Now cut down along the membrane lining of one section, then run the knife blade under the opposite side of the section to flip it into the bowl. Repeat until you've removed all the sections. Then squeeze the pulp over the bowl to salvage the remaining juices.

Ingredients	For 1 serving	For 2 servings
Red snapper fillets (5 ounces each)	1	2
Butter or margarine, melted	1½ teaspoons	1 tablespoon
Salt and pepper	to taste	to taste
Pink grapefruit, sectioned	½	1

Brush the fish on both sides with the butter or margarine and sprinkle it with the salt and pepper.

Place a heavy, 8″ (or 10″) nonstick skillet over medium-high heat for 1 to 2 minutes. Add the fillets and brown them on both sides, about 3 to 4 minutes total. Add the grapefruit sections with their juice, reduce the heat to low and bring the juice to a simmer.

Cook for 3 to 4 minutes, or until the fish is opaque throughout and firm to the touch. With a slotted spatula, remove the fish and the grapefruit sections to a warm plate and serve.

Per serving: 229 calories, 7.7 g. total fat, 4 g. saturated fat, 68 mg. cholesterol, 148 mg. sodium, 29.8 g. protein, 9.3 g. carbohydrates, 1.6 g. dietary fiber.

Rainbow Trout in Foil

Baking fish in foil saves dish washing, a benefit that's especially appreciated by male cooks. This trout recipe is basic and simple. You can make the recipe even more basic by omitting everything but the salt, pepper and trout. Or you can fancy it up with fresh herbs like tarragon, basil or thyme. You could also replace the lemon or lime with thin slices of onion and tomato. If you use frozen trout, increase the baking time. Frozen fillets will take anywhere from 12 to 20 minutes.

Ingredients	For 1 serving	For 2 servings
Rainbow trout fillets (5 ounces each)	1	2
Melted butter or olive oil	1 teaspoon	2 teaspoons
Salt and pepper	to taste	to taste
Thin lemon or lime slices	3	6
Finely chopped fresh parsley (optional)	2 teaspoons	4 teaspoons

Preheat the oven to 400°.

Brush the fillets on both sides with the butter or oil. Arrange each on a 12″ square of heavy foil. Sprinkle with the salt and pepper, cover with the lemon or lime slices and sprinkle the parsley (if using) over the top.

Fold the foil diagonally to make a triangle, then seal the edges tightly by folding and crimping them. Place the foil packets on a baking sheet and bake for 8 to 12 minutes, or until the fish is firm to the touch and opaque throughout. If the trout isn't quite done when you first check, reseal the foil and bake it a little longer. Serve the trout in the foil packet on a dinner plate.

Per serving: 206 calories, 8.7 g. total fat, 3.3 g. saturated fat, 90 mg. cholesterol, 79 mg. sodium, 29.6 g. protein, 3.1 g. carbohydrates, 0.4 g. dietary fiber.

Rigatoni alla Calabria

Everything you need to sustain life until tomorrow is in this fast pasta dish that's equally good as a cold salad or hot entrée. Pick up ready-to-cook fresh broccoli and tomato quarters from the supermarket salad bar to combine with ingredients found in most well-stocked kitchens.

Ingredients	For 1 serving	For 2 servings
Rigatoni	1 cup	2 cups
Olive oil	1½ teaspoons	1 tablespoon
Broccoli florets	⅔ cup	1⅔ cups
Garlic, crushed	1 clove	2 cloves
Diced tomatoes	1 medium	2 medium
Water-packed canned solid light tuna	3½ ounces	6½ ounces
Pepper	to taste	to taste
Parmesan cheese (optional)	2 tablespoons	¼ cup

Cook the rigatoni according to the directions on the package but without salt.

While the pasta is cooking, film a heavy, 8″ (or 10″) nonstick skillet with the oil. Add the broccoli and cook over medium-high heat for 3 minutes, stirring often. Add the garlic, then the tomatoes.

Drain the tuna, break it apart a little with a fork and add it to the skillet. Reduce the heat to low, cover the skillet and cook the mixture for 5 minutes, or until it is bubbling hot.

When the pasta has finished cooking, drain it well, turn it into a large bowl and toss it gently with the tuna mixture. Sprinkle with the pepper and Parmesan (if using). Serve hot or at room temperature.

Per serving: 595 calories, 14.6 g. total fat, 1.7 g. saturated fat, 46 mg. cholesterol, 600 mg. sodium, 41.8 g. protein, 73.9 g. carbohydrates, 3.2 g. dietary fiber.

Pan-Seared Tuna with Red Peppers & Fennel

Two types of fennel are called for here: crunchy bulb fennel (*finocchio* in Italian), with its celery-like texture and mild anise flavor, and aromatic fennel seed, which comes from a tall perennial that's grown principally for seeds used in food, perfumes and medicine. You'll find bulb fennel in the market from late winter through spring. When fresh fennel is not in season, substitute onions and double the fennel seeds. Be sure to have your fishmonger cut the tuna steaks ¾" thick.

Ingredients	For 1 serving	For 2 servings
Tuna steaks (5 ounces each)	1	2
Olive or canola oil	1½ teaspoons	1 tablespoon
Salt	to taste	to taste
Ground red or black pepper	to taste	to taste
Sweet red pepper, sliced	½ medium	1 medium
Thinly sliced fennel	½ cup	1 cup
Garlic, crushed	1 clove	2 cloves
Dry white wine	¼ cup	½ cup
Fennel seeds	¼ teaspoon	½ teaspoon

Preheat a heavy, 8" (or 10") nonstick skillet over medium heat for 2 to 3 minutes.

Brush the tuna on both sides with the oil, allowing ½ teaspoon per serving. Sprinkle with the salt and ground pepper. Add the tuna to the skillet. Cook, turning often with a broad spatula, for 5 to 8 minutes, or until the fish is opaque throughout and feels firm to the touch. (If in doubt, make a small cut in the thickest part and make sure the fish is cooked through.) Transfer the tuna to a warm plate.

Add the remaining oil to the skillet. Add the sweet peppers and sliced fennel. Cook, stirring frequently, for 2 to 3 minutes. Stir in the garlic and cook for 1 minute.

Stir in the wine and fennel seeds; raise the heat to high. Cook for 1 minute, or until the wine is syrupy and reduced by half. Spoon the vegetables around the tuna and serve.

Per serving: 317 calories, 13.9 g. total fat, 2.7 g. saturated fat, 53 mg. cholesterol, 111 mg. sodium, 34 g. protein, 5.9 g. carbohydrates, 1.5 g. dietary fiber.

Pan-Grilled Tuna Teriyaki

Any firm-fleshed fish that's large enough to cut into steaks will work in this recipe. You could try cod, halibut, grouper, rainbow trout, salmon, shark or swordfish. For the best results, make sure the steaks are at least ¾" thick. Serve the fish with hot rice and steamed snow peas.

Ingredients	For 1 serving	For 2 servings
Reduced-sodium soy sauce	1 tablespoon	2 tablespoons
Dry sherry or pineapple juice	1 tablespoon	2 tablespoons
Lime juice	1 tablespoon	2 tablespoons
Minced fresh ginger	1 teaspoon	2 teaspoons
Sugar	½ teaspoon	1 teaspoon
Garlic, smashed	1 small clove	1 large clove
Tuna steaks (5 ounces each)	1	2
Canola or peanut oil	½ teaspoon	1 teaspoon
Lime wedges	2	4

In a plastic or glass container large enough to hold the fish in a single layer, stir together the soy sauce, sherry or pineapple juice, lime juice, ginger, sugar and garlic until the sugar is dissolved. Add the fish, turning to coat it with the marinade. Cover and chill it for 2 hours or overnight; turn the fish occasionally while it marinates.

Remove the fish from the marinade and dry it thoroughly with paper towels, removing as much moisture as possible to ensure even browning. Reserve the leftover marinade.

Brush the fish on both sides with the oil.

Place a heavy, 8" (or 10") nonstick skillet over medium-high heat for 1 to 2 minutes, add the fish and cook, turning it occasionally, for 5 to 8 minutes, or until the fish is opaque throughout and feels firm to the touch.

Transfer the fish to a warm serving plate. Pour the reserved marinade into the skillet and cook over high heat for 30 seconds, or until the marinade foams up. Pour over the fish and serve garnished with the lime wedges.

Per serving: 276 calories, 9.3 g. total fat, 2 g. saturated fat, 53 mg. cholesterol, 585 mg. sodium, 34.9 g. protein, 8.6 g. carbohydrates, 0.9 g. dietary fiber.

Deviled Mackerel

Deviled mackerel tastes like a lot of work but isn't. The secret sauce is nothing more than a little mayonnaise and mustard, thinned with vermouth or lemon juice. The paprika sprinkled on top promotes browning as well as flavor. Good serve-alongs include new potatoes and coleslaw.

Ingredients	For 1 serving	For 2 servings
Mackerel fillets (5 ounces each)	1	2
Mayonnaise	1 teaspoon	2 teaspoons
Dijon mustard	2 teaspoons	1 tablespoon
Dry vermouth or lemon juice	1 tablespoon	2 tablespoons
Paprika	to taste	to taste
Salt and pepper	to taste	to taste

Preheat the broiler.

Line a small baking pan with foil, then lay the mackerel on the foil, skin side down.

In a small bowl, whisk together the mayonnaise, mustard and vermouth or lemon juice. Spread the sauce evenly over the mackerel. Sprinkle with the paprika, salt and pepper.

Broil 6" from the heat for 8 to 10 minutes, or until the mackerel is firm and the topping is well-browned.

Per serving: 194 calories, 6.2 g. total fat, 0.8 g. saturated fat, 75 mg. cholesterol, 274 mg. sodium, 28.8 g. protein, 0.2 g. carbohydrates, 0 g. dietary fiber.

Bay City Blues

Dark, flavorful fish like bluefish can handle strong seasonings like oregano, garlic, onion and wine. Serve these baked blues with a baked potato or crusty slices of sourdough bread and a green salad.

Ingredients	For 1 serving	For 2 servings
Dry white wine or white grape juice	¼ cup	½ cup
Thin onion slices	1	2
Green or sweet red pepper, coarsely chopped	⅛	¼
Garlic, crushed	½ clove	1 clove
Dried oregano	⅛ teaspoon	¼ teaspoon
Salt and pepper	to taste	to taste
Bluefish fillets (5 ounces each)	1	2

Preheat the oven to 450°.

In a blender, combine the wine or grape juice, onions, green or red peppers, garlic, oregano, salt and pepper; process until the vegetables are coarsely pureed. Pour into a small saucepan, bring it to a full boil over high heat and set aside.

Arrange each fillet, skin side down, in a shallow, 2-cup oval gratin dish or baking dish. Cover with the sauce.

Bake for 10 minutes, or until the fish is opaque throughout and firm to the touch. Serve in the baking dish set on a dinner plate.

Per serving: 201 calories, 6.1 g. total fat, 1.3 g. saturated fat, 83 mg. cholesterol, 87 mg. sodium, 28.8 g. protein, 2.6 g. carbohydrates, 0.3 g. dietary fiber.

Trim for Tenderness

The dark-red strip of flesh that runs down the midline of bluefish and other fast-swimming saltwater fish is a strong muscle that sustains continuous swimming. When cooked, it has a taste that is too strong for many people. To remove it before cooking, lay each fish fillet flat and use a sharp knife to make a shallow V-shaped incision under the red strip of muscle. Then lift it out.

Salmon Panned in Orange Sauce

This speedy orange sauce is a grand accompaniment to just about any fish, though it's best with oilier types, such as salmon, tuna and mackerel. Other possibilities are grouper, red snapper, swordfish and wahoo—the gourmet's mackerel, which has a sweet, nutty flavor.

Ingredients	For 1 serving	For 2 servings
Salmon fillets or steaks (5 ounces each)	1	2
Olive or canola oil	½ teaspoon	1 teaspoon
Salt and pepper	to taste	to taste
Orange juice	½ cup	1 cup
Butter or margarine	½ teaspoon	1 teaspoon

Place a heavy, 8″ (or 10″) nonstick skillet over medium heat for 1 to 2 minutes. Brush the salmon lightly on both sides with the oil; sprinkle it with the salt and pepper. Lay the fish in the hot skillet and cook it, turning once with a broad spatula, for 5 to 8 minutes, or until the salmon is opaque throughout. Transfer the salmon to a serving plate and keep it warm while you make the sauce.

Pour the orange juice into the skillet and rapidly boil it down over high heat until it becomes syrupy and is reduced to about half its original volume. Swirl in the butter or margarine, pour the sauce over the salmon and serve.

Per serving: 293 calories, 13.4 g. total fat, 2.9 g. saturated fat, 84 mg. cholesterol, 82 mg. sodium, 29.1 g. protein, 12.9 g. carbohydrates, 1 g. dietary fiber.

Shopping for Fresh Fish

When shopping for fish, inspect it carefully. And don't be embarrassed to use the nose test! Fresh fish has a clean, salty, almost cucumbery smell. Reject any and all with an unpleasantly strong fishy odor.

Whole fish should have eyes that are convex and shiny, not sunken and milky. The gills should be bright red, not brown. The flesh should feel firm and elastic, not soft and spongy when poked with an inquiring finger.

Fillets and cross-cut steaks should be firm and moist, not dry, yellowish or leathery. And the flesh should not look as though it's separating into chunks.

Fish and Shellfish

Salmon Sizzler
with Late-Summer Vegetables

It's not impossible, but it would certainly be tedious to limit yourself to foods containing 30 percent or less calories from fat. Besides, says the American Dietetic Association, such dietary stringency is totally uncalled for. It's your total diet, not individual foods, that counts. Salmon gets over 50 percent of its calories from fat, but it can fit very nicely into a healthy diet if you accompany it with a medium baked potato, a salad of spinach and mushrooms with low-calorie buttermilk dressing and a healthy dessert of honeydew melon or cantaloupe. You'll have a delicious dinner with all the fat percentages in the right place — comfortably below the recommended 30 percent.

Ingredients	For 1 serving	For 2 servings
Tomato	1 small	1 large
Fresh basil (optional)	3–4 leaves	6–8 leaves
Salmon fillets or steaks (5 ounces each)	1	2
Olive or canola oil	½ teaspoon	1 teaspoon
Yellow squash or zucchini, thinly sliced	1 small	2 small
Green onions, thinly sliced	1	2
Salt and pepper	to taste	to taste

Preheat the oven to 450°.

Core the tomato and cut it in half crosswise; gently squeeze the seeds from each half and cube the halves.

Stack the basil leaves (if using), roll them into a cylinder and slice across to make thin strips.

Brush the salmon with the oil; arrange each fillet on a 12″ square of heavy foil. Top with the squash or zucchini, tomatoes, green onions and basil. Sprinkle with the salt and pepper. Fold the foil diagonally over the fish to form a triangle and seal it tightly by folding and crimping the edges.

Set a heavy, 8″ (or 10″) cast-iron skillet in the oven to heat for 5 minutes.

Lay the foil packets in the skillet and bake for 10 to 15 minutes, or until the salmon is opaque at the thickest part and the vegetables are crisp-tender. Transfer the packets to dinner plates and serve.

Per serving: 265 calories, 11.8 g. total fat, 1.8 g. saturated fat, 78 mg. cholesterol, 76 mg. sodium, 30.6 g. protein, 9.3 g. carbohydrates, 3.5 g. dietary fiber.

Steamed Black Sea Bass Chinoise

Steaming is a classic Chinese technique for cooking whole fish—it produces tender, moist fish with a subtle flavor. If black sea bass is unavailable or less than fresh, choose cape shark, cod, sea trout, flounder, catfish, halibut or fresh water bass for this recipe. Serve the fish with plenty of hot rice.

Ingredients	For 1 serving	For 2 servings
Black sea bass fillets (5 ounces each)	1	2
Reduced-sodium soy sauce	1 tablespoon	2 tablespoons
Dry sherry or nonalcoholic beer	1 tablespoon	2 tablespoons
Canola oil	1 teaspoon	2 teaspoons
Minced fresh ginger	1 teaspoon	2 teaspoons
Chili sauce	1 teaspoon	2 teaspoons
Sugar	½ teaspoon	1 teaspoon
Carrot	1 small	1 medium
Snow peas	1 ounce	2 ounces
Green onions, thinly sliced	1	2

Arrange the fillets in a single layer in a shallow heat-proof bowl, folding the ends under if necessary to fit them into the bowl.

In a small mixing bowl, mix together the soy sauce, sherry or beer, oil, ginger, chili sauce and sugar; pour over the fish and let stand for 15 to 30 minutes.

Cut the carrot into 2″ lengths, then into slices about ⅛″ thick. Stack 3 or 4 slices and cut them into matchsticks.

Slice the snow peas diagonally into ¼″ strips.

Scatter the carrots, snow peas and green onions evenly over the fish.

Arrange a collapsible metal steamer in a deep skillet that's slightly larger than the bowl containing the fish. Add water to a depth of ½″ and bring rapidly to a boil.

Carefully lower the bowl containing the fish onto the steamer, cover the pan tightly and steam the fish for 8 to 10 minutes, or until the fish is opaque and firm to the touch.

With a broad spatula, transfer the fish and vegetables to a warm plate and serve.

Per serving: 249 calories, 7.5 g. total fat, 1.1 g. saturated fat, 58 mg. cholesterol, 707 mg. sodium, 29.1 g. protein, 11.8 g. carbohydrates, 2 g. dietary fiber.

Seafood Fajitas with Salsa

For variety, use small bay scallops instead of shrimp in this recipe. Both shrimp and scallops are low in fat, so you can embellish these seafood fajitas with avocado and light sour cream and still dine healthily.

Ingredients	For 1 serving	For 2 servings
Flour tortillas (8″ diameter)	2	4
Shrimp	5 ounces	10 ounces
Salsa	½ cup	1 cup
Bibb or leaf lettuce	2 leaves	4 leaves
Avocado, sliced	¼ small	½ small
Light sour cream	2 tablespoons	¼ cup
Fresh cilantro sprigs	2	4
Lime quarters	1	2

Warm the tortillas according to the package directions in a preheated oven or the microwave; cover them and keep them warm.

Peel and devein the shrimp; rinse them in cold water and drain well.

In a heavy, 8″ (or 10″) nonstick skillet over medium heat, bring the salsa to a simmer. Add the shrimp and bring the mixture back to a simmer. Reduce the heat, cover the skillet and cook for 5 to 10 minutes, or until the shrimp are curled and opaque.

Place the tortillas on dinner plates. Divide the shrimp mixture, lettuce, avocados, sour cream and cilantro among them. Roll each into a cylinder and eat with a squeeze of lime juice.

Per serving: 505 calories, 17.8 g. total fat, 3.9 g. saturated fat, 231 mg. cholesterol, 249 mg. sodium, 37.6 g. protein, 52.4 g. carbohydrates, 5.5 g. dietary fiber.

New Maryland Crab Cakes

Each of these jumbo crab cakes has less than 13 grams of fat and tastes so good that you'd eat two or three if you could. Only you can't—they're too big. Serve correctly with coleslaw, corn on the cob and ice-cold watermelon, preferably at a rustic table overlooking a considerable expanse of open water. Crab cakes reheat successfully in the microwave, so make enough for tonight and tomorrow. Or freeze them individually, tightly wrapped. Reheat them in a conventional or microwave oven.

Ingredients	For 2 servings	For 4 servings
Firm-textured white bread	1 slice	2 slices
Eggs	1	2
Mayonnaise	1 tablespoon	2 tablespoons
Dijon mustard	1 rounded teaspoon	2 rounded teaspoons
Lump crab meat	8 ounces	1 pound
Finely minced onions or shallots	1 tablespoon	2 tablespoons
Seafood seasoning	½ teaspoon	1 teaspoon
Salt	to taste	to taste
Olive oil	1 teaspoon	2 teaspoons

Preheat the oven to 400°.

Place the bread in a blender and process briefly to make coarse crumbs.

In a mixing bowl, beat the eggs until foamy, then beat in the mayonnaise and mustard.

Pick over the crab and remove any bits of cartilage. Add to the bowl. Mix in the bread crumbs, onions or shallots, seafood seasoning and salt. Gently shape the mixture into 2 (or 4) round or oval patties at least 1" thick.

Using the oil, brush circles the size of your crab cakes on a baking sheet. Arrange the crab cakes on the oiled circles and bake on the middle shelf of the oven for 15 to 20 minutes, or until the tops are dry and lightly browned.

Run a broad spatula under the crab cakes to loosen them from the baking sheet. Invert the crab cakes onto serving plates. Serve hot.

Per serving: 256 calories, 12.7 g. total fat, 2 g. saturated fat, 220 mg. cholesterol, 592 mg. sodium, 27.2 g. protein, 6.6 g. carbohydrates, 0.3 g. dietary fiber.

Scalloped Oysters

Scalloped oysters are a hallowed Southern tradition for Thanksgiving, Christmas Eve, Christmas Day, New Year's Eve or any wintry night when self-indulgence is in order. The recipe, which couldn't be simpler, has survived intact from colonial times. In the 1824 edition of *The Virginia House-Wife*, Mrs. Mary Randolph set down her grandmother's rule "to scollop oysters":

"When the oysters are opened, put them in a bowl and wash them out of their own liquor; put some in scollop shells, strew over them a few bread crumbs and lay a slice of butter on them, then more oysters, bread crumbs and a slice of butter on top; put them into a Dutch oven to brown and serve them up in the shells." Amen.

Ingredients	For 1 serving	For 2 servings
Shucked oysters with their liquor (juices)	½ pint	1 pint
Fresh bread crumbs	⅓ cup	⅔ cup
Salt and pepper	to taste	to taste
Butter or margarine	2 teaspoons	4 teaspoons

Preheat the oven to 450°.

For each serving, place about ½ cup oysters in a shallow 2-cup baking dish or oval gratin dish. Sprinkle with about 2½ tablespoons bread crumbs and then a little salt and pepper. Repeat to make a second layer and use all the oysters and bread crumbs. Pour any remaining oyster liquor over the oysters.

Dot the oysters with the butter or margarine and bake them for 15 to 20 minutes, or just until the oysters are curled and bubbling and the crumbs are lightly browned. Serve immediately.

Per serving: 278 calories, 14.3 g. total fat, 6.4 g. saturated fat, 157 mg. cholesterol, 431 mg. sodium, 18.8 g. protein, 17 g. carbohydrates, 0.4 g. dietary fiber.

Silver Lake Oyster Stew

Laura Ingalls Wilder gives us marvelous glimpses of food the way it used to be. In *On the Shores of Silver Lake*, she describes a sea treat that she savored in South Dakota during the Christmas season of 1880.

"First, there was oyster soup. In all her life, Laura had never tasted anything so good as that savory, fragrant, sea-tasting hot milk, with golden dots of melted cream and black specks of pepper on its top, and the little dark canned oysters at its bottom."

That wondrous oyster stew was made with tinned oysters; yours will be even better because you will make it with shucked fresh oysters. Eat, as Laura did, with diminutive crackers "like doll crackers."

Ingredients	For 1 serving	For 2 servings
1% low-fat milk	1 cup	2 cups
Celery salt	⅛ teaspoon	¼ teaspoon
Pepper	to taste	to taste
Shucked standard or select oysters, with their liquor (juices)	½ pint	1 pint
Butter or margarine	1 teaspoon	2 teaspoons

In a small heavy saucepan over medium heat, warm the milk, celery salt and pepper until bubbles begin to form around the edges of the pan.

While the milk is heating, warm the oysters and their juices in a heavy, 5" nonstick skillet over medium heat until the oysters begin to curl around the edges and the oyster liquor begins to bubble. Do not boil or the oysters will be tough.

Pour the oysters and liquor into the hot milk and heat the mixture another minute over low heat. Ladle the stew into deep, warm soup bowls and top each serving with a teaspoon of butter or margarine.

Per serving: 306 calories, 12.5 g. total fat, 5.5 g. saturated fat, 156 mg. cholesterol, 705 mg. sodium, 25.6 g. protein, 21.4 g. carbohydrates, 0 g. dietary fiber.

Fettuccine with Lemon-Walnut Scallops & Asparagus

Small bay scallops are sized right for this recipe; if you're using the larger sea scallops, cut them into quarters before you begin. The combination of lemon juice, walnut oil, asparagus, scallops and pasta is so cordial, you might want to turn this recipe into a romantic feast for two—with a side dish of sautéed love apples (cherry tomatoes).

Ingredients	For 1 serving	For 2 servings
Fettuccine	3 ounces	6 ounces
Asparagus	4 ounces	8 ounces
Walnut or olive oil	2 teaspoons	4 teaspoons
Bay scallops	4 ounces	8 ounces
Lemon juice	1 tablespoon	2 tablespoons
Paprika	to taste	to taste
Salt and pepper	to taste	to taste

Cook the fettuccine according to the directions on the package but without adding salt.

Gently bend each asparagus spear with both hands until it snaps—discard the tough stem ends. Wash the spears in lukewarm water, drain and cut them into 2" lengths.

Place a heavy, 8" (or 10") nonstick skillet over medium heat for 2 minutes. Add the oil, swirl the skillet to coat it evenly with the oil, then add the scallops and asparagus. Cook, stirring frequently, until the asparagus is bright green and the scallops lose their translucence. Stir in the lemon juice, paprika, salt and pepper.

Drain the fettuccine and divide it between dinner plates. Top with the scallop mixture.

Per serving: 540 calories, 12.2 g. total fat, 1.1 g. saturated fat, 45 mg. cholesterol, 239 mg. sodium, 35.4 g. protein, 74.4 g. carbohydrates, 2.2 g. dietary fiber.

Creamy Cider Scallops

In this dish, tart yogurt complements the sweet cider. Whatever you do, don't heat the sauce after the yogurt goes in or it will curdle. If you don't object to a thin sauce, you can omit the cornstarch and the liquid in which it's dissolved. Serve the scallops over scorching hot mashed potatoes and have a simple green salad ready and waiting.

Ingredients	For 1 serving	For 2 servings
Butter or margarine	1 teaspoon	2 teaspoons
Minced onions	1 tablespoon	2 tablespoons
Cider or apple juice	½ cup	1 cup
Bay scallops	5 ounces	10 ounces
Salt and pepper	to taste	to taste
Cornstarch	½ teaspoon	1 teaspoon
Brandy or cider	1 tablespoon	2 tablespoons
Low-fat plain yogurt	¼ cup	½ cup

Melt the butter or margarine in a heavy, 8" (or 10") nonstick skillet over medium heat. Add the onions and cook, stirring occasionally, for 2 minutes, or until the onions are tender but not brown.

Add the cider or apple juice and bring the mixture to a boil. Add the scallops, salt and pepper; reduce the heat to the lowest setting. Cook the mixture for 5 minutes, or until the scallops are opaque and firm. With a slotted spoon, remove the scallops to a heated bowl and keep them warm while you finish the sauce.

In a small bowl, stir the cornstarch into the brandy or cider to dissolve it; set the mixture aside.

Rapidly boil down the liquid in the skillet over high heat until it's reduced by half, then stir in the cornstarch mixture. Cook, stirring constantly, until the sauce is slightly thickened.

Take the skillet off the heat and stir in the yogurt; do not cook the sauce after the yogurt has been added. Return the scallops to the sauce and serve immediately.

Per serving: 296 calories, 5.8 g. total fat, 3 g. saturated fat, 61 mg. cholesterol, 311 mg. sodium, 27 g. protein, 24 g. carbohydrates, 0.2 g. dietary fiber.

Fish and Shellfish

Greek Shrimp in Marinara with Feta

The meatless spaghetti sauce for this recipe can come from a store-bought jar or a well-stocked freezer. Feta cheese has plenty of salt to season the dish, so look for a reduced-sodium marinara sauce or make your own with fresh tomatoes and basil. You may substitute scallops or fillets of firm-fleshed fish cut into 1" squares for the shrimp if you like. Serve this easy entrée with pilaf or plain rice.

Ingredients	For 1 serving	For 2 servings
Medium unshelled shrimp	5 ounces	10 ounces
Reduced-sodium marinara sauce	½ cup	1 cup
Feta cheese, thinly sliced	1 ounce	2 ounces

Preheat the oven to 400°.

Peel and devein the shrimp; rinse them in cold water. Drain the shrimp well and place each serving in a 2-cup ovenproof casserole.

Pour the marinara sauce over the shrimp and arrange the feta over the sauce. Cover the casseroles with lids or foil. Bake for 15 minutes, or until the shrimp are curled and opaque and the feta is softened.

Per serving: 257 calories, 8.2 g. total fat, 4.6 g. saturated fat, 222 mg. cholesterol, 539 mg. sodium, 31.9 g. protein, 11.3 g. carbohydrates, 1.7 g. dietary fiber.

China Clipper Steamed Shrimp

This is great hot-weather fare for both cook and eater. Serve the shrimp in soup bowls with the dipping sauce and peel them as you go—dip each shrimp into the sauce before you pop it into your mouth. This is very good with hot French bread, cold beer, corn on the cob and sliced tomatoes.

Consider doubling the recipe, since you can make an outstanding Chinese shrimp salad with the leftovers: Cover and refrigerate the leftover shrimp and sauce for up to 24 hours. Then peel the shrimp, heap them on shredded Chinese cabbage and sprinkle with thinly sliced green onions and the leftover sauce. Serve with lime wedges and rice cakes.

Ingredients	For 1 serving	For 2 servings
Large unshelled shrimp	5 ounces	10 ounces
Beer or nonalcoholic beer	¼ cup	½ cup
Reduced-sodium soy sauce	1 tablespoon	2 tablespoons
Rice vinegar	1 tablespoon	2 tablespoons
Sesame or canola oil	1½ teaspoons	1 tablespoon
Minced fresh ginger	1 tablespoon	2 tablespoons
Minced garlic	1 teaspoon	2 teaspoons
Red-pepper flakes	¼ teaspoon	½ teaspoon

Wash the shrimp in cold water, drain them in a colander, then spread them on paper towels to remove as much water as possible.

In a measuring cup, combine the beer, soy sauce and vinegar.

Place a heavy, 10″ nonstick skillet over high heat for 1 minute; add the oil and swirl the skillet to coat it evenly. Add the shrimp and ginger; cook, stirring constantly, for 2 minutes. Stir in the garlic and pepper flakes; cook for 1 minute.

Pour in the beer mixture, bring to a full boil, then reduce the heat to medium. Cook the shrimp for 2 to 3 minutes, or until they are tightly curled and pink. Serve the shrimp with the sauce in large soup bowls. Have handy a second bowl for the shells and plenty of paper napkins.

Per serving: 280 calories, 9.5 g. total fat, 1.5 g. saturated fat, 241 mg. cholesterol, 778 mg. sodium, 8.6 g. carbohydrates, 35 g. protein, 0.3 g. dietary fiber.

Lemony Linguine
with Scallops & Shrimp

This simple seafood pasta has a hint of lemon in the fresh tomato sauce. If shrimp or scallops are unavailable, substitute your favorite firm-fleshed fish, cut into cubes. Serve the linguine with a hearty salad of romaine lettuce or escarole.

Ingredients	For 1 serving	For 2 servings
Linguine	2 ounces	4 ounces
Scallops	3 ounces	6 ounces
Unshelled shrimp	3 ounces	6 ounces
Olive oil	1½ teaspoons	1 tablespoon
Minced onions or shallots	1 tablespoon	2 tablespoons
Minced garlic	½ teaspoon	1 teaspoon
Plum tomatoes, peeled and diced	2	4
Dried basil	¼ teaspoon	½ teaspoon
Grated lemon rind	½ teaspoon	1 teaspoon
Salt and pepper	to taste	to taste

Cook the linguine according to the directions on the package but without adding salt.

While the pasta is cooking, cut any large scallops into quarters; leave small scallops whole. Peel and devein the shrimp.

Film a heavy, 8″ (or 10″) nonstick skillet with the oil and set it over medium-high heat until the oil is rippling hot but not smoking. Add the scallops, shrimp and onions or shallots. Cook, stirring often, for 2 minutes. Stir in the garlic and cook the mixture another minute. Stir in the tomatoes, basil, lemon rind, salt and pepper.

Bring the sauce to a simmer, then reduce the heat to low. Cook, stirring often, for 4 minutes, or until the tomatoes begin to lose their shape and the seafood is opaque.

Drain the linguine well and divide between dinner plates. Top with the sauce.

Per serving: 458 calories, 10 g. total fat, 1.4 g. saturated fat, 159 mg. cholesterol, 276 mg. sodium, 39.7 g. protein, 50.3 g. carbohydrates, 1 g. dietary fiber.

Mussels Steamed in White Wine

Serve this classic French dish with plenty of crusty French bread for soaking up the garlicky broth. Should you cook more than you can eat at one sitting, remove the leftover mussels from their shells and refrigerate them, tightly covered, in the remaining broth. For a wonderful soup, add the leftover mussels and broth to white bean soup, minestrone or chicken soup.

Ingredients	For 1 serving	For 2 servings
Mussels in their shells	1 pound	2 pounds
Dry white wine	½ cup	1 cup
Water	½ cup	1 cup
Butter or olive oil	1½ teaspoons	1 tablespoon
Garlic, minced	1 clove	2 cloves
Pepper	to taste	to taste
Finely chopped fresh parsley	2 tablespoons	¼ cup

With a stiff brush or plastic pot scrubber, scrub the mussels in cold water to remove all traces of mud and grit. Pull or cut away the beards that cling to the shells. Place the mussels in a colander to drain.

In a 2-quart (or 3-quart) saucepan over medium-high heat, bring the wine, water, butter or oil, garlic and pepper to a boil. Quickly add the mussels, cover the pan and cook, shaking the pan often, for 5 minutes, or until the mussels open.

Discard any mussels that haven't opened. Stir in the parsley and divide the mussels and broth between shallow soup bowls. Serve immediately.

Per serving: 239 calories, 9 g. total fat, 4.2 g. saturated fat, 55 mg. cholesterol, 475 mg. sodium, 7.5 g. carbohydrates, 17.4 g. protein, 0.4 g. dietary fiber.

Using Mussels

Mussels are highly perishable and should be cooked the day you buy them. Live mussels, the only kind you ever want to cook and eat, usually have tightly closed shells. But changes in temperature that may occur between market and home—or between the refrigerator and the sink—can cause the shells to gape. Should gaping occur, live mussels will close if you immerse them in lightly salted ice water and gently rub the edges of their shells together between your thumb and forefinger. Discard any mussels that don't close after this treatment.

Beef, Pork

and Lamb

I know what it's like to crave red meat. Like most Americans over age 40, I was brought up on meat and potatoes. I do try to limit my consumption of beef, pork, lamb and veal because they are major sources of saturated fat. And saturated fat is the kind of fat that kicks up plaque in the arteries. When I do eat meat, I want it to be satisfying and healthy.

So rest assured that these recipes will satisfy your craving for red meat without overloading your arteries with saturated fat. You'll learn how to stretch a little meat with lots of vegetables and grains in hearty one-dish dinners, such as Orange-Glazed Pork Chops and Sweet Potatoes. You'll also learn how to stretch your food dollars by following cooking methods that get the fat out of less expensive, fattier cuts of meat. I'll tell you when to buy regular ground beef, for instance, and when it makes sense to spring for higher-priced, extra-lean ground beef. And you'll find plenty of downsized recipes for homey favorites like meat loaf, pot roast and stuffed (actually, unstuffed) cabbage.

Pan-Seared Steak
with Tomatoes & Olives

To make this Sicilian treat, buy lean round steak cut almost as thin as paper. If you can't find see-through steaks, buy eye of round cut about ½″ thick, then gently pound it between sheets of plastic wrap with a rolling pin or mallet to a thickness of ¼″ or less. Serve the steak with Italian rolls.

Ingredients	For 1 serving	For 2 servings
Onion, thinly sliced	½ small	1 small
Olive oil	1½ teaspoons	1 tablespoon
Garlic, minced	1 clove	2 cloves
Canned diced tomatoes (with juice)	½ cup	1 cup
Greek olives, pitted and quartered	4	8
Dried oregano or basil	⅛ teaspoon	¼ teaspoon
Pepper	to taste	to taste
Lean round steak, very thinly sliced	4 ounces	8 ounces

Combine the onions and 1 teaspoon (or 2 teaspoons) of the oil in a small heavy saucepan. Cook, stirring often, over medium heat, for 5 minutes, or until the onions begin to brown.

Stir in the garlic, tomatoes (with juice), olives, oregano or basil and pepper. Bring the sauce to a simmer. Cover and cook for 10 minutes. Remove the cover and cook the sauce for another 5 minutes, or until it becomes fairly thick. Keep the sauce warm while you pan-grill the steak.

Place a heavy, 8″ nonstick or cast-iron skillet over medium-high heat for 2 to 3 minutes. Brush the steak on both sides with the remaining oil, lay it in the skillet and cook it until it is seared and browned on both sides, turning as needed to prevent scorching. Do not overcook or the steak will be tough. Top the steak with the sauce and serve.

Per serving: 255 calories, 13.7 g. total fat, 2.9 g. saturated fat, 59 mg. cholesterol, 326 mg. sodium, 26.5 g. protein, 7.8 g. carbohydrates, 1.6 g. dietary fiber.

Beef, Pork and Lamb

A Better Burger

The secret of lower-fat burgers lies in strictly portioning the leanest beef possible (ground sirloin is a good choice) into 4-ounce patties, then cooking the burgers until they're well-done. Cooking them to that stage melts away the most possible fat.

There are about 3 grams of fat in every ounce of cooked burger made with extra-lean raw beef and cooked according to this recipe. Whether you broil, grill or pan-fry doesn't make much difference; U.S. Department of Agriculture figures show the same amounts of fat in burgers cooked by each of the three methods.

For a low-fat feast, serve your burger with corn on the cob instead of french fries and top off the meal with a slice of ice-cold watermelon instead of ice cream.

    4 ounces extra-lean ground beef
    Salt and pepper
    1 whole-wheat bun
    1 teaspoon brown or Dijon mustard
    1 thick sweet onion slice
    1 thick ripe tomato slice

Lightly shape the beef into a patty. Sprinkle lightly with the salt and pepper.

Place a heavy, 5″ cast-iron or nonstick skillet over medium-high heat for 2 to 3 minutes. Add the beef and pan-grill until medium-well done, turning as necessary. (Pressing the burgers with a spatula during cooking is not recommended; you're only pressing out the flavorful juices.)

Spread the bottom half of the bun with the mustard. Arrange the burger on top. Add the onion, tomato and top half of the bun. Serve immediately.

Makes 1 serving

Per serving: 315 calories, 10.8 g. total fat, 3.5 g. saturated fat, 84 mg. cholesterol, 391 mg. sodium, 32 g. protein, 22.5 g. carbohydrates, 2.7 g. dietary fiber.

Amish Baked Steak

This is a grand recipe for small households because it provides the rich flavor of pot roast and gravy for a few good meals — without an eternity of leftovers.

The next time boneless round steak is on sale, buy the amount specified in the recipe below, cut at least 1″ thick. When browning the meat, remember that because so little fat is used, your skillet must be sizzling hot when the steak hits it so that it doesn't stick. Cook enough for two meals, and you'll have enough to reheat for a hot roast beef sandwich another night.

Ingredients	For 2 servings	For 4 servings
Boneless round or chuck steak	12 ounces	1½ pounds
Salt	¼ teaspoon	½ teaspoon
Pepper	to taste	to taste
All-purpose flour	1 tablespoon	2 tablespoons
Olive or canola oil	1½ teaspoons	1 tablespoon
Water	¾ cup	1 cup

Preheat the oven to 300°.

Trim any fat from the steak. Sprinkle the meat with the salt and pepper. Sprinkle half the flour on one side of the steak and gently pound it into the meat with the rim of a heavy plate; repeat with the remaining flour on the other side of the steak.

Place a heavy, ovenproof, 8″ (or 10″) nonstick skillet with a metal handle over medium heat for 3 to 5 minutes. Film the skillet with the oil, lay the steak in the skillet and cook until it's well-browned on both sides, turning as necessary. Pour in the water. Cover the skillet with an ovenproof lid or heavy foil and set the skillet on the middle shelf of the oven.

Bake the steak for 1½ to 2 hours, or until fork-tender; check during the cooking period and add a little water if the steak begins to stick.

Per serving: 278 calories, 12.1 g. total fat, 3.2 g. saturated fat, 104 mg. cholesterol, 352 mg. sodium, 37 g. protein, 3 g. carbohydrates, 0.2 g. dietary fiber.

GARLIC

Spicy Orange Beef & Broccoli

Despite the word "fry," authentically good stir-fries can be made with very little fat—around 1½ teaspoons per serving, to be precise. Since stir-fries are usually loaded with vegetables, they're high in carbohydrates, fiber, vitamins and minerals yet relatively low in calories. So extend a little beef with a lot of flavor from broccoli and oranges in this spicy stir-fry. Boneless pork chops and chicken breast work equally well in this recipe.

Ingredients	For 1 serving	For 2 servings
Lean top or bottom round steak	4 ounces	8 ounces
Broccoli	1 small stalk	1 large stalk
Grated orange rind (optional)	1 teaspoon	2 teaspoons
Orange juice	½ cup	1 cup
Cornstarch	1½ teaspoons	1 tablespoon
Reduced-sodium soy sauce	1½ teaspoons	1 tablespoon
Red-pepper flakes (optional)	⅛ teaspoon	¼ teaspoon
Canola or peanut oil	1½ teaspoons	1 tablespoon
Minced fresh ginger	1 tablespoon	2 tablespoons
Garlic, minced	1 clove	2 cloves

Slice the steak into strips ½″ × ½″ × 2″.

Cut the broccoli into bite-size pieces.

In a 1-cup (or 2-cup) measure, combine the orange rind (if using), orange juice, cornstarch, soy sauce and pepper flakes (if using); stir until the cornstarch is dissolved.

Place a heavy, 10″ nonstick skillet over medium-high heat for 2 to 3 minutes, or until a drop of water sprinkled in the pan dances on the surface. Add the oil, then quickly add the beef strips and cook, stirring constantly, for 1 to 2 minutes.

Push the beef to the side of the pan and add the broccoli and ginger; cook and stir for 2 minutes. Stir in the garlic, then the juice mixture. Cook and stir for 1 minute, or until the sauce is thickened and translucent.

Reduce the heat to low, cover the skillet and cook the mixture for 2 to 3 minutes, or until the broccoli is crisp-tender. Serve immediately.

Per serving: 361 calories, 12.6 g. total fat, 2.3 g. saturated fat, 76 mg. cholesterol, 357 mg. sodium, 36.9 g. protein, 27 g. carbohydrates, 5 g. dietary fiber.

Braised Veal & Brown Mushrooms with Rigatoni

A few years ago I attended a heart-healthy conference at Disney World in Orlando and was served an unusually good bowl of rigatoni in a savory broth with ham and shiitake mushrooms. I've created a version with veal instead of ham to cut down the sodium. If you can't find rigatoni, any large pasta shape, such as penne, shells or rotini, will work well. Regular mushrooms are fine if crimini are unavailable. Add warm French or Italian bread and a salad of leafy greens to complete the meal.

Ingredients	For 2 servings	For 4 servings
Olive or canola oil	1½ teaspoons	1 tablespoon
Cubed lean veal	8 ounces	1 pound
Chopped onions	½ cup	1 cup
Garlic, crushed	1 clove	2 cloves
Thickly sliced crimini mushrooms	1½ cups	3 cups
Madeira or marsala wine	¼ cup	½ cup
Beef broth	2 cups	4 cups
Rigatoni	1 cup	2 cups
Salt and pepper	to taste	to taste

Heat the oil in a heavy, 10″ nonstick skillet over medium-high heat for 2 minutes. Add the veal and brown it well, turning as necessary; push it to the side of the skillet.

Reduce the heat to low and stir in the onions, garlic, mushrooms and wine. Cook and stir for 2 minutes. Add the broth and bring the mixture to a simmer. Cover and cook over low heat for 45 to 60 minutes, or until the veal is fork-tender.

Add the rigatoni to the skillet. Cover and cook for 15 minutes, or until the pasta is tender. Season with the salt and pepper. Serve the pasta hot in shallow soup bowls with some of the broth.

Per serving: 448 calories, 9.2 g. total fat, 2.3 g. saturated fat, 116 mg. cholesterol, 367 mg. sodium, 40 g. protein, 42.4 g. carbohydrates, 1.4 g. dietary fiber.

Honest Meat Loaf

Make the larger version of this meat loaf even if you live alone. I do, in order to have ample leftovers for a meat loaf sandwich, one of the great gastronomic treats of the Western world. Serve cold meat loaf on white bread with iceberg lettuce, kosher dills and just a hint of light mayo.

Ingredients	For 2 servings	For 4 servings
Extra-lean ground beef	8 ounces	1 pound
Fresh bread crumbs	¼ cup	½ cup
Egg	1 white	1 whole
Dried basil or oregano	½ teaspoon	1 teaspoon
Salt	¼ teaspoon	½ teaspoon
Pepper	pinch	pinch
Ketchup	2 tablespoons	¼ cup
Lemon juice	1 tablespoon	2 tablespoons
Onion, coarsely chopped	½ small	1 small
Garlic, crushed	½ clove	1 clove
Fresh parsley	2 sprigs	4 sprigs

Preheat the oven to 350°.

In a medium mixing bowl, combine the beef, bread crumbs, egg white (or whole egg), basil or oregano, salt and pepper.

In a blender, combine the ketchup, lemon juice, onions, garlic and parsley; process until the onions and parsley are coarsely pureed. Add the mixture to the ingredients in the mixing bowl. Knead the mixture lightly by hand until blended.

Form and pat into a loaf shape in a shallow baking pan. Bake for 40 to 50 minutes, or until the loaf is browned on top and cooked throughout. Let rest for 10 minutes before slicing.

Per serving: 297 calories, 16.5 g. total fat, 6.2 g. saturated fat, 177 mg. cholesterol, 527 mg. sodium, 24.9 g. protein, 10.9 g. carbohydrates, 0.7 g. dietary fiber.

PARSLEY

Tamale Pie Topped with Spoonbread

Regular ground beef costs considerably less than the extra-lean variety. If you're on a tight budget, it's nice to know that you can use the regular ground beef in recipes that call for the meat to be browned before other ingredients are added. That includes recipes such as spaghetti sauce and this one. According to research published in the *Journal of the American Dietetic Association*, the fat in ground beef melts during browning, after which much of it can be drained off. So save your extra-lean ground beef for recipes like meat loaf, in which beef isn't treated to an initial browning.

Ingredients	For 2 servings	For 4 servings
Ground beef	6 ounces	12 ounces
Chopped onions	¼ cup	½ cup
Chopped green peppers	2 tablespoons	¼ cup
Garlic, crushed	½ clove	1 clove
Chopped canned tomatoes (with juice)	½ cup	1 cup
Frozen corn	½ cup	1 cup
Chili powder	1 teaspoon	2 teaspoons
Cornmeal	2½ tablespoons	5 tablespoons
Salt	⅛ teaspoon	¼ teaspoon
1% low-fat milk	½ cup	1 cup
Egg	1 white	1 whole
Shredded Cheddar cheese (optional)	2 tablespoons	¼ cup

Preheat the oven to 350°.

In a heavy, 10″ nonstick skillet over medium heat, brown the beef, breaking it apart with a spoon, until no trace of pink remains. Transfer the meat to a paper towel–lined strainer over a bowl to drain off the fat.

To the skillet add the onions and peppers. Cook for 3 minutes, or until the vegetables begin to brown. Add the beef, garlic, tomatoes (with juice), corn, chili powder and ½ tablespoon (or 1 tablespoon) of the cornmeal. Bring the mixture to a simmer.

Transfer the mixture to a 1-quart (or 1½-quart) ovenproof casserole. Set aside.

Place the salt and remaining cornmeal in a 2-cup microwave-safe glass measure; stir in the milk. Microwave on high power for a total of 2½ minutes, or until the mixture comes to a boil and is thickened; stop and stir every 30 seconds during this time. (Alternatively, cook the mixture in a small saucepan over medium heat, stirring constantly, until thickened.)

In a small bowl, beat the egg white (or whole egg) until foamy. Gradually beat in the hot cornmeal, then the Cheddar. Pour over the beef mixture and bake for 25 to 30 minutes, or until the topping is slightly puffed and brown.

Per serving: 329 calories, 14 g. total fat, 5.9 g. saturated fat, 124 mg. cholesterol, 374 mg. sodium, 25.8 g. protein, 26.2 g. carbohydrates, 2.9 g. dietary fiber.

For Something Different

Substituting lean ground turkey (at 7 percent to 12 percent fat) for ground beef (10 percent to 34 percent fat) or ground pork (18 percent to 50 percent fat) is a good way to slim down your favorite recipes. Because turkey has a rather mild flavor, you may need to increase herbs and spices to compensate. Being lean, turkey also tends toward dryness, so don't overcook it.

Unstuffed Cabbage

When the wind shifts to the north—dropping temperatures and bringing rain in gusts—cabbage is wonderful comfort food. This recipe bypasses the labor required for making traditional stuffed cabbage while retaining all the traditional flavor. You can get a potful of my Unstuffed Cabbage simmering in under 15 minutes (provided your knives are sharp), then spend the next hour reading or puttering while your one-dish dinner finishes cooking. The cabbage makes a meal by itself, but you could serve it with new potatoes and peas.

Ingredients	For 2 servings	For 4 servings
Extra-lean ground beef	8 ounces	1 pound
Long-grain white rice	2 tablespoons	¼ cup
Egg	1 white	1 whole
Garlic, crushed	1 small clove	1 clove
Dried thyme	¼ teaspoon	½ teaspoon
Salt	⅛ teaspoon	¼ teaspoon
Pepper	⅛ teaspoon	¼ teaspoon
Chopped onions	⅓ cup	⅔ cup
Cabbage, shredded	½ small head	1 small head
Brown sugar	1½ teaspoons	1 tablespoon
Canned tomatoes (with juice)	1 cup	16 ounces
Beef broth or water	¾ cup	1½ cups

Preheat the oven to 350°.

In a medium mixing bowl, lightly but thoroughly mix the beef, rice, egg white (or whole egg), garlic, thyme, salt, pepper and half the onions. Shape the mixture into 4 (or 8) balls.

Spread half the cabbage in a heavy, 2-quart (or 3-quart) enameled iron or ceramic casserole that can go from stovetop to oven. Top with the remaining onions, then the meatballs. Finish with the remaining cabbage.

Sprinkle with the brown sugar and pour in the tomatoes (with juice) and broth or water. Bring the mixture to a simmer over medium heat.

Cover the casserole, move it to the oven and bake for 1 hour, or until the rice is tender and most of the liquid has been absorbed. During cooking, add a little extra broth or water if necessary to prevent sticking.

Per serving: 420 calories, 21.5 g. total fat, 8.3 g. saturated fat, 130 mg. cholesterol, 568 mg. sodium, 27.7 g. protein, 30.1 g. carbohydrates, 5.1 g. dietary fiber.

Pan-Fried Liver in Cider Vinegar

If you're a fat-watching lover of liver, you'll be overjoyed to hear that you can enjoy low-fat pan-fried liver. Cooked my way, every serving absorbs a mere teaspoon of oil. Liver is fairly low in fat to begin with—only 9 grams of fat in every 3-ounce serving. And though it is high in cholesterol, as are other "innards," such as sweetbreads, kidneys and brains, we know that saturated fat, not cholesterol, is the true dietary villain for most people. So, unless you are under strict orders to watch your cholesterol intake, allow yourself liver as an occasional treat. Serve it with hot rice or mashed potatoes and plenty of steamed vegetables.

A word of caution: Liver should be cooked quickly over brisk heat—just until it develops a brown crust but is still faintly pink within. Cooked too long, liver toughens to shoe leather and develops a bitter taste.

Ingredients	For 1 serving	For 2 servings
All-purpose flour	1 tablespoon	2 tablespoons
Beef or calf liver, cut ¼" thick	4 ounces	8 ounces
Salt and pepper	to taste	to taste
Canola oil	1 tablespoon	2 tablespoons
Cider vinegar	2 tablespoons	¼ cup
Water	2 tablespoons	¼ cup
Finely chopped shallots or onions	1 tablespoon	2 tablespoons
Honey	1 tablespoon	2 tablespoons

Spread the flour on a plate or wax paper; dip the liver in the flour to coat it. Then sprinkle with the salt and pepper.

Heat the oil in a heavy, 8" (or 10") nonstick skillet over medium-high heat until the oil is rippling hot but not smoking. Quickly add the liver and cook for 2 to 3 minutes, or until browned and crisp on one side. Flip it and cook the other side briefly. The liver should still be faintly pink inside.

Transfer the liver to a warm plate, pour off any remaining oil and quickly rub the skillet with a crumpled paper towel to remove every last bit of oil.

Return the skillet to the heat. Add the vinegar, water and shallots or onions. Cook, stirring frequently, until the liquid is reduced by half. Stir in the honey, bring the mixture to a full boil, pour the glaze over the liver and serve immediately.

Per serving: 283 calories, 9 g. total fat, 2 g. saturated fat, 400 mg. cholesterol, 86 mg. sodium, 23.2 g. protein, 29.4 g. carbohydrates, 0.3 g. dietary fiber.

Lamb Shanks Braised with Eggplant & Tomatoes

Allow about 8 ounces of eggplant per serving, roughly equal to a slender Japanese eggplant or half a small standard eggplant. Young, tender eggplants are ideal for this recipe. During the long, slow oven cooking, the eggplant literally melts into a richly flavored sauce. Before cooking, trim as much fat as possible from the lamb shank but leave the covering membrane intact; it gives body to the sauce.

Ingredients	For 1 serving	For 2 servings
Eggplant	8 ounces	1 pound
Olive oil	1 teaspoon	2 teaspoons
Lamb shank, trimmed of fat	8–10 ounces	16 ounces
Chopped onions	¼ cup	½ cup
Garlic, crushed	1 clove	2 cloves
Diced fresh or canned tomatoes	1 cup	2 cups
Beef broth or red wine	½ cup	1 cup
Dried thyme	¼ teaspoon	½ teaspoon
Red-pepper flakes	to taste	to taste

Trim the ends off the eggplant and cut into ¾" cubes.

Brush the oil evenly over the lamb. Place a heavy, 10" nonstick skillet over medium heat for 2 to 3 minutes, add the lamb and brown it quickly on all sides, about 5 minutes.

Push the lamb to one side of the skillet and add the onions. Cook, stirring constantly, for 1 minute, or until the onions begin to brown. Stir in the garlic, tomatoes, broth or wine, thyme and pepper flakes; bring the mixture to a simmer.

Stir in the eggplant. Cover and cook on low heat for 1½ hours, or until the lamb is fork-tender; turn the lamb in the vegetables occasionally as it cooks.

To serve, cool the lamb slightly, then cut it into bite-size pieces. Reheat it with the vegetables.

Per serving: 358 calories, 14.4 g. total fat, 3.9 g. saturated fat, 101 mg. cholesterol, 623 mg. sodium, 35.5 g. protein, 21.6 g. carbohydrates, 5.2 g. dietary fiber.

Ham & Scalloped Potatoes

I have taken most of the cream and butter out of this comforting homestyle dish and changed the technique a little to cut down on preparation time. Try this dish accompanied by green peas and a sliced tomato salad. For a comforting meatless main dish, omit the ham and spread some shredded Gruyère or Cheddar cheese over the potato layers before baking.

Ingredients	For 1 serving	For 2 servings
Boiling potatoes	8 ounces	1 pound
Diced ham	¼ cup	½ cup
1% low-fat milk	½ cup	1 cup
All-purpose flour	2 teaspoons	4 teaspoons
Grated nutmeg	pinch	⅛ teaspoon
Salt and pepper	to taste	to taste
Dijon mustard	¼ teaspoon	½ teaspoon
Butter or margarine	1 teaspoon	2 teaspoons

Preheat the oven to 400°.

Scrub the potatoes and cut them into the thinnest possible slices. Layer half the potato slices in the bottom of a deep 2-cup (or 1-quart) baking dish. Sprinkle the ham evenly over the potatoes, then add the rest of the potatoes.

In a blender, combine the milk, flour, nutmeg, salt, pepper and mustard. Blend the mixture until it is smooth; then pour it over the potatoes and ham.

Dot the casserole with the butter or margarine. Place the casserole on a baking sheet (in case the milk boils over) and bake for 15 (or 20) minutes.

Press the potatoes into the milk with a large spoon. Reduce the oven temperature to 350° and bake for 20 (or 25) minutes more; baste the potatoes with the sauce every 10 minutes during this time. The dish is done when the potatoes are tender and browned.

Per serving: 421 calories, 8.1 g. total fat, 4.1 g. saturated fat, 41 mg. cholesterol, 707 mg. sodium, 20 g. protein, 67.8 g. carbohydrates, 5.6 g. dietary fiber.

Orange-Glazed Pork Chops & Sweet Potatoes

Orange juice complements the flavor of pork and sweet potatoes in this autumn one-dish dinner. You can substitute butternut squash for the sweet potatoes if you like. For the best results, have the pork chops cut 1" thick. If you don't want to use sherry, double the amount of orange juice.

Ingredients	For 1 serving	For 2 servings
Lean boneless pork chops	4 ounces	8 ounces
Canola oil	½ teaspoon	1 teaspoon
Salt and pepper	to taste	to taste
Sweet potatoes	1 small	2 small
Orange juice	¼ cup	½ cup
Dry sherry	¼ cup	½ cup

Place a heavy, 8" (or 10") nonstick skillet over medium-high heat for 2 to 3 minutes. Brush the pork chops on both sides with the oil, then sprinkle them with the salt and pepper. Lay the chops in the skillet and cook for 3 minutes per side, or until well-browned.

Peel the sweet potatoes and cut them into circles ¼" thick.

Remove the chops from the skillet, reduce the heat to medium and add the orange juice and sherry. Add the sweet potatoes in a single layer. Lay the pork chops over the sweet potatoes, cover the skillet and cook for 15 to 20 minutes, or until the sweet potatoes are tender and no trace of pink shows in the center of the pork when tested with a sharp knife.

Remove the pork chops to a warm serving plate and rapidly cook the sweet potatoes and orange juice over high heat until the glaze is thick and syrupy. Arrange the sweet potatoes by the pork chops, spoon the glaze over both and serve immediately.

Per serving: 451 calories, 15 g. total fat, 5.1 g. saturated fat, 63 mg. cholesterol, 127 mg. sodium, 22.5 g. protein, 38.5 g. carbohydrates, 0.5 g. dietary fiber.

Green Beans & Pork Hunan-Style

The combination of pork cooked with dried or green beans is so good that it's repeated in recipes the world over. Here, I've hybridized a recipe from China's Hunan province: a spicy stir-fry to serve over my grandmother's cornbread. It's a cross-cultural feast that's especially good when green beans are plentifully fresh and in season. Enjoy it Southern-style, as I do, over fresh cornbread or, if you insist, over steamed brown or white rice.

Ingredients	For 1 serving	For 2 servings
Green beans	8 ounces	1 pound
Lean boneless pork chops	3 ounces	6 ounces
Dry sherry or apple juice	¼ cup	½ cup
Defatted chicken broth or water	¼ cup	½ cup
Cornstarch	1½ teaspoons	1 tablespoon
Sugar	1 teaspoon	2 teaspoons
Reduced-sodium soy sauce	1½ teaspoons	1 tablespoon
Red-pepper flakes (optional)	¼ teaspoon	½ teaspoon
Canola oil	1½ teaspoons	1 tablespoon
Minced fresh ginger	1½ teaspoons	1 tablespoon
Garlic, crushed	1 clove	2 cloves
Green onions, sliced	1	2

Snap the stem ends from the beans, then snap the beans into 2″ lengths. Immerse them in lukewarm water, then turn them into a colander to drain.

Cut the pork chops into strips about the size and shape of the green beans.

In a 1-cup (or 2-cup) measure, combine the sherry or apple juice, broth or water, cornstarch, sugar, soy sauce and pepper flakes (if using); stir to dissolve the cornstarch and sugar.

Place a heavy, 10″ nonstick skillet over medium-high heat for 2 to 3 minutes. Add the oil, then the pork and ginger. Cook, stirring constantly, for 2 minutes. Add the beans and garlic; cook and stir for 1 minute.

Stir in the broth mixture. Cook and stir for 1 minute longer, or until the sauce is translucent and thickened. Reduce the heat to low, cover the skillet and cook the mixture for 2 to 3 minutes, or until the beans are crisp-tender. Stir in the green onions and serve hot.

Per serving: 363 calories, 10.4 g. total fat, 1.7 g. saturated fat, 60 mg. cholesterol, 411 mg. sodium, 24 g. protein, 31.2 g. carbohydrates, 0.2 g. dietary fiber.

Irish Lamb Oven Stew

For their famous lamb stew, Irish cooks put all the ingredients in a pot, then put the pot in the oven, where the stew bakes unattended. With potatoes, carrots, onions and green peas, Irish stew is an easy one-dish dinner for busy cooks.

The kind of casserole you choose for baking this stew depends on whether you bring it to a simmer on the stove or in the microwave. For stove-top cooking, enameled cast-iron works best. For microwaving, choose an ovenproof glass casserole. And do not—repeat, do not—add salt to this recipe, since there's more than enough in the canned beef bouillon to season your stew.

Ingredients	For 1 serving	For 2 servings
Waxy new potatoes	6 ounces	12 ounces
Coarsely chopped onions	¼ cup	½ cup
Carrots, coarsely chopped	1 medium	2 medium
Round bone-in shoulder lamb chops (5 ounces each)	1	2
Dried thyme	¼ teaspoon	½ teaspoon
Pepper	to taste	to taste
Bay leaves	1	2
Tomato paste	1 teaspoon	2 teaspoons
Canned condensed beef bouillon	⅔ cup	1⅓ cups
Green peas	¼ cup	½ cup

Preheat the oven to 300°.

Scrub the potatoes, cut them into 1" chunks and place them in an ovenproof casserole with the onions and carrots.

Trim the fat and bones from the lamb chops and cut the meat into 1½" pieces; add to the casserole (also add the bones for extra flavor). Sprinkle with the thyme and pepper, then tuck in the bay leaves.

In a small bowl, combine the tomato paste and bouillon; pour the mixture over the lamb and vegetables. Cover the casserole, bring it to a simmer on top of the stove or in the microwave on high power, then bake it on the middle shelf of the oven for 1 hour.

Add the peas. Cover and bake for 15 minutes, or until the peas are done. Remove the bay leaves and bones before serving. Serve hot.

Per serving: 368 calories, 8.5 g. total fat, 3.1 g. saturated fat, 63 mg. cholesterol, 347 mg. sodium, 24.2 g. protein, 49.2 g. carbohydrates, 3.2 g. dietary fiber.

Vegetables

*I*nstead of giving the expected lecture on why you should eat your vegetables, I am going to let America's First Gourmet, Thomas Jefferson, do it for me. Rightly called the greatest gourmet ever to occupy the White House, Jefferson was an avid farmer who kept detailed accounts of the first and last harvest dates of every vegetable, fruit and herb grown in his considerable kitchen gardens. He was growing broccoli 200 years before George Bush revealed his loathing for the vegetable to a stunned populace.

Not quite a vegetarian, Jefferson was extremely partial to fresh seasonal fruits and vegetables. In 1819, when he was a robust 76 and still had every tooth in his head—in those days of dreadful preventive care—he credited his good health to a fondness for vegetables.

In a letter to Dr. Vine Utley, he wrote: "I have lived temperately, eating little animal food, and that not as an aliment so much as a condiment for the vegetables which constitute my principal diet."

Jefferson enjoyed robust good health right up to the end and died young at the ripe old age of 83. Today, modern science has proved what he seemed to know by instinct—that a diet based on grains, vegetables and fruits, with modest amounts of foods from animal sources, can promote good health and long life. Now, will you listen to your mother and me? Eat those vegetables!

Asparagus in Orange Sauce

This dish will make you feel like you're cheating when you're not. The creamy orange sauce is a mock hollandaise—minus the egg yolks but with just a whisper of butter or margarine for a rich flavor that pairs well with asparagus, of course, but also with chicken, pork, fish, broccoli, carrots, beets, artichokes and other vegetables. Be sure to cook enough asparagus. Half a pound per person is about right for a side dish; those who can make a meal of asparagus topped with a poached egg should allow a full pound for each person.

Ingredients	For 1 serving	For 2 servings
Asparagus spears	8 ounces	1 pound
Grated orange rind	½ teaspoon	1 teaspoon
Orange juice	½ cup	1 cup
Cornstarch	1 teaspoon	2 teaspoons
Butter or margarine	1½ teaspoons	1 tablespoon

Bend each asparagus stalk near the cut end until it breaks. Discard the tough cut ends and wash the stalks in lukewarm water.

Place about ⅓″ of water in a skillet that is large enough to hold the asparagus in a single layer. Bring it to a boil over high heat. Gather the asparagus in a bunch with your hand, tips on top, and gently lay them in the pan. Cover the pan and cook the asparagus up to 10 minutes, until it is bright green and just tender; the exact time will depend on the thickness of the spears. Drain any water that remains in the pan. Remove the asparagus to a serving dish.

In a small saucepan, mix the orange rind, orange juice and cornstarch until the cornstarch is dissolved. Cook, stirring constantly, over medium heat for 2 minutes, or until the sauce comes to a boil and is slightly thickened.

Stir in the butter or margarine. Spoon the sauce over the hot asparagus and serve.

Per serving: 58 calories, 3 g. total fat, 1.8 g. saturated fat, 7 mg. cholesterol, 30 mg. sodium, 0.5 g. protein, 7 g. carbohydrates, 0.5 g. dietary fiber.

Vegetables

Fresh Asparagus

When you're buying asparagus, look for crisp shoots with tightly closed tips. Open tips indicate tough and stringy asparagus. Size doesn't matter much. Asparagus can be fat or thin as long as all the spears are roughly the same size, so they cook in about the same time. To keep from overcooking this delicate spring treat, cook asparagus only until a stalk held horizontally by the butt end flexes ever so slightly.

Greek Green Beans & Tomatoes

These green beans are as good cold as they are hot, so make enough to enjoy hot today and cold tomorrow. (Try them in a salad topped with crumbled feta cheese and a few Greek olives.) If you're lucky enough to have fresh dill, use twice as much as the dried dill called for here and add the fresh dill at the end of the cooking process to preserve its flavor.

Ingredients	For 1 serving	For 2 servings
Onion, coarsely chopped	½ small	1 small
Olive oil	1 teaspoon	2 teaspoons
Garlic, crushed	1 clove	2 cloves
Ripe tomato, peeled and coarsely chopped	1 small	1 large
Dried dill weed	½ teaspoon	1 teaspoon
Salt and pepper	to taste	to taste
Green beans	8 ounces	1 pound

In a heavy, 10″ nonstick skillet over medium heat, cook the onions in the oil for 3 minutes, or until tender but not brown. Stir in the garlic, tomatoes, dill, salt and pepper. Cook, stirring often, for 3 minutes, or until the juices begin to run from the tomatoes.

Break the ends from the beans and cut or break them into 2″ pieces. Add to the tomato mixture. Reduce the heat to low, cover the pan and cook the beans for 10 minutes, or until they are as tender as you like them. Serve hot or cold.

Per serving: 92 calories, 2.8 g. total fat, 0.4 g. saturated fat, 0 mg. cholesterol, 92 mg. sodium, 3.3 g. protein, 16.3 g. carbohydrates, 2.1 g. dietary fiber.

Beets in Orange Juice & Rosemary

When it comes to cooked beets, roasted beets have the best flavor. But it isn't always practical to crank up the oven for an hour or so to roast a handful of beets. Fortunately, you can get very good results by steaming or microwaving beets. (Boiling leaches out a lot of flavor.)

No matter how you cook your beets, this orange-rosemary marinade brings out their best flavor. Serve them alongside poultry and pork or eat them as they are, with a thick slice of rustic bread.

Ingredients	For 1 serving	For 2 servings
Beets	4 ounces	8 ounces
Grated orange rind	¼ teaspoon	½ teaspoon
Orange juice	2 tablespoons	¼ cup
Dried rosemary	pinch	⅛ teaspoon

Cut the tops from the beets, leaving an inch or so of the stems attached to prevent bleeding.

Place a collapsible steamer basket in a saucepan and add water to a depth of 1". Lay the beets in the steamer, cover the pan and bring the water to a boil over high heat. Reduce the heat to medium and cook the beets for 25 to 35 minutes, or until they are very tender. (Alternatively, microwave the beets: Arrange them in a 1-quart casserole with their root ends pointing toward the center. Cover with vented plastic wrap and microwave on high power for a total of 6 to 10 minutes, until the beets are tender when pierced with a paring knife; stop and rotate the casserole halfway through the cooking time.)

Let the beets stand until cool enough to handle. Peel and cut them into quarters or eighths. Place in a small bowl. Add the orange rind, orange juice and rosemary. Mix well and serve hot or chilled.

Per serving: 45 calories, 0.1 g. total fat, 0 g. saturated fat, 0 mg. cholesterol, 49 mg. sodium, 1.3 g. protein, 10 g. carbohydrates, 2.3 g. dietary fiber.

ROSEMARY

Vegetables

Roasting Beets

For intensely flavored beets, roast them. Yes, roasting can take more than an hour of oven time. That's probably wasteful of energy and money, but if something else is baking at the same time, it's economical and well worth the wait. To roast beets, lightly brush well-scrubbed beets with a little oil, arrange them in a single layer in a shallow pan and roast them for 35 minutes to an hour. The exact time will depend on the size of the beets and the oven temperature you're using—it can vary anywhere from 350° to 450° and still give excellent results. The beets are done when they can be pierced easily with a sharp knife.

Vegetables

Charlene's Garlic-Braised Broccoli

My friend Charlene Davenport, who holds a Grand Diplôme from LaVarenne cooking school, recently served a perfectly roasted chicken with a mystery vegetable. It appeared to be a coarse puree of drab olive green, with a taste reminiscent of the Southern greens I love so well. But it wasn't collards or turnip greens or kale. It was broccoli, Charlene told me, when I gave up guessing.

She had slow-simmered a large bunch with plenty of garlic, a touch of olive oil and some lemon juice, which brightened the taste but did nothing for the color. Broccoli cooked Charlene's way is an entirely different vegetable from the brilliant green, tender-crisp vegetable we're used to. It's also wonderful spread on bread or pizza, particularly pizza made with caramelized onions.

Ingredients	For 2 servings	For 4 servings
Broccoli	12 ounces	24 ounces
Minced garlic	1 teaspoon	2 teaspoons
Olive oil	1½ teaspoons	1 tablespoon
Water or defatted chicken broth	1 cup	2 cups
Lemon juice	1 tablespoon	2 tablespoons
Salt and pepper	to taste	to taste

Trim the tough ends from the broccoli stalks and cut the florets from the stalks. Cut the stalks lengthwise into strips about ½" thick; stack the strips and cut them crosswise into ½" cubes. Coarsely chop the florets.

In a heavy, 10" nonstick skillet over low heat, cook the garlic in the oil for 3 minutes, or until it begins to color. Add the broccoli and water or broth. Increase the heat to high and bring the mixture quickly to a boil.

Reduce the heat to low, cover the skillet and cook, stirring occasionally, for 30 minutes; add liquid as necessary to prevent sticking.

Remove the cover and cook, stirring often, for another 15 minutes, or until most of the liquid has cooked away and the broccoli resembles a coarse puree. Stir in the lemon juice, salt and pepper. Cook for 2 to 3 minutes, until the lemon juice is absorbed.

Per serving: 86 calories, 4 g. total fat, 0.6 g. saturated fat, 0 mg. cholesterol, 47 mg. sodium, 5.4 g. protein, 11.1 g. carbohydrates, 4.8 g. dietary fiber.

Gingered Brussels Sprouts

Brussels sprouts are usually sold fresh in 10-ounce cartons or frozen in 10-ounce packages. If you like brussels sprouts, you might as well cook the whole 10 ounces, even if you're home alone. Hot gingered sprouts go nicely with grilled or roast pork, turkey and chicken.

If you have leftovers, add a splash of rice vinegar to cold gingered sprouts for an unusual salad or appetizer. If you're using frozen sprouts, shorten the cooking time; frozen vegetables have already been cooked briefly.

Ingredients	For 1 serving	For 2 servings
Brussels sprouts	5 ounces	10 ounces
Water or defatted chicken broth	½ cup	1 cup
Reduced-sodium soy sauce	1½ teaspoons	1 tablespoon
Minced fresh ginger	1 teaspoon	2 teaspoons
Garlic, crushed	1 clove	2 cloves
Sugar (optional)	½ teaspoon	1 teaspoon
Red-pepper flakes (optional)	pinch	⅛ teaspoon

Trim the stems from the brussels sprouts and pull off any wilted leaves. Immerse the sprouts in a sinkful of lukewarm water and turn them into a colander to drain.

In a heavy medium saucepan, combine the water or broth, soy sauce, ginger, garlic, sugar (if using) and pepper flakes (if using). Bring the mixture to a boil over medium-high heat and cook for 3 minutes. Add the sprouts, cover the pan and cook, stirring occasionally, for 10 minutes, or until the sprouts are crisp-tender. Serve hot or chilled.

Per serving: 74 calories, 0.8 g. total fat, 0 g. saturated fat, 0 mg. cholesterol, 303 mg. sodium, 4.6 g. protein, 16.2 g. carbohydrates, 5.9 g. dietary fiber.

Polish Cabbage & Mushrooms in Yogurt

You can use standard white mushrooms in this upscale treatment of cabbage. But you'll get a deeper, richer flavor from more exotic varieties, such as criminis, portobellos or shiitakes. For a vegetarian main course, spoon the cabbage and mushrooms over buckwheat pancakes or whole-wheat biscuits.

Ingredients	For 1 serving	For 2 servings
Butter or margarine	1 teaspoon	2 teaspoons
Finely chopped onions	2 tablespoons	¼ cup
Finely chopped mushrooms	½ cup	1 cup
Minced garlic	½ teaspoon	1 teaspoon
Dried dill weed	¼ teaspoon	½ teaspoon
Salt	⅛ teaspoon	¼ teaspoon
Pepper	to taste	to taste
Shredded cabbage	2 cups	4 cups
Water	½ cup	⅔ cup
Low-fat plain yogurt	¼ cup	½ cup

Melt the butter or margarine in a heavy, 10″ nonstick skillet over medium heat. Add the onions and cook, stirring often, for 3 minutes, or until they begin to brown. Stir in the mushrooms, garlic, dill, salt and pepper. Cover the skillet and cook the mixture for 2 to 3 minutes, or until the mushrooms begin to release their juices and look oily.

Add the cabbage and water, raise the heat to high and bring quickly to a boil. Then reduce the heat to low, cover the pan and cook the cabbage, stirring occasionally, for 10 to 15 minutes, or until it is just tender. If there is water remaining in the pan, remove the cover, raise the heat to high and cook the cabbage, stirring constantly, until most of the water has evaporated.

Remove the skillet from the heat and stir in the yogurt. Serve hot.

Per serving: 127 calories, 4.3 g. total fat, 2.4 g. saturated fat, 11 mg. cholesterol, 380 mg. sodium, 6.6 g. protein, 18.5 g. carbohydrates, 4.4 g. dietary fiber.

Sweet & Sour Red Cabbage with Apples

This enlightened old favorite is excellent with roast, baked, broiled or grilled meats, poultry and—surprisingly—fish. Actually, cole (cabbage) slaw is a long-time favorite companion to fish, so it makes good eating sense to pair this cabbage with any simply cooked fish. Canned applesauce works fine in this dish and saves time.

Ingredients	For 1 serving	For 2 servings
Defatted chicken broth or water	½ cup	¾ cup
Chopped onions	2 tablespoons	¼ cup
Brown sugar	1½ teaspoons	1 tablespoon
Cider vinegar	1½ teaspoons	1 tablespoon
Caraway seeds (optional)	¼ teaspoon	½ teaspoon
Bay leaf	½	1
Shredded red cabbage	1¼ cups	2½ cups
Applesauce	¼ cup	½ cup
Salt and pepper	to taste	to taste

In a heavy 2-quart (or 3-quart) saucepan, combine the broth or water, onions, brown sugar, vinegar, caraway seeds (if using) and bay leaf. Bring quickly to a boil over high heat. Stir in the cabbage and applesauce. Bring to a simmer.

Reduce the heat to medium, cover the saucepan and cook for 15 to 20 minutes, or until the cabbage is tender.

Remove the cover, increase the heat to high and rapidly cook away any remaining water, stirring the cabbage to prevent scorching. Season with the salt and pepper. Serve hot or chilled.

Per serving: 82 calories, 0.6 g. total fat, 0.1 g. saturated fat, 1 mg. cholesterol, 125 mg. sodium, 1.8 g. protein, 19.6 g. carbohydrates, 2.6 g. dietary fiber.

Candied Carrots & Parsnips

Cider (or orange juice) and just a spoonful of honey turn everyday carrots and parsnips into something special. If you have carrots but no parsnips, or vice versa, use double the amount of whichever vegetable you do have.

Ingredients	For 1 serving	For 2 servings
Carrots	1 medium	2 medium
Parsnip	1 small	1 medium
Cider or orange juice	½ cup	1 cup
Honey	1 teaspoon	2 teaspoons

Peel the carrots and parsnip and trim off the tops and ends. Cut them into pieces about 2" long. Cut vertically to make uniform pieces.

Combine the cider or orange juice and honey in a small heavy saucepan and bring to a boil over high heat. Stir in the carrots and parsnips. Bring the mixture back to a boil.

Reduce the heat to low, cover the saucepan and cook the vegetables for 10 to 15 minutes, or until crisp-tender. Remove the cover, raise the heat to high and continue cooking until the liquid is syrupy and reduced to about 1½ tablespoons (or 3 tablespoons). Serve hot.

Per serving: 175 calories, 0.4 g. total fat, 0 g. saturated fat, 0 mg. cholesterol, 37 mg. sodium, 1.9 g. protein, 42.9 g. carbohydrates, 6.5 g. dietary fiber.

Oven-Barbecued Root Vegetables

On impulse, I brushed a simple barbecue sauce over some carrots, potatoes and onions that I was roasting with a meat loaf. The results were wonderful; the vegetables came out of the oven looking as if they were grilled, thanks to the charring effects of the sugar in the sauce.

Carrots, red onions, new potatoes, sweet potatoes, turnips and parsnips are good candidates for oven-roasting. Peel the vegetables (except tiny white turnips and new potatoes) before anointing them with sauce. To ensure that the vegetables are all done at the same time, it is important to cut them to about the same size. I cut carrots and parsnips into 2″ lengths, then into halves or quarters; sweet potatoes into 2″ chunks; potatoes and turnips into halves, quarters or eighths; onions into halves or quarters. Leave small turnips, onions and potatoes whole.

Enjoy these vegetables hot with meat loaf or as a main course in their own right with Cheddar cheese and thick slices of whole-grain bread. They're good cold, too, for lunch or for nibbling like bonbons in front of the TV.

Ingredients	For 2 servings	For 4 servings
Root vegetables, peeled and cut into uniform pieces	1¼ pounds	2½ pounds
Ketchup	¼ cup	½ cup
Dark brown sugar	1 tablespoon	2 tablespoons
Grated lemon rind	1 teaspoon	2 teaspoons
Lemon juice	2 tablespoons	¼ cup
Dijon mustard	1½ teaspoons	1 tablespoon
Olive or canola oil	1½ teaspoons	1 tablespoon

Preheat the oven to 400°.

Line an 8″ × 8″ (or 9″ × 13″) baking pan with heavy foil and arrange the vegetables on top of the foil in a single layer.

In a small bowl, whisk together the ketchup, brown sugar, lemon rind, lemon juice, mustard and oil. Brush the mixture evenly over the vegetables.

Bake on the middle shelf of the oven. Roast the vegetables about 1 hour, until they are charred outside and tender inside. (During roasting, turn the vegetables every 20 minutes and baste with any remaining sauce and pan juices.)

Per serving: 266 calories, 3.8 g. total fat, 0.5 g. saturated fat, 0 mg. cholesterol, 382 mg. sodium, 4 g. protein, 57.5 g. carbohydrates, 4.9 g. dietary fiber.

Barbecue-Sauced Cauliflower

Nature doesn't package all her vegetables for small families. Take cauliflower, for example. One small head breaks down into more than 4 cups of florets, which is more cauliflower than most singles or couples bargained for. Slice up some of the extra to toss in a spectacularly good salad with iceberg lettuce, red onions, avocado, a few crumbles of blue cheese and Red French Dressing. Or buy just the amount you need from the supermarket salad bar.

Ingredients	For 2 servings	For 4 servings
Water	¼ cup	½ cup
Barbecue sauce	2½ tablespoons	⅓ cup
Cauliflower florets	2 cups	4 cups
Chopped fresh parsley (optional)	1 tablespoon	2 tablespoons

In a heavy, 8″ (or 10″) nonstick skillet, combine the water and barbecue sauce, stirring to blend.

Bring the mixture to a boil over medium heat and add the cauliflower; turn the pieces in the sauce to coat them evenly. Reduce the heat to low, cover and cook for 5 minutes, or until crisp-tender.

Transfer the cauliflower to a serving dish and sprinkle it with the parsley (if using). Serve hot or chilled.

Per serving: 39 calories, 0.5 g. total fat, 0.1 g. saturated fat, 0 mg. cholesterol, 175 mg. sodium, 2.4 g. protein, 7.6 g. carbohydrates, 2.7 g. dietary fiber.

New-Wave Corn on the Cob

For an easy way to cook corn on the cob, zap it right in nature's wrappings. The moisture in the husks steams microwaved corn to juicy sweetness, and the silks are easy to strip off afterward. Cooked this way, fresh corn tastes so good, you won't need salt or butter. But if you insist on some sort of spread for your corn, try one or more of the following: freshly ground pepper, salsa, mustard, lemon juice, snipped fresh chives, thyme or dill.

Ingredients	For 1 serving	For 2 servings
Unhusked corn	1 ear	2 ears

Position the unhusked corn in the center of the microwave (place 2 ears side by side). Microwave on high power for a total of 3 to 4 (or 5 to 7) minutes; flip and reposition the ears halfway through the cooking time.

Let the corn stand at room temperature for 2 to 3 minutes, then strip off the husks and silks.

Per serving: 83 calories, 1 g. total fat, 0.2 g. saturated fat, 0 mg. cholesterol, 13 mg. sodium, 2.6 g. protein, 19.3 g. carbohydrates, 2.9 g. dietary fiber.

Microwaving Fresh Vegetables

The microwave is at its best when you are cooking vegetables for one or two. It squeezes cooking times dramatically when servings are small, though this is not the case for family-size amounts. The microwave also does a beautiful job of retaining, even enhancing, the flavor of vegetables. Sometimes it does too good a job, as in the case of cruciferous vegetables—the strong flavors of cabbage, cauliflower, brussels sprouts and broccoli, for instance, can become a little too pronounced for some tastes.

Following are appropriate cooking times and instructions for most common vegetables. Weights and sizes are given according to what you would purchase. Microwaving times are for the amount of clean, prepped vegetables you will end up with.

Microwave ovens vary, so you may have to do a little experimenting to find the precise time and procedure to suit yours.

To cook larger amounts of vegetables, extend the microwaving time slightly and check often for doneness. You can always microwave a little longer, but once food is overcooked, that's the end of the ball game. Another reason to undercook is that microwaved food continues to cook after it comes out of the oven. If you have a turntable, it isn't necessary to rotate vegetables for even cooking, though you will need to stir (as for shredded cabbage) or turn (as for potatoes) when indicated.

Always use containers that you know are microwave-safe, such as glass or microwaveable plastic. For sliced or cut-up vegetables, an 8" or 9" glass pie plate works especially well. It's large enough to hold vegetables in a single layer for even cooking.

When a cover is specified, use casseroles with snugly fitted lids. Lacking a lid, cover the container tightly with plastic wrap and either cut vents in several places with a paring knife or turn back one corner of the plastic so that steam can escape. When using plastic wrap, choose containers deep enough to keep the wrap from coming in contact with foods, except corn in the husk.

For a special touch, sprinkle vegetables with a pinch of your favorite herb before microwaving. Don't salt them because salt can cause black spots; add salt after cooking, if at all. The flavors of microwaved vegetables are so intense that you may find salt entirely unnecessary.

Always let any microwaved food, including vegetables, stand at least 3 to 5 minutes before you serve it to finish cooking and to cool ever so slightly. Instructions given here are for fresh vegetables; frozen and canned vegetables take less time.

Times and Techniques

Artichokes. Place a medium artichoke in a deep bowl with only the water that clings from washing, cover the bowl and microwave on high for 6 to 7 minutes, rotating the artichoke halfway through cooking. For 2 artichokes, increase the cooking time to 8 to 10 minutes.

Asparagus spears. Align ⅓ pound asparagus spears on a glass pie plate with tips in the same direction, add 2 teaspoons water, cover and microwave on high for 1½ to 2 minutes. For 2 servings, double the amount of asparagus, add 2 tablespoons water and increase the time to 2 to 3 minutes.

Beans, green or wax. Align ⅓ pound beans in a single layer on a glass pie plate, add 2 teaspoons water, cover and microwave on high for 3 to 4 minutes. For 2 servings, double the amount of beans, add 1 tablespoon water and microwave on high for 5 to 8 minutes.

Beets. Place 2 medium beets in a 2″-deep casserole, cover and microwave on high for 6 to 8 minutes; halfway through cooking, turn each beet and rotate the casserole. For 2 servings, double the amount of beets and microwave on high for 8 to 12 minutes.

Broccoli. Cut 2 medium broccoli stalks with buds into uniform, bite-size pieces and spread evenly in a glass pie plate with 1 tablespoon water. Cover and microwave on high for 1 to 2 minutes, rotating the dish halfway through cooking. For 2 servings, double the amount of broccoli and water; increase the time to 3 to 4 minutes.

Brussels sprouts. Arrange ⅓ pound brussels sprouts in a 1-quart casserole with 2 tablespoons water, cover the casserole and microwave on high for 3 to 4 minutes, stirring halfway through cooking. For 2 servings, double the amount of brussels sprouts, add 3 tablespoons water and microwave on high for 5 to 7 minutes.

Cabbage. Coarsely shred a quarter of a small head of cabbage. Place in a 1-quart casserole with 1 tablespoon water, cover and microwave on high for 2 to 4 minutes, stirring halfway through cooking. For 2 servings, double the amount of cabbage and water; microwave on high for 5 to 7 minutes.

Carrots. Spread ¼ pound peeled, sliced carrots on a glass pie plate with

(continued)

2 tablespoons water, cover and microwave on high for 3 to 4 minutes, stirring halfway through cooking. For 2 servings, double the amount of carrots and water; increase the cooking time to 5 to 7 minutes.

Cauliflower. Break a quarter of a small head into florets. Spread in a glass pie plate with 1 tablespoon water, cover and microwave on high for 2 to 3 minutes. For 2 servings, double the amount of cauliflower and water; microwave on high for 4 to 5 minutes.

Corn on the cob. Wrap 1 medium unhusked ear of corn tightly in plastic wrap and microwave on high for 3 to 4 minutes, turning halfway through cooking. Let stand for 3 minutes. Peel away the husks and silks. For 2 servings, double the amount of corn and microwave on high for 5 to 6 minutes.

Greens. Place ½ pound washed, trimmed greens (such as collards, kale, mustard greens or turnip greens) in a 1½-quart casserole with ⅓ cup water. Cover and microwave on high for 5 to 7 minutes, stirring halfway through cooking. For 2 servings, double the amount of greens and water, use a 3-quart casserole and microwave on high for 8 to 12 minutes.

Onions, baby. Peel ⅓ pound baby onions and spread them in a glass pie plate with 1 tablespoon water, cover the plate and microwave on high for 2 to 4 minutes, stirring halfway through cooking. For 2 servings, double the amount of onions and water; increase cooking time to 4 to 7 minutes.

Onions, regular. Slice 1 medium onion and spread the slices in a glass pie plate with 1 tablespoon water, cover and microwave on high for 2 to 4 minutes, stirring halfway through cooking. For 2 servings, double the amount of onions and water; microwave on high for 5 to 7 minutes.

Peas, green. Place 1 cup shelled peas in a 1-quart bowl with 1 tablespoon water, cover and microwave on high for 2 to 3 minutes, stirring halfway through cooking. For 2 servings, double the amount of peas and water, use a 2-quart bowl and microwave on high for 3 to 5 minutes.

Potatoes, all-purpose. Peel a medium potato, cut into 1" chunks and place in a 1-quart glass measure with ¼ cup water. Cover and microwave on high for 5 to 6 minutes, stirring halfway through cooking. For 2 servings, use 2 medium potatoes, spread them in a glass pie plate, add ⅓ cup water and microwave on high for 6 to 9 minutes.

Potatoes, small new. Scrub ⅓ pound small new potatoes. Peel a narrow strip around the middle of each potato and place the potatoes in a 2-cup glass measure with 1 tablespoon water. Cover and microwave on high for 3 to 4 minutes, stirring halfway through cooking. For 2 servings, double the amount of potatoes and water, use a 4-cup measure and increase the time to 5 to 7 minutes.

Spinach. Wash ⅓ pound fresh spinach. Place in a 1½-quart bowl with only the water that clings to the leaves, cover and microwave on high for 1 to 2 minutes, stirring halfway through cooking. For 2 servings, double the amount of spinach, use a 2-quart bowl and microwave on high for 2 to 4 minutes.

Squash, acorn. Pierce a small squash in several places with a fork; place the squash on a paper towel on the floor of the oven. Microwave on high for 6 to 7 minutes, turning the squash halfway through cooking. Let stand for 5 minutes, then cut in half and remove the seeds and pulp. For 2 servings, use a medium squash and microwave on high for 8 to 9 minutes.

Squash, summer, or zucchini. Cut ⅓ pound summer squash or zucchini into ⅓" slices and spread evenly in a glass pie plate with 1 teaspoon water. Cover and microwave on high for 2 to 4 minutes, stirring once; let stand for 3 minutes before serving. For 2 servings, double the amount of squash and water and microwave on high for 3 to 5 minutes.

Sweet potatoes. Pierce 1 medium (8 to 10 ounces) sweet potato in several places with a fork, place on a paper towel on the floor of the oven and microwave on high for 4 to 6 minutes, turning the potato halfway through cooking. For 2 servings, use 2 medium sweet potatoes and microwave on high for 6 to 8 minutes.

Swiss chard. Wash and coarsely shred ⅓ pound Swiss chard and place in a 1½-quart bowl with only the water that clings from washing. Cover and microwave on high for 2 to 3 minutes, stirring halfway through cooking. For 2 servings, double the amount of chard, use a 2-quart bowl and microwave on high for 4 to 6 minutes.

Turnips, white. Wash ⅓ pound turnips. Peel any large turnips; leave the peel on small tender ones. Cut into ½" slices and spread evenly in a glass pie plate with 1 tablespoon water. Cover and microwave on high for 3 to 4 minutes, stirring halfway through cooking. For 2 servings, double the amount of turnips and water; increase cooking time to 5 to 8 minutes.

Turnips, yellow (rutabagas). Peel half a small rutabaga and cut into ¾" cubes. Place in a glass pie plate with ⅓ cup water or beef bouillon, cover and microwave on high for 6 to 9 minutes, stirring halfway through cooking. For 2 servings, double the amount of rutabaga, add ½ cup liquid and cook for 9 to 12 minutes.

Nanaw's Cream-Style Corn

The French Prince of Gastronomes, Curnonsky, once noted: "Cuisine is when foods taste like themselves." No food ever tasted more like itself than the cream-style corn cooked by my grandmother. Nanaw's secret to great corn cuisine lay in the way she cut the kernels from each ear. Sitting on the back porch steps with a large mixing bowl in her lap, she'd run the tip of a paring knife worn thin from use down the center of each row of kernels before she first cut, then scraped the corn from the cob.

When you're lucky enough to find fresh-picked sweet corn, buy extra for this recipe. Use the leftovers in salads, soups and pancakes. If you use salt, leave it out until the very end of the cooking process; salt added too soon will toughen fresh corn.

Ingredients	For 1 serving	For 2 servings
Unhusked corn	1 ear	2 ears
Water	1 tablespoon	2 tablespoons
Sugar (optional)	⅛ teaspoon	¼ teaspoon
Salt and pepper	to taste	to taste

With a sharp knife, slice off the top of each ear, then shuck it by pulling downward on the husks and silks.

Working with a large mixing bowl (to catch corn juices), cut each row of kernels in half by slicing down the center with a sharp paring knife. Cut the kernels from the cob, then scrape out remaining juices by scraping the dull side of the knife blade down the cob.

Transfer the corn and milky juices to a heavy, 8″ (or 10″) nonstick skillet. Mix in the water. Cover and cook over medium heat for 5 to 8 minutes, or until the corn is tender.

Stir in the sugar (if using), salt and pepper just before serving.

Per serving: 85 calories, 1 g. total fat, 0.2 g. saturated fat, 0 mg. cholesterol, 13 mg. sodium, 2.6 g. protein, 19.8 g. carbohydrates, 2.9 g. dietary fiber.

Succulent Succotash

Certainly, you can use frozen corn instead of fresh, but true succulence in succotash comes from fresh corn, cut from the cob the way my Nanaw used to do it. I'm a fanatic about using fresh corn when it's available, but frozen baby lima beans taste fine because they survive freezing better than delicate corn.

Ingredients	For 1 serving	For 2 servings
Water	½ cup	1 cup
Fresh or frozen baby lima beans	½ cup	1 cup
Fresh or frozen corn	½ cup	1 cup
Salt and pepper	to taste	to taste

In a medium saucepan, quickly bring the water to a boil over high heat. Add the beans and return the mixture to a boil. Reduce the heat to low, cover the saucepan and cook for 15 minutes.

Add the corn and cover the saucepan. Cook for 5 to 10 minutes, or until the vegetables are tender. Stir in the salt and pepper. Serve immediately.

Per serving: 112 calories, 0.7 g. total fat, 0.1 g. saturated fat, 0 mg. cholesterol, 112 mg. sodium, 5.8 g. protein, 22.8 g. carbohydrates, 6.3 g. dietary fiber.

New Light Greens

When I was growing up in Georgia, we had 3 or 4 vegetables and some sort of hot bread for dinner at least once a week. Strictly speaking, our vegetable suppers weren't vegetarian, since ham hocks poked out of the crowder peas, and fatback lubricated the fried yellow squash. Southern-style vegetables like those, seasoned with lots of love and fat, need to be lightened up before they can count as healthy food.

I've done just that by omitting the pork fat and seasoning our aggressive Southern greens with minced garlic, red pepper and a hint of olive oil. Even collards, the toughest of greens, can be cooked by this method in minutes rather than hours. Serve these greens with hot-pepper vinegar (if your market carries it) and fresh cornbread.

Ingredients	For 1 serving	For 2 servings
Kale, collard, turnip or mustard greens	8 ounces	1 pound
Olive oil	1 teaspoon	2 teaspoons
Garlic, minced	2 cloves	4 cloves
Red-pepper flakes	⅛ teaspoon	¼ teaspoon
Hot-pepper or regular vinegar	to taste	to taste

Leave young, tender greens whole. Trim out and discard the thick center stems of large tough greens like collards or kale, then roll them into cylinders containing 4 or 5 leaves each. Slice across the cylinders to make 1" strips.

Wash the greens in tepid water, changing the water until no trace of sand or dirt is left behind; drain in a colander.

Fill a 2-quart (or 3-quart) saucepan with water and bring it to a boil over high heat. Carefully add the greens to the rapidly boiling water and cook for 2 to 3 minutes, only until wilted.

Drain the greens, reserving about ½ cup (or 1 cup) of the cooking liquid.

Heat the oil in a heavy, 10" nonstick skillet over medium heat; stir in the garlic and cook for 1 minute, or until it begins to color.

Stir in the greens, sprinkle with the pepper flakes and add the reserved cooking liquid. Cover and cook for 5 minutes, tossing the greens every minute or so with tongs. Serve hot or at room temperature, sprinkled with the vinegar.

Per serving: 122 calories, 5.4 g. total fat, 0.7 g. saturated fat, 0 mg. cholesterol, 56 mg. sodium, 4.7 g. protein, 14.9 g. carbohydrates, 7.6 g. dietary fiber.

The Big Cheese Onion

For a savory meatless entrée, bake an onion or two, then devour them with pan-toasted whole-grain bread and a green salad. Or skip the cheese and have the roasted onion alongside a pan-grilled steak or some roast chicken or turkey.

Ingredients	For 1 serving	For 2 servings
Large Bermuda onions (10–12 ounces)	1	2
Sherry or apple juice	1 tablespoon	2 tablespoons
Salt and pepper	to taste	to taste
Soft bread crumbs	2 tablespoons	¼ cup
Butter or margarine, melted	1 teaspoon	2 teaspoons
Thinly sliced Gruyère or Cheddar cheese	2 tablespoons	¼ cup

Preheat the oven to 400°.

Peel the onions and cut a thin slice from the root end of each so they will stand upright. Cut a ½" slice from the top of each onion and place the onions in a round 2-cup baking dish (or a 4" × 8" loaf pan).

Drizzle with the sherry or apple juice and sprinkle with the salt and pepper. Cover the baking dish with foil and bake for 40 to 45 minutes, or until the onions can be easily pierced with a thin paring knife.

In a small bowl, toss the bread crumbs with the butter or margarine.

Remove the foil from the pan and sprinkle the Gruyère or Cheddar evenly over the onions. Then sprinkle the bread crumbs over the cheese.

Bake, uncovered, for 10 to 15 minutes, until the cheese is melted and the crumbs are browned. Serve hot.

Per serving: 234 calories, 9.5 g. total fat, 5.1 g. saturated fat, 26 mg. cholesterol, 124 mg. sodium, 8.1 g. protein, 28.3 g. carbohydrates, 4.7 g. dietary fiber.

Green Peas Braised in Garden Lettuce

Plenty of people are passionate about peas. Thomas Jefferson was; he competed every year with neighboring gentlemen farmers to bring the first dish of peas to the table. For those of us who are equally passionate about peas but don't have a bounteous pea patch, a pound of fresh green peas, weighed in the pod, yields 1 to 1½ cups after shelling, depending on maturity. (The peas', not yours.)

Look for large, bright-green, well-filled, velvety pods. To shell peas, arrange yourself comfortably with yesterday's newspaper opened in your lap to catch the shelled pods and a bowl to hold the peas. With your thumbs, snap each pod open along the outer edge and run your thumb down the inside to pop the peas into the bowl.

Ingredients	For 1 serving	For 2 servings
Butter or margarine	½ teaspoon	1 teaspoon
Leaf lettuce, shredded	2 large leaves	4 large leaves
Peas	¾ cup	1½ cups
Salt and pepper	to taste	to taste

In a heavy, 8″ nonstick skillet over low heat, melt the butter or margarine. Spread half the lettuce in the skillet, add the peas and cover them with the remaining lettuce.

Cover the skillet and cook the mixture for 10 to 15 minutes, or until the peas are just tender; during cooking, add 1 or 2 teaspoons of water as necessary to prevent the vegetables from scorching. Season with the salt and pepper just before serving.

Per serving: 109 calories, 2.4 g. total fat, 1.3 g. saturated fat, 5 mg. cholesterol, 27 mg. sodium, 6.3 g. protein, 16.7 g. carbohydrates, 0.4 g. dietary fiber.

Vegetables

Roasted Greek Potatoes

These lovely lemony potatoes are often a main dish for my vegetarian daughters. They prefer waxy boiling potatoes, which have more sugar than starch, because starchy baking potatoes have a tendency to collapse into mush when used for this recipe. Cooking tip: Be sure to line your baking pan with foil as indicated or be prepared to spend a lot of time scouring the pan.

Ingredients	For 2 servings	For 4 servings
Water	3 cups	3 cups
Waxy boiling potatoes	8 ounces	1 pound
Lemon juice	2 tablespoons	¼ cup
Olive oil	1 teaspoon	2 teaspoons
Minced garlic	½ teaspoon	1 teaspoon
Dried oregano	½ teaspoon	1 teaspoon
Salt and pepper	to taste	to taste

Preheat the oven to 450°.

Bring the water to a boil over high heat in a 2-quart saucepan or a tea kettle.

Scrub the potatoes but do not peel them. Cut the small ones in half; cut larger ones vertically into thick wedges.

Line a 1-quart casserole (or 8″ × 8″ baking pan) with heavy foil, pressing the foil to fit. Add the lemon juice, oil, garlic, oregano, salt and pepper. Add the potatoes, turning to coat them well, then pour in enough boiling water to equal a depth of ½″.

Bake for 20 minutes. Turn the potatoes in the dish, reduce the oven temperature to 400° and bake them 40 minutes longer, or until the water is absorbed and the potatoes are tender and browned (turn the potatoes every 15 to 20 minutes during this stage).

Per serving: 151 calories, 2.4 g. total fat, 0.3 g. saturated fat, 0 mg. cholesterol, 143 mg. sodium, 2.8 g. protein, 30.7 g. carbohydrates, 2.8 g. dietary fiber.

Mashed Potatoes

The microwave is great for squaring up a meal for one or two with starchy side dishes like potatoes. For example, you can scratch-cook mashed potatoes—possibly the greatest of all comfort foods—in about the time it takes to pan-grill a chop or a chicken breast. If you don't mind little brown flecks in your mashed potatoes, scrub your potatoes and leave the peels on. For the creamiest results, choose high-starch russet or baking potatoes.

Ingredients	For 1 serving	For 2 servings
Baking potatoes, cut into 1" cubes	8 ounces	1 pound
Water	¼ cup	½ cup
Butter or margarine	1 teaspoon	2 teaspoons
1% low-fat milk	¼ cup	½ cup
Salt	⅛ teaspoon	¼ teaspoon
Pepper	to taste	to taste

Place the potatoes and water in a 4-cup microwave-safe glass measure. Cover with vented plastic wrap and microwave on high power for a total of 5 to 6 (or 8 to 9) minutes, or until the potatoes are very tender; stop and stir the potatoes halfway through the cooking time.

Drain the potatoes. Add the butter or margarine, milk, salt and pepper. Beat until fluffy and smooth with a hand-held mixer on low speed (or mash them by hand with a potato masher, then beat vigorously with a serving spoon).

Just before serving, reheat the finished potatoes by microwaving them, uncovered, on high power for 30 seconds (or 1 minute). Stir and serve.

Per serving: 254 calories, 4.7 g. total fat, 2.8 g. saturated fat, 13 mg. cholesterol, 347 mg. sodium, 5.9 g. protein, 48.3 g. carbohydrates, 2.5 g. dietary fiber.

Tatties & Neeps

This is the Scottish name for a simple, earthy dish of mashed potatoes and turnips that is delicious with roasted meat and poultry and equally good on its own. Buying tip: For each cup of cubed yellow turnips or potatoes, buy about 6 ounces.

Ingredients	For 1 serving	For 2 servings
Peeled and cubed yellow turnips (rutabagas)	1 cup	2 cups
Peeled and cubed potatoes	1 cup	2 cups
Salt	¼ teaspoon	½ teaspoon
Pepper	pinch	⅛ teaspoon
Butter or margarine	1 teaspoon	2 teaspoons
1% low-fat milk	¼ cup	½ cup
Finely chopped fresh parsley or chives	1½ teaspoons	1 tablespoon

Place the turnips in a medium saucepan with enough water to cover them; bring to a boil, cover and cook for 10 minutes over medium heat. Add the potatoes and cook for 10 minutes, or until the vegetables are very tender. Drain well.

Add the salt, pepper, butter or margarine and milk to the saucepan with the vegetables. Set over low heat until the milk begins to bubble. Remove from the heat and beat the mixture until smooth with a hand-held mixer (or mash it by hand with a potato masher). Stir in the parsley or chives and serve immediately.

Per serving: 153 calories, 4.3 g. total fat, 2.8 g. saturated fat, 13 mg. cholesterol, 664 mg. sodium, 4.4 g. protein, 25.6 g. carbohydrates, 3.3 g. dietary fiber.

Gratin of Potato & Tomato

When you already have the oven going for a roast, chicken or fish, add a bake-along—a small casserole of sliced tomatoes and potatoes. Tuck whole cloves of garlic to roast between the sliced vegetables. Garlic cooked this way is surprisingly mild in flavor. To eat, hold each garlic clove by the stem end, then pull it between your teeth as if you were nibbling a leaf from an artichoke. (Or scrape out the garlic with the flat side of a knife and spread it over hot French bread instead of butter.)

Ingredients	For 1 serving	For 2 servings
Medium tomatoes	1	2
Waxy potatoes	1 small	2 small
Unpeeled garlic	3 cloves	6 cloves
Olive oil	1 teaspoon	2 teaspoons
Salt and pepper	to taste	to taste

Preheat the oven to 400°.

Slice the stem and core ends from the tomatoes and cut each tomato into 5 or 6 slices.

Slice the potatoes as thinly as possible.

For each serving, alternate the potatoes and tomatoes in a 2-cup oval gratin dish. Tuck in the garlic, drizzle the oil over the vegetables and season with the salt and pepper.

Bake for 30 minutes, or until the potatoes are tender. Serve immediately.

Per serving: 172 calories, 5 g. total fat, 0.7 g. saturated fat, 0 mg. cholesterol, 19 mg. sodium, 3.6 g. protein, 30.2 g. carbohydrates, 3.6 g. dietary fiber.

Vegetables

Sweets in a Flash

Daughter Joan recently raved about sweet potatoes that she dined on at a friend's house. Odd, during all the years that Joan's care and feeding was up to me, she wouldn't touch sweet potatoes with a 10-foot pole. "What's so special about Linda's sweet potatoes?" I asked.

"She bakes them until the skins are crispy and serves them with little bowls of crumbled Gorgonzola cheese and chopped chives, with turnip greens on the side," came the reply.

For a satisfying main course, serve them the way Linda does. For a simple but delicious dessert, drizzle a baked sweet potato with maple, sorghum or ribbon cane syrup; add a few toasted pecans and a dash of cinnamon or nutmeg. While you're baking the sweet potatoes, do a few extras for a ravishing sweet potato salad with walnut vinaigrette.

No matter what else you intend to do with the sweet potatoes, this straight-forward recipe will get you started.

Ingredients	For 1 serving	For 2 servings
Sweet potatoes (10 ounces each)	1	2

Preheat the oven or toaster oven to 450°.

Scrub the potatoes, dry them with a paper towel and puncture them in several places with the tines of a fork to prevent steam-induced explosions during cooking. Microwave on high power for 5 (or 8) minutes.

Transfer the sweet potatoes to the oven and bake for about 15 minutes, or until they are tender when pierced with a sharp paring knife.

Per serving: 233 calories, 0.2 g. total fat, 0 g. saturated fat, 0 mg. cholesterol, 23 mg. sodium, 3.9 g. protein, 55.1 g. carbohydrates, 6.8 g. dietary fiber.

Sweet Potato Salad

Enhance the earthy flavor of this unusual potato salad with a touch of walnut oil. Sure, it's expensive, but it's worth the cost for the rich, nutty flavor it adds to vinaigrettes and dressings. A small bottle will last 6 months—remember to keep it in the refrigerator after you open it so it doesn't go rancid. (If you don't have walnut oil, replace it with canola oil.)

Do not overcook the sweet potatoes for this recipe—they should be just tender, not mushy and soft. Serve the salad on radicchio or red-leaf lettuce for the greatest color impact.

Ingredients	For 2 servings	For 4 servings
Cooked sweet potatoes	8 ounces	1 pound
Diced celery	2½ tablespoons	⅓ cup
Finely chopped red onions	2 tablespoons	¼ cup
Orange juice	1 tablespoon	2 tablespoons
Walnut oil	1 tablespoon	2 tablespoons
Red wine vinegar	1½ teaspoons	1 tablespoon
Salt	⅛ teaspoon	¼ teaspoon

Cut the sweet potatoes into ¾" cubes. Place them in a medium mixing bowl and add the celery and onions.

In a small bowl, whisk together the orange juice, oil, vinegar and salt; pour the dressing over the vegetables and toss well to coat. Cover and chill for 2 hours or overnight.

Per serving: 184 calories, 7 g. total fat, 0.5 g. saturated fat, 0 mg. cholesterol, 153 mg. sodium, 2.1 g. protein, 29.4 g. carbohydrates, 3.7 g. dietary fiber.

Best Picks for Beta-Carotene

Beta-carotene is what makes carrots orange, peppers red, winter squashes yellow-orange and kale deep-green. Our bodies convert beta-carotene to the antioxidant vitamin A when we need it. People who eat plenty of foods rich in beta-carotene seem to be less prone to developing cancer, but more research is needed to prove (or disprove) the theory. Meanwhile, it won't hurt to pack your meals with beta-carotene, which is found only in plants. Best sources are dark-green leafy vegetables (such as kale, collards, spinach, turnip greens and mustard greens), broccoli and deep-orange or yellow fruits and vegetables (such as sweet potatoes, carrots, pumpkin, winter squash, cantaloupe, apricots, mangoes, papayas, peaches and oranges).

Spinach with Sesame Seeds & Soy

Stemming and washing spinach takes far more time than cooking it. So if you have more money than time, pick up spinach that's already prepped from the supermarket salad bar. That way, you'll cut your kitchen time for this Japanese version of Popeye's favorite to 5 minutes or less.

Ingredients	For 1 serving	For 2 servings
Spinach leaves, lightly packed	4 cups	8 cups
Sesame seeds	1 teaspoon	2 teaspoons
Reduced-sodium soy sauce	1½ teaspoons	1 tablespoon

Pick over the spinach, pinch off the stems and discard any wilted leaves. Wash in several changes of lukewarm water until no trace of grit or dirt remains; drain the spinach in a colander.

Pan-toast the sesame seeds in a heavy, 10" nonstick skillet over medium heat, shaking the skillet constantly, until the seeds begin to color, about 2 minutes. Add the spinach with only the water that clings from washing. Cover the skillet and cook for 1 to 2 minutes, or until the spinach is barely wilted (if necessary, flip the spinach with tongs during cooking to be sure that it cooks evenly). Sprinkle with the soy sauce. Serve hot or cold.

Per serving: 122 calories, 7.7 g. total fat, 1.1 g. saturated fat, 0 mg. cholesterol, 392 mg. sodium, 7.3 g. protein, 9.4 g. carbohydrates, 6.5 g. dietary fiber.

Sauté of Spinach & Cucumber

If you like cucumbers but they don't like you, you'll really appreciate this burpless but luscious combination. For each serving, pick up about 2 cups prepped spinach at the salad bar. Or skip the spinach altogether and make sautéed cucumbers; use a whole cucumber for each serving. This two-toned sauté is excellent with fish or chicken.

Ingredients	For 1 serving	For 2 servings
Cucumber	½ large	1 large
Butter or margarine	1 teaspoon	2 teaspoons
Spinach leaves, lightly packed	2 cups	4 cups
Salt	pinch	⅛ teaspoon
Pepper	to taste	to taste

Peel the cucumber and cut it in half lengthwise. Scoop out the seeds with a teaspoon. Slice crosswise into ¼" pieces.

Melt the butter or margarine in a heavy, 10" nonstick skillet over medium heat. Add the cucumbers and cook, stirring often, for 2 minutes, or until they become translucent. Add the spinach, salt and pepper. Cook, stirring occasionally, for 2 minutes, or until the spinach is wilted. Serve immediately.

Per serving: 65 calories, 4.2 g. total fat, 2.4 g. saturated fat, 10 mg. cholesterol, 374 mg. sodium, 3 g. protein, 5.9 g. carbohydrates, 3.2 g. dietary fiber.

Apple-Stuffed Acorn Squash

Medium squash, weighing slightly less than a pound, work best here. They're large enough to accommodate a filling, yet small enough to comfortably coexist with other dinner components. For best results, use a crisp cooking apple such as Granny Smith or Winesap. And cut the squash in half lengthwise, from stem to tip.

Ingredients	For 1 serving	For 2 servings
Acorn squash, halved lengthwise	½ medium	1 medium
Apple, cubed	½ medium	1 medium
Honey or maple syrup	1 teaspoon	2 teaspoons
Butter or margarine	½ teaspoon	1 teaspoon
Grated nutmeg or ground cinnamon	pinch	⅛ teaspoon

Preheat the oven to 400°.

Scoop out and discard the seeds and strings from the squash. Place the squash, cut side up, in a deep 2-cup casserole (or 4½″ × 8½″ loaf pan). Fill the center with the apples, cover with foil and bake for 30 minutes.

In a small microwave-safe bowl, combine the honey or maple syrup and butter or margarine. Microwave on high power for 20 seconds, or until liquefied.

Remove the foil from the squash and drizzle it with the syrup mixture. Sprinkle with the nutmeg or cinnamon. Bake for 15 minutes, or until the squash and apples are tender. Serve hot.

Per serving: 186 calories, 4.2 g. total fat, 2.6 g. saturated fat, 5 mg. cholesterol, 27 mg. sodium, 2 g. protein, 39.4 g. carbohydrates, 4.5 g. dietary fiber.

Zucchini Panned with Red Peppers

In this recipe, zucchini and sweet red peppers cook in a covered heavy skillet without any liquid and only the merest hint of oil. The method is called sweating. Subjected to low but steady heat, the vegetables sweat out their juices and cook in them for intense flavor. Many other vegetables, including yellow summer squash, onions, even tiny new potatoes, can be cooked this way with outstanding results. Try these vegetables alongside fish or over pasta.

Ingredients	For 1 serving	For 2 servings
Sweet red or green pepper	¼ small	½ small
Zucchini	8 ounces	1 pound
Olive oil	1 teaspoon	2 teaspoons
Finely chopped onions	2 tablespoons	¼ cup
Minced garlic (optional)	¼ teaspoon	½ teaspoon
Dried basil	¼ teaspoon	½ teaspoon
Salt	⅛ teaspoon	¼ teaspoon
Pepper	to taste	to taste

Cut the red or green pepper into strips about ½" wide, stack the strips and cut them across to make ½" squares.

Trim the ends from the zucchini and cut into thin rounds.

Add the oil to a heavy, 8" (or 10") nonstick skillet set over medium heat. Stir in the peppers and onions; cook, stirring often, for 3 minutes, or until the vegetables are tender but not brown. Stir in the garlic, zucchini, basil, salt and pepper.

Reduce the heat to low and cover the skillet. Cook, stirring occasionally, for 10 to 15 minutes, or until the zucchini is just tender.

Per serving: 90 calories, 4.9 g. total fat, 0.7 g. saturated fat, 0 mg. cholesterol, 275 mg. sodium, 3.3 g. protein, 10.7 g. carbohydrates, 4.1 g. dietary fiber.

Desserts

*M*any of the desserts that I've included in this chapter—like Lemon Sponge Pudding, Blueberry Flummery and Deep-Dish Cherry Cobbler—hark back to carefree times, when dessert followed dinner as surely as night follows day. Others, like Frozen Strawberry Yogurt, are fairly recent additions to the dessert lineup. In any case, most are fruit-based, to help you pile on vitamins, minerals and fiber in a most enjoyable way.

Believe it or not, dessert isn't forbidden when you're watching your waistline. Some dieters even report better luck taking off those stubborn pounds when they top off their low-fat dinners with a little something sweet. The operative words here, of course, are "a little something." There's a big difference between gracefully capping off the meal with a refreshing fruit sorbet and giving it the coup de grâce with double-chocolate mousse buried under a mountain of whipped cream.

Many of the recipes make more than one serving per person. There's no point in going to the trouble of preparing a crisp or cobbler—not to mention cupcakes, biscotti or quick bread—for only one portion. Besides, all these items keep well and will healthfully satisfy tomorrow's sweet tooth.

Sally's Left Bank Apple Crisp

My daughter Sally spent 5 years apprenticing as a chef in Paris, where she was employed in kitchens that ranged from the upscale Hôtel Plaza Athénée to an oddball health food restaurant on the Left Bank, where she baked a higher-fat version of this homey apple crisp. It's very good served warm for dessert, possibly with vanilla yogurt, and equally good for breakfast reheated in the microwave. For best results, use good baking apples like Granny Smith or Golden Delicious.

Ingredients	For 2 servings	For 4 servings
Apples	2 medium	4 medium
Cider	2 tablespoons	¼ cup
Light brown sugar, packed	¼ cup	½ cup
Rolled oats	2 tablespoons	¼ cup
Ground cinnamon	¼ teaspoon	½ teaspoon
Butter or margarine, softened	1 tablespoon	2 tablespoons

Preheat the oven to 375°.

Peel, halve and core the apples, then cut each half into 6 or 8 slices. Place the slices in a 4½" × 8" loaf pan (or an 8" × 8" baking dish) and sprinkle them with the cider.

In a small bowl, using your fingertips, rub together the brown sugar, oats, cinnamon and butter or margarine until the mixture feels crumbly; sprinkle it evenly over the apples. Bake for 30 to 35 minutes, or until the topping is browned and the apples are tender. Serve warm.

Per serving: 278 calories, 6.4 g. total fat, 3.7 g. saturated fat, 15 mg. cholesterol, 67 mg. sodium, 1.1 g. protein, 49.1 g. carbohydrates, 2.7 g. dietary fiber.

Handmade Applesauce

Making your own applesauce is not quick and easy, but it's a good confidence-building exercise for a beginning cook. Peeling, coring and slicing a pound of apples is tedious work that, even with a swivel-bladed vegetable peeler and a sharp paring knife, takes up to 15 minutes for 2 servings. You won't save money either: A 1-pound jar of runny, corn syrup–sweetened applesauce costs less than the Granny Smith, Gravenstein or McIntosh apples that it takes to make a pound of thick, lumpy, luscious applesauce.

Why bother? Because homemade applesauce tastes so much better than store-bought. It keeps well, too—up to 10 days in the refrigerator in a tightly covered container. Savor it all by itself, as a spread for whole-grain toast or as a winter's shortcake with Triple-Ginger Cupcakes and vanilla yogurt.

Ingredients	For 2 servings	For 4 servings
Crisp cooking apples	1 pound	2 pounds
Cider or water	¼ cup	½ cup
Brown or granulated sugar	2 tablespoons	¼ cup
Ground cinnamon or grated nutmeg (optional)	¼ teaspoon	½ teaspoon

Peel, halve and core the apples, then cut each half into 4 slices. Place the apple chunks in a heavy 1-quart (or 2-quart) saucepan. Add the cider or water, cover the pan and bring the mixture to a boil over medium-high heat.

Reduce the heat to low and cook the apples, stirring occasionally, for 20 minutes, or until they are mushy but still chunky. Stir in the sugar and cinnamon or nutmeg (if using). Serve warm or chilled.

Per serving: 295 calories, 0.9 g. total fat, 0.2 g. saturated fat, 0 mg. cholesterol, 8 mg. sodium, 0.3 g. protein, 57.2 g. carbohydrates, 4.4 g. dietary fiber.

Deep-Dish Cherry Cobbler

Cherry cobbler was one of the most popular recipes ever to appear in my newspaper column for single cooks. Readers have been especially pleased with the ease of preparation. As one put it, "Last night I tried my hand at that cherry cobbler, and it was so easy and delicious I surprised the heck out of myself."

This is an updated version of that recipe and is, I think, every bit as delicious as the original, though it has less than half the fat. Serve it warm, plain or topped with frozen vanilla yogurt.

Ingredients	For 2 servings	For 4 servings
Canned water-packed pitted sour cherries (with liquid)	1 cup	16 ounces
Sugar	¼ cup	½ cup
Cornstarch	1 teaspoon	2 teaspoons
Almond extract (optional)	⅛ teaspoon	¼ teaspoon
Reduced-fat biscuit mix	⅓ cup	⅔ cup
1% low-fat milk	2 tablespoons	¼ cup

Preheat the oven to 400°.

Drain the cherries, reserving the liquid. Measure the liquid and add water, if necessary, to make ½ cup (or 1 cup); set aside.

Spread the cherries in the bottom of a 3-cup shallow casserole (or an 8″ × 8″ baking pan).

In a small saucepan, mix the sugar and cornstarch. Stir in the liquid reserved from the cherries. Place over medium heat and bring the mixture to a boil, stirring constantly. Stir in the almond extract (if using) and pour the thickened liquid over the cherries.

In a small mixing bowl, stir together the biscuit mix and milk until just blended. Divide the dough into 2 (or 4) biscuits and spoon over the cherries.

Bake the cobbler for 15 minutes, or until the biscuits are browned and the cherries are bubbling. Serve warm or at room temperature.

Per serving: 194 calories, 2.8 g. total fat, 1.8 g. saturated fat, 1 mg. cholesterol, 127 mg. sodium, 2.2 g. protein, 42.6 g. carbohydrates, 0.5 g. dietary fiber.

Strawberry-Rhubarb Cobbler

Rhubarb has a tart-sweet taste that's a mirror image and magnifier of the sweet-tart taste of strawberries. I think that "pieplant," as rhubarb is sometimes called, is at its best when paired with strawberries, though blueberries aren't bad companions either. Make enough of this deep-dish cobbler to have some tonight and more tomorrow for breakfast.

Ingredients	For 2 servings	For 4 servings
Strawberries	1 cup	2 cups
Rhubarb stalks	4 ounces	8 ounces
Sugar	½ cup	1 cup
Cornstarch	4 teaspoons	2½ tablespoons
Reduced-fat biscuit mix	½ cup	1 cup
1% low-fat milk	3 tablespoons	6 tablespoons

Preheat the oven to 425°.

Wash the strawberries and drain them well. Remove the stems and cut large berries in half, but leave small berries whole. Cut the rhubarb stalks into ½" slices. Combine the strawberries and rhubarb in a medium mixing bowl.

In a small bowl, mix the sugar and cornstarch until lump-free, then toss the mixture gently with the fruit.

Turn the mixture into a 9" × 5" loaf pan (or an 8" × 8" baking pan) and cover the pan with foil.

Set the pan on a baking sheet and bake for 15 to 20 minutes, or until the fruit filling begins to look translucent.

In a small mixing bowl, stir together the biscuit mix and milk to make a stiff dough (add a little extra milk, if necessary).

Spoon the biscuit dough evenly over the filling. Bake, uncovered, for 10 minutes, or until the biscuits are browned and cooked through. Serve warm or at room temperature.

Per serving: 278 calories, 5 g. total fat, 1.2 g. saturated fat, 1 mg. cholesterol, 388 mg. sodium, 3.8 g. protein, 80.1 g. carbohydrates, 2.4 g. dietary fiber.

Old-Fashioned Strawberry Shortcake with Biscuits

Save this recipe to use again and again with all sorts of fresh fruits as they come into season: peaches, blueberries, raspberries, even apples handmade into sauce. Slice or crush fresh fruit for shortcake, then sweeten it to taste and serve at room temperature over warm split biscuits. Reheat leftover cold biscuits in the microwave for a few seconds or wrap them loosely in foil and heat briefly in a 350° oven.

To turn this recipe into blueberry shortcake, substitute 1 to 2 cups blueberries for the strawberries. For peach shortcake, use 1½ to 3 cups peeled and sliced peaches.

Ingredients	For 2 servings	For 4 servings
Strawberries	1 pint	1 quart
Sugar	3 tablespoons	6 tablespoons
Nonfat plain yogurt	½ cup	1 cup
Honey or dark brown sugar	1 tablespoon	2 tablespoons
Reduced-fat biscuit mix	½ cup + 1 tablespoon	1 cup + 2 tablespoons
Grated nutmeg (optional)	dash	⅛ teaspoon
1% low-fat milk	2–3 tablespoons	⅓ cup

Preheat the oven to 400°.

Wash the strawberries and drain them well. Remove the stems and cut the berries in half. Place in a medium mixing bowl. Add 1½ tablespoons (or 3 tablespoons) of the sugar, toss well and set aside.

In a small bowl, whisk the yogurt with the honey or brown sugar.

In another medium mixing bowl, combine the biscuit mix, nutmeg (if using) and the remaining sugar. Stir in the milk to form a stiff dough. Spoon the dough onto an ungreased baking sheet, making 2 (or 4) drop biscuits. Flatten each biscuit slightly with the palm of your hand. Bake the biscuits for 12 to 15 minutes, or until they are golden brown.

Split the hot biscuits. Place the bottom halves on individual plates. Spoon on some of the sweetened berries; replace the biscuit tops and spoon on the rest of the berries. Serve warm with the sweetened yogurt.

Per serving: 229 calories, 5.9 g. total fat, 1.5 g. saturated fat, 2 mg. cholesterol, 127 mg. sodium, 7.6 g. protein, 65.9 g. carbohydrates, 4.3 g. dietary fiber.

Peach Dumplings

Peach dumplings may sound down-home, but this luxurious and quickly made dessert is in reality a variation of an uptown theme devised by Chef Gary Danko of San Francisco's swank Ritz-Carlton. Chef Danko used strawberries in his dumplings as a salute to the Golden State's vast strawberry fields. I used peaches, as a salute to the Peach State, my Georgia home. For something entirely different, try blueberry dumplings. Substitute blueberries for the peaches, increase the water to ⅓ cup for each 2 servings and omit the almond extract.

Ingredients	For 2 servings	For 4 servings
Peeled and sliced peaches	1½ cups	3 cups
Light brown sugar, packed	⅓ cup	⅔ cup
Water	¼ cup	½ cup
Almond extract (optional)	⅛ teaspoon	¼ teaspoon
Reduced-fat biscuit mix	½ cup	1 cup
Sugar	1 tablespoon	2 tablespoons
1% low-fat milk	3 tablespoons	6 tablespoons

In a heavy, 8″ (or 10″) nonstick skillet, combine the peaches, brown sugar, water and almond extract (if using). Bring to a simmer over medium heat. Cover and cook for 3 to 5 minutes, or until the juices run freely from the peaches.

In a small mixing bowl, stir together the biscuit mix and sugar. Stir in the milk to form a stiff dough. Drop the dough onto the simmering peaches to make 4 (or 8) dumplings. Cook over medium heat for 5 minutes. Then cover the skillet and cook for 10 to 12 minutes, or until the dumplings are cooked through. Serve warm in shallow soup bowls, with the peaches spooned over the dumplings.

Per serving: 263 calories, 4.9 g. total fat, 1.3 g. saturated fat, 1 mg. cholesterol, 400 mg. sodium, 4 g. protein, 76.3 g. carbohydrates, 2.4 g. dietary fiber.

Blueberry Flummery

When good bread goes stale, give thanks and turn it into flummery, which is nothing more than lightly buttered bread soaked in simmered blueberries (or blackberries or raspberries). Chilled and eaten blissfully with low-fat yogurt or sour cream, flummery tastes like a minimalist cobbler. If fresh berries are out of season, use unsweetened frozen ones. Don't overlook this time-honored dessert just because it sounds (and is) so simple to make.

Ingredients	For 2 servings	For 4 servings
Blueberries	1 cup	2 cups
Sugar	¼ cup	½ cup
Water	1 tablespoon	2 tablespoons
Thinly sliced stale white bread	3 slices	6 slices
Butter or margarine, softened	1 tablespoon	2 tablespoons

In a small heavy saucepan, mix the blueberries, sugar and water. Place over medium heat and bring to a boil, stirring often. Cook for 2 to 4 minutes, or until the berries begin to burst. Remove the pan from the heat and set it aside.

Remove the crusts from the bread. Spread the top side of each slice with 1 teaspoon of the butter or margarine. Arrange 1 slice, buttered side up, in the bottom of a 1-quart casserole (or arrange 2 slices in a small loaf pan). Pour half the hot berries over the bread. Top with 1 slice (or 2 slices) of bread. Add the remaining berries. Top with the remaining bread, buttered side down. Cover with plastic wrap. Press the bread into the berries by placing a small can of pineapple or tuna on top of the plastic wrap.

Chill the flummery for 2 hours or overnight. Serve cold.

Per serving: 273 calories, 7.3 g. total fat, 3.9 g. saturated fat, 15 mg. cholesterol, 240 mg. sodium, 3.4 g. protein, 51 g. carbohydrates, 2.3 g. dietary fiber.

Old-Time Bread Pudding

Here's comfort food for you: a downsized version of an old-time treat, bread pudding. Use the recipe as a basic pattern for creating your own bread puddings; try substituting brown sugar for white sugar, grated orange rind or lemon rind for the cinnamon, low-fat chocolate milk for white milk and so forth. As for your bread choice, it can be white, French, whole-wheat, whole-grain, oat or even rye or pumpernickel.

Ingredients	For 2 servings	For 4 servings
Cubed stale bread	1½ cups	3 cups
Sugar	2 tablespoons	¼ cup
Raisins (optional)	1 tablespoon	2 tablespoons
Ground cinnamon or grated nutmeg	⅛ teaspoon	¼ teaspoon
Egg	1 white	1 whole
1% low-fat milk	½ cup	1 cup
Butter or margarine, melted	1 teaspoon	2 teaspoons

Preheat the oven to 325°.

Place the bread in a medium mixing bowl and sprinkle with the sugar, raisins (if using) and cinnamon or nutmeg.

In a small mixing bowl, beat together the egg white (or whole egg), milk and butter or margarine. Pour over the bread and stir well.

Transfer the mixture to a shallow 3-cup (or 1-quart) baking dish or casserole. Bake on the middle shelf of the oven for 20 to 25 (or 25 to 30) minutes, or until lightly browned and slightly puffed. Serve warm or cold.

Per serving: 243 calories, 6.6 g. total fat, 2.7 g. saturated fat, 114 mg. cholesterol, 281 mg. sodium, 8.8 g. protein, 37.8 g. carbohydrates, 1.3 g. dietary fiber.

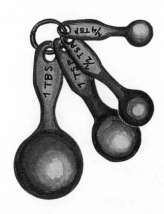

Rice Custard

This is the best recipe for rice pudding I know. Of course, it's cut down considerably from the original, which was an old Stouffer's quantity recipe for 50 servings. My prototype recipe dates back to the 1940s and 1950s, when Stouffer's was a restaurant chain with Irish waitresses and freshly made homestyle desserts like this one.

Ingredients	For 2 servings	For 4 servings
1% low-fat milk	1¼ cups	2½ cups
Long-grain white rice	2½ tablespoons	⅓ cup
Ground cinnamon	dash	⅛ teaspoon
Salt (optional)	dash	⅛ teaspoon
Eggs	1	2
Sugar	2 tablespoons	¼ cup
Vanilla	¼ teaspoon	½ teaspoon
Seedless raisins (optional)	1 tablespoon	2 tablespoons

In a small heavy saucepan, mix the milk, rice, cinnamon and salt (if using). Bring the mixture to a simmer over medium heat, then reduce the heat to low and cook, stirring occasionally, for 20 minutes, or until the rice is tender.

In a medium mixing bowl, beat together the eggs, sugar and vanilla; beat in the hot rice mixture, then transfer the mixture back to the saucepan. Cook, stirring, for 2 minutes longer. Stir in the raisins (if using) and pour the pudding into serving dishes. Cover with plastic wrap and chill for 2 hours or overnight.

Per serving: 225 calories, 4.4 g. total fat, 1.9 g. saturated fat, 113 mg. cholesterol, 256 mg. sodium, 10.4 g. protein, 36.2 g. carbohydrates, 0.4 g. dietary fiber.

Chocolate Pudding

Chocolate pudding, that innocent treat of the nursery school set, acquires grown-up sophistication in this new low-fat treatment. Made with cocoa instead of chocolate, it tastes so rich you'll never guess that it has dropped most of the fat.

Ingredients	For 2 servings	For 4 servings
1% low-fat milk	¾ cup	1½ cups
Sugar	¼ cup	½ cup
Unsweetened cocoa powder	2½ tablespoons	⅓ cup
All-purpose flour	1½ tablespoons	¼ cup
Egg	1 yolk	1 whole
Vanilla	¼ teaspoon	½ teaspoon

Place the milk in a 2-cup (or 4-cup) microwave-safe glass measure. Microwave on high power for 2 to 4 minutes, or until a skin begins to form on top of the milk, but the milk is not quite boiling.

In a medium glass bowl, whisk together the sugar, cocoa and flour. Gradually whisk in the hot milk and stir until smooth. Microwave on high for 1 to 2 minutes, or until the mixture thickens; stop and stir every 30 seconds during this time.

In a cup, lightly beat the egg yolk (or whole egg) and vanilla. Slowly whisk into the hot chocolate mixture. Microwave on high for 30 seconds (or 1 minute) longer.

Cover the surface of the pudding with plastic wrap to prevent a skin from forming and chill for 2 hours or overnight. Serve cold.

Per serving: 200 calories, 4.3 g. total fat, 1.4 g. saturated fat, 110 mg. cholesterol, 54 mg. sodium, 6.5 g. protein, 8.2 g. carbohydrates, 0.2 g. dietary fiber.

Lemon Sponge Pudding

Lemon sponge dates back to the 1950s and is a combination soufflé, sponge cake and custard. Try it served with a handful of fresh raspberries or blueberries scattered over the top.

Ingredients	For 2 servings	For 4 servings
Eggs, separated	1	2
1% low-fat milk	½ cup	1 cup
Grated lemon rind	1 teaspoon	2 teaspoons
Lemon juice	2 tablespoons	¼ cup
Butter or margarine, melted	1½ teaspoons	1 tablespoon
Sugar	⅓ cup	⅔ cup
All-purpose flour, unsifted	2½ tablespoons	⅓ cup
Baking powder	¼ teaspoon	½ teaspoon

Preheat the oven to 350°.

In a small mixing bowl, beat the egg yolks and milk until well-blended. Then beat in the lemon rind, lemon juice and butter or margarine.

In a medium bowl, sift together the sugar, flour and baking powder. Add to the egg mixture and beat until smooth.

In a clean, dry bowl, beat the egg whites until stiff but not dry. Fold them into the lemon mixture. Divide evenly among 8-ounce custard cups.

Set the cups in a baking pan on the middle shelf of the oven. Pour enough boiling water into the pan to reach a depth of ½". Bake for 20 to 25 minutes, or until the puddings are browned and slightly cracked on top. Serve warm or chilled.

Per serving: 246 calories, 6 g. total fat, 2.9 g. saturated fat, 117 mg. cholesterol, 133 mg. sodium, 6.1 g. protein, 43.6 g. carbohydrates, 0.3 g. dietary fiber.

Sweet Potato Pudding

What a glorious way to eat your vegetables! Beyond fiber, sweet potato spoonbread packs a powerful punch of beta-carotene thanks to the deep-orange sweet potatoes. If you don't have a kitchen scale (and most folks don't), weigh the sweet potatoes on the store's scales when you buy them.

Ingredients	For 2 servings	For 4 servings
Sweet potatoes	6 ounces	12 ounces
Butter or margarine	½ teaspoon	1 teaspoon
1% low-fat milk	½ cup	1 cup
Brown sugar, packed	¼ cup	½ cup
Eggs	1	2
Ground cinnamon	¼ teaspoon	½ teaspoon
Salt	¼ teaspoon	½ teaspoon
Vanilla	1½ teaspoons	1 tablespoon
Pecan halves	6	12

Preheat the oven to 350°.

Prick the sweet potatoes in several places with a fork and place them on a microwave-safe plate. Microwave on high power for 6 to 8 minutes, or until tender. (Alternatively, bake the sweet potatoes in a conventional oven at 375° for 1 hour.) Let cool.

Grease 2 (or 4) 1-cup ovenproof custard cups or gratin dishes with the butter or margarine.

Peel the sweet potatoes, cut them into large chunks and put them in a blender. Add the milk, brown sugar, eggs, cinnamon, salt and vanilla. Blend the mixture until it is smooth.

Pour about ¾ cup of the sweet potato mixture into each custard cup. Arrange 3 pecan halves on top of each spoonbread. Place the dishes on a baking sheet and bake for 25 to 30 minutes, or until the mixture is browned around the edges and slightly puffed. Serve warm or chilled.

Per serving: 288 calories, 5.7 g. total fat, 1.4 g. saturated fat, 109 mg. cholesterol, 391 mg. sodium, 7.3 g. protein, 52.5 g. carbohydrates, 2.8 g. dietary fiber.

New-Age Soft Custard

If you won't drink your milk, eat it in delicious desserts like this creamy custard. Made without fuss in less than 10 minutes using a microwave, this is the ultimate comfort food. Enjoy it chilled and unadorned as a dessert or use it as a scrumptious sauce over strawberries, blueberries or sliced peaches, kiwis or bananas.

Ingredients	For 2 servings	For 4 servings
1% low-fat milk	¾ cup	1½ cups
Sugar	2 tablespoons	¼ cup
Eggs	1	2
Vanilla	¼ teaspoon	½ teaspoon

In a 2-cup (or 4-cup) microwave-safe glass measure, combine the milk and sugar. Microwave on high power for 3 (or 5) minutes, or until the milk just comes to the boiling point.

In a glass mixing bowl, whisk together the eggs and vanilla until foamy. Gradually whisk in the hot milk.

Microwave on medium-low power (50%) for 1 minute, or until the custard just begins to thicken; stop and stir after 30 seconds. Do not overcook or the custard will curdle.

Immediately pour the custard into a refrigerator container and cool it uncovered to lukewarm. (The custard will continue to thicken as it cools.) Cover the container and chill for 2 hours or overnight before serving.

Per serving: 129 calories, 3.6 g. total fat, 1.4 g. saturated fat, 110 mg. cholesterol, 85 mg. sodium, 6.8 g. protein, 17.6 g. carbohydrates, 0 g. dietary fiber.

Biscotti Allegro

Don't attempt this recipe without an electric mixer or a strong arm because, in the true Italian tradition, the biscotti depend on air bubbles beaten into the eggs for leavening power. With a hand-held or stationary mixer, these twice-baked cookies are easy to make. They're even easier to eat, especially late in the afternoon when you get that "I can't wait 'til dinner" sensation. It really takes no more time or trouble to make a double batch. And since these biscotti keep almost indefinitely in a tightly closed container, you might want to make the larger amount.

Ingredients	For 12 biscotti	For 24 biscotti
Eggs	2	4
Sugar	10 tablespoons	1¼ cups
Anise seeds	2 teaspoons	4 teaspoons
All-purpose flour, unsifted	1¼ cups	2½ cups

Preheat the oven to 375°.

Lightly butter and flour 1 (or 2) 9″ × 5″ loaf pans and set aside.

Combine the eggs and sugar in a medium mixing bowl. Beat on high speed with an electric mixer for 10 minutes, scraping down the bowl several times. Beat in the anise seeds. Reduce the mixer speed to low and gently fold in the flour just until incorporated. Do not overmix once you've added the flour—this can make the cookies tough.

Turn the batter into the prepared pans and bake for 25 minutes, or until the top looks crusty and pale gold. Turn the biscotti loaves out of the pans onto a wire rack and cool them for 15 minutes.

Using a serrated knife, cut each loaf into 12 slices about ¾″ thick. Arrange the slices in a single layer on an ungreased baking sheet. Bake for 7 minutes. Flip the cookies and bake them another 7 minutes, or until the biscotti are very crisp and golden beige on both sides.

Transfer the cookies to a wire rack and cool to room temperature. Store in an airtight container.

Per biscotti: 98 calories, 1 g. total fat, 0.3 g. saturated fat, 35 mg. cholesterol, 11 mg. sodium, 2.4 g. protein, 20.1 g. carbohydrates, 0.4 dietary fiber.

Triple-Ginger Cupcakes

I've been hooked on ginger ever since I was 8 or 9 years old, when my daddy used to bring me chocolate-covered candied ginger from New York. I've used three varieties of ginger here in these moist cupcakes: grated fresh ginger, candied ginger and ground ginger. (If necessary, you could leave out one or two and still enjoy them.) Have these spicy, single-serving cakes plain or with applesauce or a spoonful of Chocolate Glaze. And for the ultimate peach shortcake, split the warm cupcakes and layer them with lightly sweetened fresh peach slices. These cupcakes freeze well and will last for up to 3 months.

Ingredients	For 8 cupcakes	For 16 cupcakes
Light brown sugar, packed	¼ cup	½ cup
Eggs	1	2
Low-fat plain yogurt	6 tablespoons	¾ cup
Molasses	¼ cup	½ cup
Canola oil or melted butter (optional)	2 tablespoons	¼ cup
Candied ginger	1 tablespoon	2 tablespoons
Grated fresh ginger	1½ teaspoons	1 tablespoon
All-purpose flour, unsifted	¾ cup + 2 tablespoons	1¾ cups
Ground ginger	½ teaspoon	1 teaspoon
Baking soda	½ teaspoon	1 teaspoon

Preheat the oven to 375°.

Line muffin cups with fluted paper liners. (If your muffin tin holds more cupcakes than you are making, pour water into the empty cups until they are half-full. This will help distribute heat evenly in your pan and keep your cupcakes from scorching.)

In a medium mixing bowl, combine the brown sugar, eggs, yogurt, molasses and oil or butter (if using). Beat until smooth. Stir in the candied ginger and grated ginger.

In another medium mixing bowl, sift together the flour, ground ginger and baking soda. Add to the egg mixture and stir only to blend. Do not overmix or the cupcakes will be tough; the batter should be a little lumpy.

Fill each muffin cup ⅔ full of batter. Bake for 15 to 20 minutes, or until the cupcakes are browned on top and no imprint remains when the top of a cupcake is lightly pressed.

Cool for 5 minutes in the pan on a wire rack, then remove the cupcakes from the pan and finish cooling them on the rack.

Per cupcake: 148 calories, 4.4 g. total fat, 0.6 g. saturated fat, 27 mg. cholesterol, 71 mg. sodium, 2.8 g. protein, 24.7 g. carbohydrates, 0.4 g. dietary fiber.

Caramel-Glazed Bananas

Choose bananas tinged with green for this simple dessert. Turn it into a luscious hot banana split by adding frozen vanilla yogurt and a spoonful of Chocolate Glaze.

Ingredients	For 1 serving	For 2 servings
Bananas	1	2
Melted butter or margarine	1 teaspoon	2 teaspoons
Dark or light brown sugar	1 tablespoon	2 tablespoons
Orange juice or rum	1 tablespoon	2 tablespoons
Ground cinnamon or grated nutmeg (optional)	dash	⅛ teaspoon

Preheat the oven to 400°.

Peel the bananas, cut in half lengthwise and place each banana in an individual shallow oval baking dish or gratin dish.

In a small bowl, combine the butter or margarine, brown sugar, orange juice or rum and cinnamon or nutmeg (if using); pour the mixture over the bananas.

Bake for 10 to 12 minutes, or until the syrup is bubbling and the bananas are slightly browned. Serve hot or warm.

Per serving: 222 calories, 4.3 g. total fat, 2.6 g. saturated fat, 10 mg. cholesterol, 44 mg. sodium, 1.2 g. protein, 40 g. carbohydrates, 3.7 g. dietary fiber.

Chocolate Glaze

This delectably dark and shiny glaze is wonderful on Pears Poached in Red Wine, Triple-Ginger Cupcakes and Banana Loaf. (This amount is enough for a small Banana Loaf; double it to glaze a larger loaf.) Because it gets its rich chocolate flavor mainly from cocoa powder, it's fairly low in fat.

⅓ cup confectioners' sugar

1½ tablespoons unsweetened cocoa powder

½ ounce unsweetened chocolate

2 tablespoons water

Sift the sugar and cocoa into a small mixing bowl.

Place the chocolate and water in a microwave-safe cup. Microwave on high power for 1 minute, or until the chocolate is softened (it might not look melted; do not overheat). Stir rapidly to make a smooth paste, then stir the chocolate paste into the cocoa mixture until smooth. Use the glaze while it is warm, for easy spreading.

Makes ⅓ cup

Per tablespoon: 44 calories, 1.7 g. total fat, 0 g. saturated fat, 0 mg. cholesterol, 2 mg. sodium, 0.7 g. protein, 8.8 g. carbohydrates, 0 g. dietary fiber.

Banana Loaf

This loaf freezes successfully, so you needn't worry about making too much. Although it's delicious as is, it's even better with Chocolate Glaze. You can glaze the whole loaf and serve it on successive days. Or you can freeze individual slices of the banana bread and glaze them after they thaw.

Ingredients	For 8 slices	For 16 slices
Sifted all-purpose flour	1¼ cups	2½ cups
Baking powder	½ teaspoon	1 teaspoon
Baking soda	¼ teaspoon	½ teaspoon
Sugar	⅓ cup	⅔ cup
Eggs	1	2
Butter or margarine, softened	2 tablespoons	¼ cup
Mashed ripe bananas	½ cup	1 cup
Low-fat plain yogurt	2 tablespoons	¼ cup
Chopped pecans or walnuts (optional)	¼ cup	½ cup

Preheat the oven to 350°.

Grease and flour a 4½″ × 8″ (or 9″ × 5″) loaf pan.

In a medium mixing bowl, sift together the flour, baking powder and baking soda.

In another medium mixing bowl, beat the sugar, eggs and butter or margarine until fluffy. Slowly beat in the bananas and yogurt. Add the flour mixture and mix just until blended. Do not overmix or the cake will be tough. Stir in the pecans or walnuts (if using).

Spoon the batter into the prepared pan and bake on the middle shelf of the oven for 35 to 40 (or 50 to 60) minutes, or until a wooden toothpick inserted in the center of the cake comes out clean.

Cool the cake in the pan on a wire rack for 5 minutes, then invert the pan onto the rack and let cool completely. Wrap tightly in plastic wrap and let stand overnight to mellow the flavors.

Per slice: 186 calories, 6.2 g. total fat, 2.2 g. saturated fat, 34 mg. cholesterol, 86 mg. sodium, 3.6 g. protein, 30.6 g. carbohydrates, 1.2 g. dietary fiber.

Pears Poached in Red Wine

I've pared down a Cordon Bleu classic. Make it a day ahead to give the pears a chance to soak up the ruby-red syrup. If it pleases you, serve these pretty pears with a dollop of low-fat frozen yogurt and a spoonful of Chocolate Glaze. If you can't find stick cinnamon, try 4 to 8 whole allspice berries. Be sure to use firm pears. Bosc and D'Anjou are especially good choices.

Ingredients	For 2 servings	For 4 servings
Dry red wine	1 cup	2 cups
Water	½ cup	1 cup
Sugar	2½ tablespoons	⅓ cup
Cinnamon stick	½ medium	1 medium
Vanilla	½ teaspoon	1 teaspoon
Firm pears, peeled	2 medium	4 medium

Pour the wine and water into a saucepan wide enough to hold the pears in a single layer. Add the sugar, cinnamon and vanilla and bring to a simmer over medium heat; stir occasionally to dissolve the sugar.

Add the pears and turn to coat them on all sides. Bring the mixture back to a simmer. Cover the saucepan and cook the pears for 20 to 30 minutes, or until they can be easily pierced with a sharp knife and are just tender; occasionally turn the pears in the liquid so they color evenly.

With a slotted spoon, transfer the pears to a bowl. Rapidly boil down the syrup until it's reduced by half; pour the syrup over the pears. Let cool to room temperature, then cover and chill overnight before serving.

Per serving: 217 calories, 0.6 g. total fat, 0 g. saturated fat, 0 mg. cholesterol, 7 mg. sodium, 0.7 g. protein, 41.2 g. carbohydrates, 3.7 g. dietary fiber.

Desserts

Chalet Suzanne Broiled Grapefruit

This particular broiled grapefruit is a signature dish at Chalet Suzanne, a well-frequented resort of the rich and famous near Lake Wales, Florida. Chalet Suzanne is run by the Hinshaw family and still serves grapefruit the way the original founder, Bertha Hinshaw, used to. This is basically Bertha's recipe, minus most of the butter. It's appropriate for an appetizer as well as a dessert.

Ingredients	For 1 serving	For 2 servings
Grapefruit, halved crosswise	½ medium	1 medium
Butter or margarine, softened	1 teaspoon	2 teaspoons
Sugar	1 tablespoon	2 tablespoons
Ground cinnamon	¼ teaspoon	½ teaspoon

Preheat the broiler.

Trim out the center of each grapefruit half. Loosen the sections of the grapefruit by running a paring knife around each segment to separate it from the rind and the membrane. For each serving, place 1 teaspoon of the butter or margarine and 1 teaspoon of the sugar in the center of the grapefruit.

Mix the remaining sugar with the cinnamon and sprinkle evenly over the halves. Place the grapefruit on a broiler pan and broil 3″ to 4″ from the heat source for 5 minutes, or until bubbling hot and lightly browned.

Per serving: 117 calories, 3.9 g. total fat, 2.4 g. saturated fat, 10 mg. cholesterol, 39 mg. sodium, 0.7 g. protein, 21.7 g. carbohydrates, 1.6 g. dietary fiber.

Oranges Alhambra

This Spanish dessert makes a light ending to a meal. The inspiration came from a dessert I once had at the end of a meal of tapas—delicious snacks that frequently accompany drinks in Spain. And although this dessert is luxurious, it's wonderfully good, simple to make and very low in fat.

Ingredients	For 1 serving	For 2 servings
Navel oranges	1 large	2 large
Orange marmalade	1 tablespoon	2 tablespoons
Cream sherry	1 tablespoon	2 tablespoons
Toasted slivered almonds	1 tablespoon	2 tablespoons

Peel the oranges, removing all the white pith. Cut crosswise into thick slices. Arrange in a serving dish.

Place the marmalade in a microwave-safe, 1-cup glass measure and microwave on high power for 30 to 60 seconds, just until the marmalade melts. Stir in the sherry and spoon the mixture evenly over the orange slices. Cover and chill for 2 hours or overnight to blend the flavors. Just before serving, sprinkle with the almonds.

Per serving: 191 calories, 4 g. total fat, 0.4 g. saturated fat, 0 mg. cholesterol, 3 mg. sodium, 3.1 g. protein, 36.2 g. carbohydrates, 5 g. dietary fiber.

Strawberry Bleeding Hearts

This is a romantic dessert to serve at the close of an intimate dinner, though there's no reason you can't enjoy it when you're alone. For an elegant effect, spoon the strawberries into crystal goblets. And if you're in the mood for indulgence, place a single chocolate truffle—the best and most expensive you can find—alongside.

Ingredients	For 1 serving	For 2 servings
Frozen raspberries in syrup, thawed	5 ounces	10 ounces
Cassis (black currant liqueur), optional	1 tablespoon	2 tablespoons
Strawberries	1 cup	1 pint

Combine the raspberries (with syrup) and cassis (if using) in a blender and puree on high speed, stopping several times to scrape down the sides. Strain the raspberries into a mixing bowl, pressing down with the back of a spoon to extract as much pulp and juice as possible; set the liquid aside and discard the seeds.

Wash the strawberries, drain well and remove the stems. Slice them in half lengthwise to get the heart shape. Mix gently with the pureed raspberries. Serve immediately or cover and refrigerate for up to 2 hours before serving.

Per serving: 236 calories, 0.8 g. total fat, 0 g. saturated fat, 0 mg. cholesterol, 3 mg. sodium, 1.9 g. protein, 51.8 g. carbohydrates, 10.1 g. dietary fiber.

Frozen Strawberry Yogurt

No need to make a special trip to the frozen yogurt bar when you get a hankering for frozen yogurt. Make it in your blender, 1 or 2 healthy low-fat servings at a time. You can use strawberries, as I do here, or replace them with frozen peaches, blueberries or bananas.

Ingredients	For 1 serving	For 2 servings
Partially frozen strawberries	1 cup	2 cups
Sugar	1 tablespoon	2 tablespoons
Low-fat plain yogurt	½ cup	1 cup

Place the strawberries in a blender and sprinkle them with the sugar. Allow them to thaw briefly, for 15 to 20 minutes.

Add the yogurt, cover and blend the mixture on high speed for 30 seconds, or until smooth and about the consistency of soft-serve ice cream. Serve immediately in chilled dishes or crystal goblets.

Per serving: 169 calories, 1.9 g. total fat, 1.1 g. saturated fat, 7 mg. cholesterol, 83 mg. sodium, 6.6 g. protein, 33.6 g. carbohydrates, 3.9 g. dietary fiber.

Fruit Sorbet

You don't need an ice cream maker to whip up refreshing fruit sorbet. All you really need is a blender—and some frozen fruit and a shot of simple syrup. Simple syrup gives sorbet a creamy consistency and just the right amount of sweetness.

To make ¼ cup of simple syrup—enough for 2 servings of sorbet—mix 3 tablespoons sugar and 3 tablespoons water in a small saucepan. Bring the mixture to a boil, then let it cool before using. Because simple syrup keeps indefinitely in the refrigerator, you might want to prepare a larger batch and keep it on hand.

You can make any flavor sorbet you like. Strawberry is wonderful, but so are raspberry, peach, blueberry or blackberry. You can even mix flavors—try raspberry and cantaloupe for a really refreshing combination.

Ingredients	For 1 serving	For 2 servings
Frozen fruit	1 cup	2 cups
Simple syrup	2 tablespoons	¼ cup

Place the fruit in a blender and let it stand for 15 to 20 minutes to thaw slightly. Add the simple syrup and blend on medium speed until the fruit is pureed, stopping the motor as necessary to scrape down the sides of the blender. Serve immediately in chilled dishes or crystal goblets.

Per serving: 119 calories, 0.2 g. total fat, 0 g. saturated fat, 0 mg. cholesterol, 4 mg. sodium, 0.6 g. protein, 31.6 g. carbohydrates, 3.9 g. dietary fiber.

Frozen Fruit When You Want It

To prepare your own frozen yogurt or fruit sorbets, you can use commercially frozen peaches, blueberries, strawberries, raspberries or melon balls. Or you can freeze your own seasonal fruits when they're plentiful, cheap and at their peak of flavor.

First prep the fruit as though you were going to eat it. Peel peaches, nectarines and bananas, then thinly slice them. Pit and stem sweet cherries. Remove the caps from strawberries. Peel, seed and cube cantaloupe and honeydew melons. Pick over blueberries, raspberries, blackberries and other small berries; wash them only if they need it.

Spread well-drained prepared fruit in a single layer in a baking pan, then freeze just until the pieces are firm. Transfer the fruit to heavy-duty, resealable plastic bags and return them to the freezer until you crave sorbet or frozen fruit yogurt.

Use the fruits singly or create interesting combinations. Highly recommended are blueberries with honeydew, strawberries with raspberries and white peaches with raspberries or blackberries.

I wouldn't recommend using fibrous fruits like pineapple and mango. They tend to get hung up in the blender blades when you try to process them.

Healthy

MENU
Pumpkin Clam Chowder
Southern Skillet Cornbread
Broccoli Slaw
Triple Gi

Menus

*T*he menus in this chapter are flexible; they are meant to give you ideas for simple, inviting meals that will add variety and flavor to your diet without extra fat. There are times when you may want to treat yourself by preparing a feast that includes several courses, and I've given menus for those occasions. But a meal can also be as simple as soup accompanied by a crusty slice of good bread and followed by a succulent piece of fresh fruit. I've included lots of such no-fuss menus.

If you are trying to get more fruits and vegetables into your diet, take my advice: Treat yourself to the best. You're worth it, and if a bowl of tiny strawberries can tempt you away from salty, fattening and expensive snacks, they're worth it, too.

Here are a few things to keep in mind as you use this chapter.

* The menus include recipes you will find in this book (in bold-face type) plus other basic foods, such as milk, oranges and French bread. If you do not see a page number following a menu item, it is not a recipe that you will find in this book.
* Nutrient amounts given are for one serving of the size indicated in that recipe, unless otherwise noted; in these menus, I sometimes reduce the size of a serving of soup or salad when it accompanies other foods. In general, you will find the portions in this book are generous and filling.
* Values are given for calories, total grams of fat and grams of saturated fat.

The Skinny on Fat

In spite of all the talk about dietary fat, to most Americans a gram of fat remains as mysterious as a quark. The United States is one of the few countries in the world to use ounces, pounds and quarts as units of measurement rather than milligrams, grams and liters, which is why we have so much trouble visualizing fat in grams. So, just how much—or how big—is a gram of fat? Slightly less than a fifth of a teaspoon.

Picture 5 grams of fat as a level teaspoon of solid white lard. (You vegetarians can picture vegetable shortening.) Though 5 grams of pure fat will fill a teaspoon, nothing in life is completely pure, including fat. So the actual numbers are slightly lower: 1 teaspoon of butter or stick margarine has 3.8 grams of fat; 1 teaspoon of lard, vegetable shortening or beef tallow contains around 4.2 grams of fat. Vegetable oils are slightly higher in fat, averaging 4.5 grams per teaspoon.

Unfortunately, fat isn't packaged exclusively in easy-to-recognize fats and oils. Almost every edible known to man, including lettuce, contains fat in amounts that range from infinitesimal to a whole heap, depending on the food. Before you can make meaningful food choices and plan menus that are balanced for good nutrition as well as fat, you need to know how many teaspoons of fat you're allotted daily. Most experts agree that a healthy diet gets 30 percent or less of its calories from fat. Here's an easy way to translate that into a number that you can use and understand.

Divide your ideal weight by two; the answer is your daily allotment of fat in grams.

A woman who weighs (or wants to weigh) 120 pounds would have a daily fat allotment of 60 grams. (At approximately 5 grams of fat per teaspoon, that comes to 12 teaspoons.) A man weighing 180 pounds would be allowed 90 grams (18 teaspoons). This method is easy to use but a little oversimplified; you will probably need to adjust your answer according to your sex, age, health and exercise habits. Check with your doctor before making any big changes in your diet.

Now that you have a ballpark figure of your allotted fat intake, use food labels, menus such as those in this chapter and nutrient analyses such as the ones accompanying my recipes to help yourself keep a running total of your fat consumption.

Menu	Calories	Total fat	Saturated fat
		(grams)	*(grams)*

Fast Breakfasts & Leisurely Brunches

Menu	Calories	Total fat	Saturated fat
Breakfast in a Glass (page 20)	300	1.6	0.3
1 toasted whole-wheat bagel	163	1.4	0
1 tablespoon cherry jam	55	0	0
Total	**518**	**3.0**	**0.3**
¾ cup fresh orange juice	83	0.4	0
Irish Fruit & Fiber (page 23)	126	1.0	0.2
1 cup nonfat yogurt	127	0.4	0.3
Total	**336**	**1.8**	**0.5**
1 tangerine, sectioned	37	0.2	0
Pecan Brancakes with Cider Syrup (page 26)	344	11.5	2.3
Total	**381**	**11.7**	**2.3**
Strawberry-Banana Smoothie (page 20)	213	0.7	0.2
Apple-Walnut Bran Muffin (page 24)	115	4.1	0.6
Total	**328**	**4.8**	**0.8**
1 cup blueberries	81	0.6	0.1
Apricot & Almond Granola (page 22)	204	6.9	0.8
1 cup nonfat yogurt	127	0.4	0.3
Total	**412**	**7.9**	**1.2**
1 wedge honeydew melon	49	0.4	0
Fried Green Tomatoes with Country Gravy (page 130)	158	8.8	5.3
1 ounce pan-sizzled deli ham	66	4.8	2.3
2 reduced-fat biscuits	210	4.0	1.0
Total	**483**	**18.0**	**8.6**
Greengrocer's Frittata (page 146)	305	19.3	5.3
1 slice seven-grain bread, toasted	68	0.8	0
1 cup strawberries	55	0.7	0
1 cup nonfat yogurt sweetened with honey	131	0	0
Total	**559**	**20.8**	**5.3**

Menu	Calories	Total fat	Saturated fat
		(grams)	*(grams)*

Summer Lunches & Dinners

Menu	Calories	Total fat	Saturated fat
Corn & Red Pepper Chowder (page 69)	183	7.1	4.2
2 dinner rolls	168	2.8	1.1
Peach Dumplings (page 265)	263	4.9	1.3
Total	**614**	**14.8**	**6.6**
Mauve Decade Borscht (page 63)	101	0.8	0.3
Epicurean Roast Beef Salad (page 115)	237	4.6	1.5
2 slices French baguette	88	1.0	0
Old-Fashioned Strawberry Shortcake with Biscuits (page 264)	229	5.9	1.5
Total	**655**	**12.3**	**3.3**
½ serving Green & White Minestrone (page 66)	78	2.0	0.3
Personalized Pizza (page 39)	295	11.6	3.8
1 cup dark sweet cherries	82	0.4	0
Total	**455**	**14.0**	**4.1**
New Maryland Crab Cakes (page 196)	256	12.7	2.0
New-Wave Corn on the Cob (page 237)	83	1.0	0.2
Thin and Creamy Coleslaw (page 93)	83	2.1	1.2
1 thick slice watermelon	111	0.9	0
Total	**533**	**16.7**	**3.4**
Shaved Fennel & Parmesan Cheese (page 96)	144	11.2	3.7
Roasted Eggplant Parmesan (page 131)	248	13.6	4.2
2 slices crusty Italian bread	56	0.2	0
Peach slices sweetened with 1 tablespoon honey	122	0.2	0
1 Biscotti Allegro (page 273)	98	1.0	0.3
Total	**668**	**26.2**	**8.2**

Menu	Calories	Total fat	Saturated fat
		(grams)	*(grams)*
Fire & Ice Bisque (page 61)	90	0.6	0.1
Big Easy Salad of Red Beans & Rice (page 113)	487	9.4	1.4
1 slice French bread	44	0.5	0.1
Banana Loaf (page 277) with **Chocolate Glaze** (page 276)	230	7.9	2.2
Total	**851**	**18.4**	**3.8**
Texas Caviar (page 50)	127	4.1	0.6
Pan-Fried Catfish (page 180)	253	10.8	2.0
Polenta from the Microwave (page 129)	126	0.6	0.1
New Light Greens (page 244)	122	5.4	0.7
Peach Dumplings (page 265)	263	4.9	1.3
Total	**891**	**25.8**	**4.7**
Country-Style Cucumbers (page 101)	21	2.8	0
China Clipper Steamed Shrimp (page 202)	280	9.5	1.5
1 French roll	156	1.6	0.5
1 cup blueberries with ¼ cup nonfat lemon yogurt	192	0.8	0.2
Total	**649**	**14.7**	**2.2**
Gazpacho Salad (page 102)	97	4.2	0.6
Fettuccine with Spinach & Feta (page 125)	449	20.1	9.6
1 slice toasted French bread	44	0.5	0
Fruit Sorbet (page 282)	119	0.2	0
Total	**709**	**25.0**	**10.2**
½ serving **Curried Bisque of Summer Squash** (page 60)	68	3.0	1.6
Smoked Turkey & Fruit Salad (page 108)	209	6.6	1.0
1 whole-wheat pita	44	0.5	0
Frozen Strawberry Yogurt (page 282)	169	1.9	1.1
Total	**490**	**12.0**	**3.7**

Menu	Calories	Total fat	Saturated fat
		(grams)	*(grams)*

Fall Lunches & Dinners

Menu	Calories	Total fat	Saturated fat
Salmon Panned in Orange Sauce (page 192)	293	13.4	2.9
Nanaw's Cream-Style Corn (page 242)	85	1.0	0.2
½ cup steamed broccoli	40	0.5	0
1 whole-wheat roll	150	2.8	0.9
1 fresh peach	58	0.2	0
Total	**626**	**17.9**	**4.0**
Autumn Vegetables with Balsamic Sauce (page 140)	254	7.5	0.8
1 slice cracked-wheat toast with 1 ounce Cheddar cheese	172	9.8	4.8
Chocolate Pudding (page 269)	200	4.3	1.4
Total	**626**	**21.6**	**7.0**
Esau's Pottage of Lentils & Leeks (page 136)	421	5.6	0.8
Beefsteak Tomato & Sweet Onion Salad (page 100)	152	7.8	1.1
Oranges Alhambra (page 280)	191	4.0	0.4
Total	**764**	**17.4**	**2.3**
Couscous with Sweet Potatoes & Yellow Squash (page 138)	668	10.4	1.4
2 slices whole-wheat French bread	102	1.2	0.6
1 cup fresh pineapple chunks	76	0.6	0
Total	**846**	**12.2**	**2.0**
Luau Turkey Loaf (page 172)	211	12.3	0.5
Pineapple Chutney (page 173)	72	0.1	0
Mashed sweet potatoes	291	1.0	0
1½ cups shredded cabbage with **Creamy Peanut Dressing** (page 104)	112	5.5	1.0
Rice Custard (page 268)	225	4.4	1.9
Total	**911**	**23.3**	**3.4**

Menu	Calories	Total fat	Saturated fat
		(grams)	*(grams)*
2 **Basic Quesadillas** (page 43)	278	12.4	5.4
with **Salsa Rapida** (page 45)	148	4.4	0.6
Triple-Ginger Cupcakes (page 274)			
Total	426	16.8	6.0
Orange-Scented Bisque of Acorn Squash (page 72)	210	7.6	4.5
Bistro Sandwich (page 42)	301	14.4	6.5
1 D'Anjou or Bartlett pear	101	0.7	0
Total	612	22.7	11.0
Carrots in Lemon-Walnut Vinaigrette (page 92)	78	4.7	0.4
Braised Mushrooms & Plum Tomatoes over			
Pan-Grilled Polenta (page 128)	373	10.2	1.4
Handmade Applesauce (page 261)	295	0.9	0.2
Total	746	15.8	2.0
Pumpkin-Clam Chowder (page 71)	150	4.1	0.7
Southern Skillet Cornbread (page 28)	196	4.1	1.4
Broccoli Slaw (page 94)	61	1.2	0.2
Triple-Ginger Cupcakes (page 274)			
with **Chocolate Glaze** (page 276)	192	6.1	0.6
Total	599	15.5	2.9
Moroccan Orange Salad (page 90)	154	6.7	1.0
Downsized Roast Turkey (page 168)	115	0.6	0.2
Good Gravy (page 177)	25	1.8	0.5
¼ cup cranberry sauce	101	0.1	0
Tatties & Neeps (page 249)	153	4.3	2.8
Gingered Brussels Sprouts (page 231)	74	0.8	0
1 whole-wheat dinner roll	119	3.0	0.5
Sweet Potato Pudding (page 271)	288	5.7	1.4
Total	1,029	23.0	6.4

Menu	Calories	Total fat	Saturated fat
		(grams)	(grams)

Winter Lunches & Dinners

Menu	Calories	Total fat	Saturated fat
Russian Vegetable Soup (page 73)	124	0.5	0.1
Skillet Casserole of Bulgur & Crimini Mushrooms (page 137)	128	6.8	3.8
2 slices dark pumpernickel bread	158	0.4	0
New-Age Soft Custard (page 272) with banana slices	247	3.9	1.4
Total	**657**	**11.6**	**5.3**
Chili non Carne (page 84)	231	4.8	0.6
8 saltine crackers	96	2.6	0
Vegetable Slaw with Spa Dressing (page 95)	78	5.2	0.6
Stewed apricots with 1 ounce Neufchâtel cheese	208	6.9	3.4
Total	**613**	**19.5**	**4.6**
White Bean & Tomato Soup with Rosemary (page 67)	177	3.1	0.4
Southern Skillet Cornbread (page 28)	196	4.1	1.4
Sally's Left Bank Apple Crisp (page 260)	278	6.4	3.7
Total	**651**	**13.6**	**5.5**
Potato Pancakes with Apple Puree (page 132) and yogurt cheese	225	5.2	0.4
Beets in Orange Juice & Rosemary (page 228)	45	0.1	0
1 slice dark rye bread	61	0.3	0
Chocolate Pudding (page 269)	200	4.3	1.4
Total	**531**	**9.9**	**1.8**
Amish Baked Steak (page 210)	278	12.1	3.2
Mashed Potatoes (page 248)	254	4.7	2.8
Sweet & Sour Red Cabbage with Apples (page 233)	82	0.6	0.1
1 whole-wheat dinner roll	119	3.0	0.5
Rice Custard (page 268)	225	4.4	1.9
Total	**958**	**24.8**	**8.5**
New Boston Baked Beans (page 143)	248	1.0	0
2 ounces pan-grilled Canadian bacon	108	5.0	2.8
Thin and Creamy Coleslaw (page 93)	83	2.1	1.2
2 slices Steamed Boston Brown Bread (page 30)	236	1.4	0.4
½ serving Handmade Applesauce (page 261)	148	0.5	0.1
Total	**823**	**10.0**	**4.5**

Menu	Calories	Total fat	Saturated fat
		(grams)	*(grams)*
Baked Potato Soup with Broccoli & Cheddar (page 80)	241	6.8	4.2
2 slices dark rye bread	122	0.6	0
Waldorf Salad with Creamy Lime Dressing (page 103)	212	8.8	2.7
Total	**575**	**16.2**	**6.9**
Hopping John Risotto (page 134)	306	7.6	2.8
Southern Skillet Cornbread (page 28)	196	4.1	1.4
Pears Poached in Red Wine (page 278)	217	0.6	0
Total	**719**	**12.3**	**4.2**
Scalloped Oysters (page 197)	278	14.3	6.4
Spoonbread Soufflé (page 32)	303	8.5	3.4
Broccoli Slaw (page 94)	61	1.2	0.2
Chalet Suzanne Broiled Grapefruit (page 279)	117	3.9	2.4
Total	**759**	**27.9**	**12.4**

Spring Lunches & Dinners

Asparagus in Orange Sauce (page 226)	58	3.0	1.8
Deviled Chicken Breasts (page 158)	301	8.7	1.9
New Potato Salad with White-Wine Vinaigrette (page 97)	152	4.7	0.6
Old-Fashioned Strawberry Shortcake with Biscuits (page 264)	229	5.9	1.5
Total	**740**	**22.3**	**5.8**
Rainbow Trout in Foil (page 186)	206	8.7	3.3
Roasted Greek Potatoes (page 247)	151	2.4	0.3
Greek Green Beans & Tomatoes (page 227)	92	2.8	0.4
Strawberry Bleeding Hearts (page 281)	236	0.8	0
Total	**685**	**14.7**	**4.0**
Pan-Grilled Tuna Teriyaki (page 189)	276	9.3	2.0
1 cup steamed brown rice	232	1.2	0.4
Spinach with Sesame Seeds & Soy (page 254)	122	7.7	1.1
1 cup fresh pineapple chunks	75	0.6	0
Total	**705**	**18.8**	**3.5**
Carolina Casserole (page 154)	387	8.0	4.2
Warm Spinach Salad Chinoise (page 89)	130	8.9	1.3
1 baked sweet potato with 2 tablespoons maple syrup	333	0.2	0
Total	**850**	**17.1**	**5.5**
Poached Cod with Creamy Cucumber Sauce (page 182)	180	7.0	4.0
1 baked potato	173	0.2	0
Green Peas Braised in Garden Lettuce (page 246)	109	2.4	1.3
Lemon Sponge Pudding (page 270)	246	6.0	2.9
Total	**708**	**15.6**	**8.2**
Irish Lamb Oven Stew (page 222)	368	8.5	3.1
Beets in Orange Juice & Rosemary (page 228)	45	0.1	0
2 slices French baguette	88	1.0	0
1 cup salad greens with Skinny Dip (page 53)	51	0.7	0.3
Old-Time Bread Pudding (page 267)	243	6.6	2.7
Total	**795**	**16.9**	**6.1**

Index

D

Rigatoni
  Braised Veal and Brown Mushrooms with
    Rigatoni, 212
  Rigatoni alla Calabria, 187
Russian Vegetable Soup, 73
Rutabagas. *See* Turnips

S

Salad bars, <u>161</u>
Salad dressings
  Creamy Peanut Dressing, 104
  fat calories in, 87
  Pink Grapefruit Vinaigrette, 107
  Red French Dressing, 106
Salads
  Beefsteak Tomato and Sweet Onion Salad,
    100
  Beet and Endive Salad with Goat Cheese
    Toasts, 119
  Big Easy Salad of Red Beans and Rice,
    113
  Black and White Salad, 99
  Broccoli Slaw, 94
  Carrots in Lemon-Walnut Vinaigrette, 92
  Classic Green Salad with New Vinaigrette,
    88
  Country-Style Cucumbers, 101
  Cucumber Raita, 56
  Curried Chicken and Bulgur Salad, 111
  Downsized Tabbouleh, 112
  Epicurean Roast Beef Salad, 115
  Gazpacho Salad, 102
  Marinated Mushroom and Celery Salad,
    98
  Moroccan Orange Salad, 90
  New Potato Salad with White-Wine
    Vinaigrette, 97
  Shaved Fennel and Parmesan Cheese, 96
  Shrimp Salad Remoulade, 117
  Smoked Turkey and Fruit Salad, 108

Spicy Sesame Noodles, 118
  Sweet Potato Salad, 252
  Tavern-Style Carrots, 47
  Thin and Creamy Coleslaw, 93
  Tuna Salad Monterey, 116
  Vegetable Slaw with Spa Dressing, 95
  Waldorf Salad with Creamy Lime
    Dressing, 103
  Warm Spinach Salad Chinoise, 89
Salmon
  Chowder of Salmon and Green Peas, 70
  Salmon Panned in Orange Sauce, 192
  Salmon Sizzler with Late-Summer
    Vegetables, 193
Salsa
  Green Tomato Salsa, 44
  Salsa Rapida, 45
  Seafood Fajitas with Salsa, 195
  Thai Peach Salsa, <u>167</u>
Sandwiches. *See also* Spreads
  Bistro Sandwich, 42
  Brighton Beach Eggplant, 52
Sauces. *See also* Dips; Dressings
  Green Tomato Salsa, 44
  Pesto of Sun-Dried Tomatoes and Salt-
    Cured Olives, 48
  Pineapple Chutney, 173
  Salsa Rapida, 45
  Thai Peach Salsa, <u>167</u>
  Turkey in the Straw, 174
Scallops
  Creamy Cider Scallops, 200
  Fettuccine with Lemon-Walnut Scallops
    and Asparagus, 199
  Seafood Fajitas with Salsa, 195
Scottish-style dishes
  Tatties and Neeps, 249
Seafood. *See* Fish; Shellfish